# IT'S THE END
# OF THE CHURCH
## AS WE KNOW IT

# IT'S THE END
# OF THE CHURCH
## AS WE KNOW IT

## THE 166 FACTOR

MARC LAWSON

DESTINY IMAGE® PUBLISHERS, INC.
P.O. Box 310, Shippensburg, PA 17257-0310

*"Speaking to the Purposes of God for this Generation and for the Generations to Come."*

This book and all other Destiny Image, Revival Press, Mercy Place, Fresh Bread, Destiny Image Fiction, and Treasure House books are available at Christian bookstores and distributors worldwide.

For a U.S. bookstore nearest you, call 1-800-722-6774. For more information on foreign distributors, call 717-532-3040.
Or reach us on the Internet: www.destinyimage.com

ISBN 10: 0-7684-2499-2

ISBN 13: 978-0-7684-2499-7

For Worldwide Distribution, Printed in the U.S.A.

1  2  3  4  5  6  7  8  9  10  11  /  09  08  07

Marc Lawson has taken a bold, innovative, and courageous step in writing *It's the End of the Church as We Know It*. With innovative insight, I believe Marc has captured the heart of the matter as to why the typical church today is thought to be irrelevant to the individual and to society as a whole.

It seems that the church is in the same place today as the synagogues were in the time of Jesus. All too often, I see churches that are more like country clubs than places for spiritual reformation and worship of the only God. I am afraid that it could also be said that the church today shuts off the Kingdom of Heaven from people. Leaders do not enter in themselves, nor do they allow those who want to enter to go in. In light of this, I am sure some will gnash at Marc with their teeth, but I am also sure he will find it worth it when he stands before the Lord on that great day.

John Paul Jackson
Streams Ministries International
New Hampshire

*It's the End of the Church as We Know It* is an exciting book that everyone who seriously loves the Church should read. It is a book full of hope. It presents compelling insights into the new day dawning for the Church of Jesus Christ—one of great power, revelation knowledge, and great fruitfulness beyond which we have already known and experienced. It is a book full of promise— the promise of a victorious Church that has profound, transforming impact on the world. As I was reading, I wanted to shout, "Amen!" It is a book for the courageous, for those who are willing to stand up and say, "No" to ineffective and non-biblical church structures and traditions. It is a book for those who are willing to be discipled and to disciple others (which is one of the functions of the church). While mostly written to an American audience, these same influences discussed here—both good and bad—are evident in churches worldwide. I commend Marc Lawson for daring to write this book and speaking boldly, challenging believers to stand up without compromise and usher in the Kingdom of God on this earth. Having been in Marc's church on several occasions, I know that this book is not just talk—it was birthed out of his heart after many years of seeking God and leading a radically different church.

Dr. John N. Chacha, President
Teamwork Ministries International

If we are going to change our world, we must first change our minds. Thanks, Marc, for helping us to change *both* through this book.

Ray Hughes Selah Ministries
Hendersonville, Tennessee

This is a timely book exposing the dangers of complacency and releasing the delights of walking in the supernatural as a lifestyle. I recommend Marc Lawson's book to all who are hungry to break out of the mundane religious mindset.

Bobby Conner
Eagle's View Ministries
Bullard, Texas

If you like the security of living in a "church box," then this book is not for you. But, if you are looking for what God is doing in these days and are prepared to break out of the box, then this book will explode your vision and bring a sense of adventure and excitement back into your Christianity.

David and Kathie Walters
Good News Ministries
Macon, Georgia

Marc Lawson leads a church that is in passionate pursuit of displaying an authentic gospel. This passion has spilled over into the streets with miracles, signs, and wonders. I am certain that *It's the End of the Church as We Know It* will stir your hearts to pursue the same lifestyle that Jesus inspired in them.

Bill Johnson,
Author, *When Heaven Invades Earth*

# CONTENTS

## PREFACE

My wife, Linda, and I have faithfully, yet imperfectly, attempted to advance and mature the Church over the past 28 years. Because we've experienced the ups and downs of leading a church and the rigors of pastoral ministry, we have a keen understanding of the issues and situations that most pastor's face during their service to the Lord. Even through difficult times, we have retained the faith and idealism about the Church that the Lord placed in both of us when we were first born again. Subsequent times of refreshing and renewal have made us even more resolved to do our part so that the Church will be all that God intends for her to be—all the while continuing to love her in spite of her failings.

Although in this book I criticize and even indict the church (as a whole) in the United States for its present condition, I believe there are some churches that are solidly following God's plan. Many others, though, have significant shortcomings that are due to an immaturity perpetuated by the current church "system." For the system to change, believers have to change first!

To bring about these radical and critical changes, we must take a hard look at her deficiencies to bring reformation—even revolution! As my friend Rick Joyner says, "It only takes one working eye to see what's wrong with anything." This discernment comes out of a love proven over years. What the church has been must die to bring forth new life.

*Truly, truly, I say to you, unless a grain of wheat falls into the earth and dies, it remains by itself alone; but if it dies, it bears much fruit* (John 12:24).

The things I am seeing and declaring in this book foretell and prophesy a New Day dawning for the Church of Jesus Christ—a day of great power, immense fruitfulness, and advancement of the Kingdom beyond anything we've yet seen or heard. I believe that the new form that the Church must take will supersede anything we've even imagined (see Eph. 3:20), and I sense that when it begins to emerge, we will understand why only God's handprints are on this long-awaited expression on the earth.

From the fall of man in the garden to David's generation where the Lord was supposedly "contained" in the Ark, to Jesus' miraculous ministry, death, and resurrection, to the birth of the New Testament church, through the Dark Age, the Protestant Reformation, and the 21st century church today, God has always desired for people to view and experience Him in ways that are not always defined and confined. Man's religious systems, wrong teachings, cultural traditions, fear, and unbelief have all contributed to limiting God's scope of operation in a typical believer's life to approximately two hours a week on Sunday morning.

Why do God's people seem content to confine Him? Why is it that believers often view their Creator through a diffused filter? Why is it that we tend to tie God's hands in so many areas? Although most believe that God can move any place and any time, they haven't significantly changed their thinking or altered their lifestyles to fully accommodate this belief. Most people would rather keep things the way they are, even if unfulfilling.

But God has never wanted His glory and power to be limited to parochial church experiences hidden behind stained glass and within four walls. Traditions of men, doctrines of demons, and plain old unbelief hold us back from entering into the life in the Spirit most of us say we live for and want. There just *has* to be something better for us than we have seen so far!

This book is titled, *It's the End of the Church as We Know It—The 166 Factor*. The number 166 describes the number of hours remaining in a week after the average Christian has attended a two-hour Sunday church service. The word *factor* is defined as "one that contributes in the cause of an action." In other words, the 166 Factor is the time available in every believer's week when unexplored opportunities can be discovered and the Kingdom of God shared with a lost world.

This book is not about bashing American Christianity or looking for scapegoats for the failures of the Church. It is also not about reinventing how to "do" Sunday morning worship or church meetings. Instead, it is about envisioning the people of God, so they can  use the other 166 hours in their week to further His Kingdom on earth.

While some sacred religious cows will be barbequed, my primary purpose is to honestly assess our fruitfulness, or lack of it, and then begin to encourage and motivate believers to boldly go where no (or few) Christians have gone before—into a new adventure in God!

I dedicate this book to John Wimber, a 20th century apostle who blazed a trail of signs, wonders, and miracles, and was committed to equipping the saints. He believed and taught that the average believer could walk in the miraculous power of Heaven. He paved the way for a generation who would live and walk in the miraculous. I thank him for pioneering a new and living walk of Christian experience.

I believe the 21st century Church is called to experience the supernatural things of God in a way that will provoke to jealousy even the church of Acts!

If you are hungry for:

- A fruitful Christian life,
- A lifelong, God-powerful adventure,
- The supernatural to be a normal and routine part of your daily experience,
- God to be released from religious boxes and mental limitations,
- God to invade the streets, neighborhoods, schools, and marketplaces,
- Every day filled with authentic supernatural living....

Then, read on!

**CHAPTER 1**

# THE THREE DREAMS

Recently, our family was wonderfully blessed by a sudden, even abrupt, move into a brand new home. Because we had lived in our former home for 15 years—the longest we had ever lived in one home—we had accumulated a lot of memories there. During those years our three oldest children each married a wonderful mate and moved out to begin their lives together. We also experienced the births of four beautiful grandchildren during our time in that house. While we did have a few difficult seasons living there, overall, our memories are good.

But the most incredible aspect about our move was that the home we moved into is the exact same house I saw in three different dreams over a five-month period, 10 years previously! The dreams came during a time when our church was located in another area of town and had just begun to experience a move of God. Many of us in the church were having vivid and detailed prophetic dreams, visions, and the like.

In my dreams, I saw the front porch, the two-story foyer, the hardwood floors on the first level, and the wall of windows in the family room overlooking a deck. In addition, specific details about the house were revealed; and in one dream I was even having a conversation with someone about the builder of the house.

At the time, we knew much less about how to interpret dreams, so we wondered if the dream was allegorical. We thought maybe the dream was about a "type of the house of

God." Or for example, the hardwood floors, a "solid foundation" and the "builder" was perhaps the Lord Himself. While at the time we didn't fully know the interpretation, I was arrested by the specificity and details in the dreams and knew they were from God.

We searched for the house in areas near the church for the next few years. When we couldn't find that specific house, we stretched the interpretation to mean that maybe we should look for land for the church. After another few years, we finally gave up any thought that it would be found.

After the church went through a major shaking, we relocated, clearly led by the Lord, to an area of town 14 miles away and nearer to my home. It became obvious that the former region was not where the ministry was to be located long-term, and we gave up thinking that the dream would ever be fulfilled. We learned a lot about the importance of being in God's assigned geographical location through that church move.

While our family's move was only five miles north and even in the same zip code, this new area, located near pasture with rolling hills, streams, and meadows, seems as if we have moved to another state. The air even seems clearer because we are miles away from heavily traveled roads, and it is mostly quiet and peaceful.

We learned several prophetic lessons during the church and home geographical moves; some of these lessons were very significant. First and foremost, I learned that God can bring a *sudden* manifestation of those things we've hoped and dreamed of for years, in a matter of moments. It doesn't matter if we have largely "let go" of those things or even wondered if they would ever materialize, God has a way of moving things quickly to bring about the change.

Remember Joseph? He had a dream from the Lord that was an actual "vision" of the future. Joseph's dream, though allegorical and needing interpretation, was a picture of what would happen. While Joseph's dream needed interpretation, some do not.

> *Then Joseph had a dream, and when he told it to his brothers, they hated him even more. He said to them, "Please listen to this dream which I have had; for behold, we were binding sheaves in the field, and lo, my sheaf rose up and also stood erect; and behold, your sheaves gathered around and bowed down to my sheaf." Then his brothers said to him, "Are you actually going to reign over us? Or are you really going to rule over us?" So they hated him even more for his dreams and for his words. Now he had still another dream, and related it to his brothers, and said, "Lo, I have had still another dream; and behold, the sun and the moon and eleven stars were bowing down to me." He related it to his father and to his brothers; and his father rebuked him and said to him, "What is this dream that you have had? Shall I and your mother and your brothers actually come to bow ourselves down before you to the ground?" And his brothers were jealous of him, but his father kept the saying in mind* (Genesis 37:5-11).

Most dreams need interpretation, but some are literal snapshots of future events. In the New Testament another man named Joseph, the earthly father of Jesus, had more than one dream in which an angel of the Lord spoke to him. In one of his dreams, Joseph was told that Mary would conceive a child supernaturally; in the second dream, Joseph was warned to go to Egypt to flee Herod. Dreams, long forgotten, can be quickly remembered and brought to pass in ways we could never imagine. Scripture reveals how suddenly the Lord can make changes.

> *But the multitude of your enemies shall become like fine dust, and the multitude of the ruthless ones like the chaff which blows away; and it shall happen instantly, suddenly* (Isaiah 29:5).

Another good example is found in Isaiah 60:1-22 which begins with the light of God arising on His people and ends with: *"I, the Lord, will hasten it in its time."*

The second valuable lesson we discovered as we found and then bought this house, was that while we didn't have to go very far to find our dream, we had to know where to look. We learned there is peace and rest near us right now *if* we are willing to look for and possess it. We must ask, seek, and knock to appropriate these things that God has for us. Exercising bold faith is not optional but mandatory, if we want to succeed. Many in the Body are expecting God to drop their "promised land" into their laps, and He won't. I believe that God only gives to those who are willing to believe.

> *And without faith it is impossible to please Him: for he who comes to God must believe that he is, and that He is a rewarder of them who diligently seek Him* (Hebrews 11:6).

> *So I say to you, ask, and it will be given to you; seek, and you will find; knock, and it will be opened to you. For everyone who asks, receives; and he who seeks, finds; and to him who knocks, it will be opened* (Luke 11:9-10).

We know the move into our new house was a prophetic sign of what we can all experience as we possess the places God has for us. It was only five months ago when our church purchased our first building, yet that act was the beginning of a shift bringing us into places of promise the Lord has destined for many of us.

The third lesson we received from this experience was that the Lord wants us to take ownership and responsibility when receiving what He has for us. In other words, ownership creates responsibility. The more the Body of Christ takes ownership and responsibility for sharing the gospel, declaring the Kingdom, and fulfilling our ministry, we will grow in authority.

Both Isaiah and Jeremiah speak of the Lord's desire to put God's people in their own land:

> ...the Lord will have compassion on Jacob...and again choose Israel, and settle them in their own land... (Isaiah 14:1).

> "Therefore, behold, the days are coming," says the Lord, "when they shall no longer say, 'As the Lord lives who brought up the children of Israel from the land of Egypt,' but, 'As the Lord lives who brought up and led the descendants of the house of Israel from the north land and from all the countries where I had driven them.' And they will live on their own soil" (Jeremiah 23:7-8).

These passages specifically declared that Israel would have its own land, and the prophecies were fulfilled in 1948. In the aftermath of World War II and the Holocaust, when Nazi Germany nearly succeeded at their attempt to exterminate the Jews, Israel became a sovereign nation with overwhelming worldwide support. In addition to the fulfillment, the Bible clearly states that the natural precedes a spiritual fulfillment.

> *However, the spiritual is not first, but the natural; then the spiritual* (1 Corinthians 15:46).

The Bible also declares that the things that occurred in the Old Testament happened for our instruction.

> *Now these things happened to them as an example, and they were written for our instruction, upon whom the ends of the ages have come* (1 Corinthians 10:11).

So even as Israel represents the Church and their land represents our spiritual inheritance, we must also understand that God prophetically speaks to us today—sometimes through dreams.

## Three Dreams

Within a matter of five weeks I had three dreams. I felt the Lord wanted me to share them in this book to unveil important revelation to the Body of Christ, about the new look of the Church and the 166 Factor.

During the fourth watch of the night (3-6 A.M.), I was awakened by the obvious presence of an angel who rouses me. However, when I am awake the angel does not communicate with me; only after I go back to sleep does he seem to escort me through the different scenes—beside me, but out of sight. After the first dream about our home, the second dream was about a city building. I am carried to an old tenement building that could occupy the inner city of Atlanta, Chicago, New York, or any of a dozen other major cities. These large housing projects, most built with government money in the 1960s and '70s, were

built with the hope of helping lift people out of poverty
Unfortunately, the plan was unsuccessful.

## The Tenement

The building I see is about six stories tall, old and run
down with graffiti painted on the outside walls. The next thing,
I know I am inside a common area of the building like—a type
of community area or recreation room. I see a lot of people
milling about wearing filthy, dirty clothes. The floor is covered
with an old, gold-colored shag carpet that has been so well trod-
den that it's completely flat from the crushed-in food, drink,
dirt, and wear. Gross.

Signs on the walls instruct the residents about paying
their rent on time and taking care of the property. "Clean Up
Room After Use" one screams in bold black letters on a faded
gold piece of cardboard. But like the carpet, the signs go unno-
ticed.

There are restrooms over in the corner, but I don't go
over there. They are probably as filthy as the people and the
room. I remember the saying, "Everyone's responsibility is no
one's." The signs were an attempt to motivate "everyone" to
take care of the room, to clean up after each event; but "everyone" thought "someone else" would do it.

Before I leave the room, I notice that there are dirty old
rags, almost like towels, on the floor that are being trampled on,
almost as if they are part of the flooring. No one stoops down
to pick them up. I am troubled. Is this place hell? Maybe the
"outer darkness"? I sensed no evil among the people there, only
apathy, boredom, fear, and even depression and hopelessness.
"What is this place?"

Then I woke up, more than a little upset and disturbed by what I saw. I asked the Lord, "What was that place and why I have seen it?" The Scripture in Isaiah comes to me:

> *You meet him who rejoices and does righteousness, Who remembers You in Your ways. You are indeed angry, for we have sinned; In these ways we continue; And we need to be saved. But we are all like an unclean thing, And all our righteousnesses are like filthy rags; We all fade as a leaf, And our iniquities, like the wind, Have taken us away. And there is no one who calls on Your name, Who stirs himself up to take hold of You...* (Isaiah 64:5-7 NKJV).

I also remember Revelation 3:5: *"He who overcomes shall be clothed in white garments, and I will not blot out his name from the Book of Life; but I will confess his name before My Father and before His angels"* (NKJV).

Then I wonder and ask the Spirit, "Is this a real place here in Atlanta? Or is this a vision of something else?" As I begin to receive an interpretation from the Lord for this vision, a peace comes over me that removes the anxiety I felt at the meaning of the dream. The interpretation comes with more and more clarity as Scriptures, insights, and a sense of understanding overcomes me.

> *The unfolding of Thy words gives light; It gives understanding to the simple* (Psalms 119:130).

> *Make your ear attentive to wisdom, Incline your heart to understanding; For if you cry for discernment, Lift your voice for understanding; If you seek her as silver, And search for her as for hidden treasures; Then you*

*will discern the fear of the Lord, And discover the knowledge of God. For the Lord gives wisdom; From His mouth come knowledge and understanding* (Proverbs 2:2-6).

Scripture is clear that God has *all* wisdom and understanding because He *is* wisdom and understanding! I personally believe that wisdom and understanding are combined as one of the seven Spirits of God revealed in Zechariah 4:10, Isaiah 11:2, and Revelation 1:12,20; 2:1.

Many Christians believe the best way to evangelize the lost is to present them with a God they can easily understand. While the motives are admirable, the premise is completely wrong. First of all, in our quest to know God we are told in Scripture that in Him alone is *understanding*, and God will not allow us to fully understand Him.

*With Him are wisdom and might; To Him belong counsel and understanding* (Job 12:13).

The Word even says that God prevents people from understanding because they just won't believe. God hardened Pharaoh's heart.

*For You have kept their heart from understanding...* (Job 17:4).

We are commanded to believe in Him and even turn from our own ways of thinking. The presupposition is that God and His ways are beyond understanding and that to merely try to "figure God out" like a math equation is impossible. It requires faith to come to Him, not understanding! After we believe, we are told to ask for understanding and wisdom and they will be given to us.

*Make your ear attentive to wisdom, Incline your heart to understanding; For if you cry for discernment, lift your voice for understanding; If you seek her as silver, and search for her as for hidden treasures; then you will discern the fear of the Lord, And discover the knowledge of God. For the Lord gives wisdom; From His mouth come knowledge and understanding. He stores up sound wisdom for the upright; He is a shield to those who walk in integrity, guarding the paths of justice, and He preserves the way of His godly ones* (Proverbs 2:2-8).

## Tentative Responsibility

The dream I had isn't about physical buildings, but what they represent. The tenement in my dream represents the habitation of God offered to the Body by most of the forms of church we see today. While people are offered a low-rent place to dwell, they know they don't own it so no one takes care of it. *Neglect* describes the scene I saw.

The tenement was a vivid picture of the impotent church where those at the top (the landlords or leaders) take care of you if you live in their dwelling, obey their rules, and accept their view of your responsibility. The landlords assume that the tenants, the renters, will be satisfied and grateful for the low rent and that they will take responsibility for their dwelling.

They are wrong; everyone's responsibility becomes no one's. Everyone assumes that those at the top are taking care of the basics, but they probably are not. Remember the bathrooms? The tenement also depicts the church which has taken on a form of religion (filthy rags, dirty clothes) and irrelevant activities rather than being an overcoming force of power and righteousness on the earth.

This dream accurately describes why most people in the Body of Christ are *tentative* about taking responsibility for their life and ministry. By only offering the Body a position as a *tenant* in the tenement, folks will not be motivated to take personal responsibility in working out their own salvation. When it comes to taking personal responsibility, they are tentative and reluctant. They don't own it, so they don't care about it.

It is not enough to just say, "We should all attend church and live godly lives in the world." We have to take responsibility for our own lives and ministries and actually follow through. We need to learn what it is to co-labor with Him in order to fulfill His will for our lives.

*And working together with Him...* (2 Corinthians 6:1).

*Grace and peace be multiplied to you in the knowledge of God and of Jesus our Lord, as His divine power has given to us all things that pertain to life and godliness, through the knowledge of Him who called us by glory and virtue, by which have been given to us exceedingly great and precious promises, that through these you may be partakers of the divine nature, having escaped the corruption that is in the world through lust* (2 Peter 1:2-4 NKJV).

*Preach the word! Be ready in season and out of season. Convince, rebuke, exhort, with all longsuffering and teaching. For the time will come when they will not endure sound doctrine, but according to their own desires, because they have itching ears, they will heap up for themselves teachers; and they will turn their ears away from the truth, and be turned aside to fables. But you be watchful in all things, endure afflictions, do the work of an evangelist, fulfill your ministry* (2 Timothy 4:2-5 NKJV).

Instead of winning the lost and preaching an authentic gospel, many have bought into the premise that if we can "get them to attend church, then we have them." That concept is simply wrong.

According to George Barna, a Christian pollster, after the 9-11 terrorist attacks many unbelievers flocked into the church for about 6-8 weeks.[1] They looked around, saw what was happening and said essentially, "No thanks, I have more reality in my own little world than there is in here." Although we thought we "had them," they apparently didn't like or want what they saw.

The tenement dream, or revelation, also illustrates how leadership must begin to fundamentally change the infrastructure and makeup of the Church so the Body truly has ownership and authority, and begins to take responsibility not just for their own salvation, but also their life and ministry. The Body can no longer hope that "someone else will take care of them." Someone else must be *you* and *me*.

We must take responsibility to do what God is telling us and no longer blame the system. On the other hand, church leadership needs to realize that the Body is now beginning to see through the "spectator" and "meeting-centric" mentality of most churches. As more and more believers recognize that their churches only provide crumbs and prevent them from fulfilling God's vision, they will become dissatisfied. In time, many will leave to fulfill the call God placed in their hearts. Churches that don't equip and release the saints will become less relevant, and eventually empty, religious institutions.

God's Kingdom work doesn't rely on the hermeneutical or oratory skills of a few highly influential leaders with large ministries. But instead His work is accomplished when each person fulfills his or her call, one day at a time. It is entirely possible that within 20 years, as future leaders look back and observe this time in Christian history, we could find that much of what is passing as the greatest ministries today may be found to have had little or no impact advancing the Kingdom.

We can't declare Jesus and His Kingdom and also embrace shameless self-promotion of our own brand of Christian fad or buzzword. While this message may be coming from well-intentioned people, if they are preaching their own kingdom, declaring their own gospel and declaring another Jesus than the One in the Book, the effort will profit nothing. While it may scratch itchy ears for awhile, when it does nothing to manifest the results of the demonstrative gospel it will inevitably be seen as hollow and worthless.

Because we are either advancing the Kingdom of God or another kingdom, those who proclaim Christ and His Kingdom will grow in authority and power; while those catering to prestige and desiring to accumulate influence will become only motivational speakers, not gospel ministers. No matter how gifted a person is they are still called to preach His gospel—the gospel of the Kingdom of God.

**Endnote**

1. George Barna, *The Year's Most Intriguing Findings, From Barna Research Studies,*12-17-01 The Barna Group, www.barna.org.

CHAPTER 2

# WHAT'S WRONG WITH THIS PICTURE?

## The Wrong Prescription

It seems to me that the Church makes the mistake of thinking, "if we just had a new oxcart we could bring in the glory." There is a sense in America and in the church that *new* is better. Numbers from the Barna Research Group support that theory: Each year, one out of every seven adults changes churches. In addition one out of every six adults attends a carefully chosen handful of churches on a rotating basis. This statistic rings true because the church in the United States runs *behind* what God is actually communicating to us prophetically. This is unfortunate. Because we haven't been listening to what the Lord is saying, we miss many opportunities He gives us to advance. Part of the problem is *no one stays in one place long enough*. God is always speaking, but unless we have "ears to hear" we will miss what He is saying.

Some in the media and the arts are hearing what the Spirit is saying more clearly than the Church; yet they don't have (or seek) a biblical grid to understand what is being said and why. A few of the latest offerings from musicians and filmmakers are more "in tune" with what God is really saying than what is heard from some pulpits.

*Relevant* and *pertinent* is what the Lord's Word is. And because the Church is so desperate to be relevant and timely, sometimes we jump at any new method we think may bring God's presence closer. The problem is our methods and our ways. Any method we use to bring God's presence to the lost that God didn't prescribe won't work and can even cause problems. There is a lot going on in the Body that God is blessing, but not inhabiting. God only glorifies and honors that which He prescribes. Just because He is honoring the faith of some, doesn't mean it is His prescription for all.

God's means has always included a demonstration of His message.

> *Now the ark of the Lord was in the country of the Philistines seven months.*
>
> *And the Philistines called for the priests and the diviners, saying, "What shall we do with the ark of the Lord? Tell us how we should send it to its place."*
>
> *So they said, "If you send away the ark of the God of Israel, do not send it empty; but by all means return it to Him with a trespass offering. Then you will be healed, and it will be known to you why His hand is not removed from you."*
>
> *Then they said, "What is the trespass offering which we shall return to Him?" They answered, "Five golden tumors and five golden rats, according to the number of the lords of the Philistines. For the same plague was on all of you and on your lords.*
>
> *"Therefore you shall make images of your tumors and images of your rats that ravage the land, and you shall give glory to the God of Israel; perhaps He will lighten His hand from you, from your gods, and from your land.*

*"Why then do you harden your hearts as the Egyptians and Pharaoh hardened their hearts? When He did mighty things among them, did they not let the people go, that they might depart?*

*"Now therefore, make a new cart, take two milk cows which have never been yoked, and hitch the cows to the cart; and take their calves home, away from them.*

*"Then take the ark of the LORD and set it on the cart; and put the articles of gold which you are returning to Him as a trespass offering in a chest by its side. Then send it away, and let it go.*

*"And watch: if it goes up the road to its own territory, to Beth Shemesh, then He has done us this great evil. But if not, then we shall know that it is not His hand that struck us; it happened to us by chance."*

*Then the men did so; they took two milk cows and hitched them to the cart, and shut up their calves at home.*

*And they set the ark of the LORD on the cart, and the chest with the gold rats and the images of their tumors.*

*Then the cows headed straight for the road to Beth Shemesh, and went along the highway, lowing as they went, and did not turn aside to the right hand or the left. And the lords of the Philistines went after them to the border of Beth Shemesh.*

*Now the people of Beth Shemesh were reaping their wheat harvest in the valley; and they lifted their eyes and saw the ark, and rejoiced to see it* (1 Samuel 6:1-13).

Look at the terrible consequences for the Philistines when they attempted, with their own wisdom, to bring God's presence:

> *Then He struck the men of Beth Shemesh, because they had looked into the ark of the Lord. He struck down 50,070 men, and the people mourned because the Lord had struck the people with a great slaughter* (1 Samuel 6:19).

> *So they set the ark of God on a new cart, and brought it out of the house of Abinadab, which was on the hill; and Uzzah and Ahio, the sons of Abinadab, drove the new cart. And they brought it out of the house of Abinadab, which was on the hill, accompanying the ark of God; and Ahio went before the ark. Then David and all the house of Israel played music before the Lord on all kinds of instruments of fir wood, on harps, on stringed instruments, on tambourines, on sistrums, and on cymbals. And when they came to Nachon's threshing floor, Uzzah put out his hand to the ark of God and took hold of it, for the oxen stumbled. Then the anger of the Lord was aroused against Uzzah, and God struck him there for his error; and he died there by the ark of God* (2 Samuel 6:3-7 NKJV).

Okay, it is obvious something was wrong. When we examine Israel's attempt to bring the ark back into Israel, we see that the Lord killed a multitude of men along with Uzzah. Because David went along with every detail of the Philistine witches' plan to bring the ark into Israel except the use of a new oxcart, God clearly objected! Because David foolishly attempted to transport it using a plan other than God's, people died; and he had to go back to the Lord for His plan.

Scripture is clear that after David sought the Lord, he remembered God's plan to move the ark only using the Levites and to have it carried in on poles. Here is what David found as He sought the Scriptures:

> *It was because you, the Levites, did not bring it up the first time that the Lord our God broke out in anger against us. We did not inquire of him about how to do it in the prescribed way* (1 Chronicles 15:13 NIV).

What the Philistines got for mishandling God's power and presence was rats, tumors, and the death of over 50,000 men! And when Israel attempted to move the ark while only suffering one death, David wisely shut everything down till he understood what was happening and why.

It is interesting to note that the name of the deceased, *Uzzah*, means "strength." Uzzah reached out his hand to "steady" the ark, as if his own strength could steady or somehow help the situation. The days of the church attempting to come up with our own plans and strategies to do what God has clearly prescribed needs to quickly come to an end. We need more leaders like David who are risk-takers but also have enough fear of God that they will drop back and punt when they realize they need to change course in obedience to God. His ways are not our ways, and we must learn this lesson quickly.

> *Let the wicked forsake his way, And the unrighteous man his thoughts; And let him return to the Lord, And He will have compassion on him; And to our God, For He will abundantly pardon. "For My thoughts are not your thoughts, Neither are your ways My ways," declares the Lord. "For as the heavens are higher than the earth, So are My ways higher than your ways, And My thoughts than your thoughts* (Isaiah 55:7-9).

It is important to note that it says here, *"Let the **wicked forsake his way and the unrighteous man his thoughts**.*" In doesn't say, let the wicked forsake his *sins* or the unrighteous man his *deeds*. Isaiah exposes the root problem that man has apart from God—his *ways* and his *thoughts*. While sins are things we do to violate God's law, our ways and thoughts are the things that cause us to go ahead and do and say evil things. When a man forsakes his own way and comes to the Lord, his every way must change. Man's ways and plans, unless initiated and continued by the breath of the Spirit are meaningless.

> *And He was also telling them a parable: "No one tears a piece from a new garment and puts it on an old garment; otherwise he will both tear the new, and the piece from the new will not match the old." And no one puts new wine into old wineskins; otherwise the new wine will burst the skins, and it will be spilled out, and the skins will be ruined. But new wine must be put into fresh wineskins. And no one, after drinking old wine wishes for new; for he says, 'The old is good enough'* (Luke 5:36-39).

This parable clearly reveals the trait of human nature that loves to keep things the way they are. Given a choice, we will always choose the old rather than the new. A friend of mine questioned an expert in the science of wine who told him that the main difference between old wine and new is that the old tastes smooth and mellow, is soft on the palate, and easy to enjoy. On the other hand, new wine is strong and pungent, with little of the smoothness of the old. Most think it's too strong to drink. Nevertheless, we need new wine! Something new and strong is needed to shock the church of Jesus Christ from where she is to the next level that God intends for Her. That may seem quite a stretch considering what the church looks like presently—little does it resemble what we read about in the Book of Acts.

## A Revolution of Resolve!

We need a revolution of thinking, where our resolve to bring reform is unshakeable and immovable. Resolve means you will re-solve the problem over and over until you solve it.

*Needed: Revolution of the Spirit*

> *And when the day of Pentecost had come, they were all together in one place. And suddenly there came from heaven a noise like a violent, rushing wind, and it filled the whole house where they were sitting. And there appeared to them tongues as of fire distributing themselves and they rested on each one of them. And they were all filled with the Holy Spirit and began to speak with other tongues, as the Spirit was giving them utterance. Now there were Jews living in Jerusalem, devout men, from every nation under heaven. And when this sound occurred, the multitude came together, and were bewildered because they were each one hearing them speak in his own language. And they were amazed and astonished..."we hear them in our own tongues speaking of the mighty deeds of God."*
> *..."For these men are not drunk, as you suppose, for it is only the third hour of the day;"* (Acts 2:1-15).

Renowned evangelist Billy Graham said, "The church has everything but God." I agree. We have programs, methods, websites, state-of-the-art graphics and digital equipment, but without the Spirit, we have no life! In the last decade, the American church has spent billions for buildings, programs, and gimmicks, with few tangible results or fruit!

*"It is the Spirit who gives life; the flesh profits nothing; the words that I have spoken to you are spirit and are life"* (John 6:63). Corporate marketing and new mission statements can't accomplish what the Spirit can. The Spirit is what the men received on the day of Pentecost, and it was evident to all as they *all* spoke in other tongues and received power!

Unfortunately, today, the nearly powerless church would still rather debate whether the gifts of the Holy Spirit are "for today" or "have ceased." Why don't evangelicals welcome the Spirit? Why don't they want the supernatural empowerment only the Spirit brings? Why don't Christians want the "whole enchilada"

They have books that tell them that miracles were for ignorant, foolish people of the past, and because some leaders say that because we now have the Bible, we no longer need the supernatural. Our theology has been largely built on the absence of God doing things rather than what scripture declares. Until we realize that powerlessness is inexcusable we won't see the power we want!

I believe that Jesus addressed this issue: *"You search the Scriptures because you think that in them you have eternal life; it is these that testify about Me; and you are unwilling to come to Me so that you may have life"* (John 5:39-40).

Because many pastors and teachers have convinced their congregations that tongues, healings, prophecy, and miracles are either not for today's believer or are part of the occult, new age, or not necessary, many church members no longer believe in the power of God. The evangelical church and much of the Pentecostal and Charismatic church have sophisticated methods and programs that perpetuate more of the same. Just ask anyone who ever served in government how hard it is to kill a program that has already begun!

There are pastors and congregations who believe and preach in the name of the Father, Son, and the Holy Bible, but won't give the Holy Spirit more than a vague mystical reference. They declare that now that we have the Bible, we don't need miracles or signs and wonders anymore.

The American church as a whole is not preaching the gospel of the Kingdom that Jesus preached: *"THE SPIRIT OF THE LORD IS UPON ME, BECAUSE HE ANOINTED ME TO PREACH THE GOSPEL TO THE POOR. HE HAS SENT ME TO PROCLAIM RELEASE TO THE CAPTIVES, AND RECOVERY OF SIGHT TO THE BLIND, TO SET FREE THOSE WHO ARE DOWNTRODDEN, TO PROCLAIM THE FAVORABLE YEAR OF THE LORD." And He closed the book, and gave it back to the attendant, and sat down; and the eyes of all in the synagogue were fixed upon Him. And He began to say to them, "Today this Scripture has been fulfilled in your hearing"* (Luke 4:18-21).

Without a humbling encounter with the Holy Spirit and openness to the new, we won't have life and won't ever enter into all that God has for us. God, if He is anything, is *real!* And He is supernatural.

## Needed: Revolution Among the Youth

But this is what was spoken of through the prophet Joel:

*It will come about after this that I will pour out My Spirit on all mankind; and your sons and daughters will prophesy, your old men will dream dreams, your young men will see visions. Even on the male and female servants I will pour out My Spirit in those days. I will display wonders in the sky and on the earth, blood, fire and columns of smoke. The sun will be turned into darkness and the moon into blood before the great and awesome day of the Lord comes. And it will come about that whoever calls on the name of the Lord will be delivered...*(Joel 2:28-32).

I need not explain the dilemma we face with our youth, but suffice it to say God's heart has always been to go after the next generation. Whatever this generation is doing for God, I want to be in the middle of it!

## Needed: Revolution in Lifestyle

*And with many other words he solemnly testified and kept on exhorting them, saying, "Be saved from this perverse generation!" So then, those who had received his word were baptized; and there were added that day about three thousand souls. And they were continually devoting themselves to the apostles' teaching and to fellowship, to the breaking of bread and to prayer. And everyone kept feeling a sense of awe; and many wonders and signs were taking place through the apostles. And all those who had believed were together, and had all things in common; and they began selling their property and possessions, and were sharing them with all, as anyone might have need. And day by day continuing with one mind in the temple, and breaking bread from house to house, they were taking their meals together with gladness and sincerity of heart, praising God, and having favor with all the people. And the Lord was adding to their number day by day those who were being saved* (Acts 2:40-47).

What if the average lifestyle of the typical Christian more resembled what we read in this Scripture than what it really is? Wouldn't it be great if Christians were seen by society as truthful people rather than hypocrites? Wouldn't it be great if Christians lived out their Christian life in power and truth rather than talk, talk, talk?

## Needed: Revolution of Power

> *Now Peter and John were going up to the temple at the ninth hour, the hour of prayer. And a certain man who had been lame from his mother's womb was being carried along, whom they used to set down every day at the gate of the temple which is called Beautiful, in order to beg alms of those who were entering the temple. When he saw Peter and John about to go into the temple, he began asking to receive alms. But Peter, along with John, fixed his gaze upon him and said, "Look at us!" And he began to give them his attention, expecting to receive something from them. But Peter said, "I do not possess silver and gold, but what I do have I give to you: In the name of Jesus Christ the Nazarene—walk!" And seizing him by the right hand, he raised him up; and immediately his feet and his ankles were strengthened. With a leap, he stood upright and began to walk; and he entered the temple with them, walking and leaping and praising God* (Acts 3:1-8).

Dr. Paul Yonggi Cho, pastor of the world's largest church said, "Much prayer, much power; little prayer, little power; no prayer, no power!" These early Christians knew that supernatural power didn't come from them but from the Spirit of God flowing through them to heal, save, and deliver.

Jesus also tells us in John 14 that *we* can expect even much *more* power to change lives; *"Truly, truly, I say to you, he who believes in Me, the works that I do, he will do also; and greater works than these he will do..."* (John 14:12).

## Needed: Revolution of Integrity and Reality

During the past few years, sexual abuse scandals surfaced concerning the Catholic priesthood; financial impropriety forced the resignation of the leader of one of the largest African-American denominations; and, a pastor of one of the Bible Belt's largest churches began teaching universalism, the belief that all men will be saved and none perish.

While God's desire is for all people to come to a knowledge of the Truth, it's clear in the Scriptures that not all will be saved. To teach otherwise is heresy. Barna released the results of their poll about divorce on December 21, 1991.[1] They had interviewed 3,854 adults from the 48 contiguous states. The margin of error is within 2 percentage points. The survey found:

- 11% of the adult population is currently divorced.
- 25% of adults have had at least one divorce during their lifetime.

Divorce rates among conservative Christians were significantly higher than for other faith groups, and for atheists and agnostics.[2]

These facts clearly reveal that the essence of what the church presently believes and practices is in great need of overhaul. While reformation brings change, we now need more than cosmetic or structural change. We need foundational change and that will look more like a revolution than a mild reformation.

The Bible is clear that the church is built on the revelation of Jesus Christ (see Matt. 16:17-18) and that this unveiling and understanding of His nature and character is the foundation of the church. (See Ephesians 2:20.) We need a revelation of Jesus Christ to bring about this revolution. Nothing less than a total overhaul of the current religious system will make a difference!

So this is where we are today. While it is not pretty, I believe there is great hope in what God has in store for us, and I believe God is up to something big. We need to open our eyes to see it.

### Endnotes

1. "Church Hopping" by Amand Phifer, "Faithworks" used by permission.

2. George Barna, The Year's Most Intriguing Findings, divorce poll, 12-21-1999, The Barna Group, www.barna.org.

**CHAPTER 3**

---

# WE ARE IN THE MATRIX

The number one blockbuster movie of 1999 was *The Matrix*. The movie was so successful that it spawned two sequels that were released four years later within six months of each other.

The movie's dark fantasy tells of a future world where machines have consigned humanity to live in a computer-generated, artificial world where few ever discover that the "life" they were living wasn't real. Humankind was enslaved in a "matrix" while the machines used their bodies for energy.

The story unfolds around a small band of resistance fighters who are convinced that a man named Neo is the one who was prophesied about to come and liberate them from bondage. The big dilemma in the story line—Neo has to be convinced that this is his mission. After the resistance unplugs him from the Matrix, he quickly discovers the world he lives in is not real, just as he had been told. While this realization is difficult for him to believe, he finally understands. Convincing him that he is some sort of superhero, though, is much harder to do and for him to accept. Ultimately, Neo believes. The key scene in the first movie is when Neo realizes that he truly is what he has been prophesied to be. This is the turning point of the movie.

## Where We Are Today

In a similar way today, the American church is in its own matrix. The church operates in a realm of unreality and fantasy that is very similar to the movie. Operating in an artificial world of services, meetings, and functions, the church by and large looks foreign to how the Bible describes the church. The problem is, no one seems to want to "pull the plug"—everyone seems content to stay in the matrix.

Is it possible that the American church's fascination with "getting results" has produced a harvest of millions of converts who aren't really converted? The Bible is clear what true conversion looks like. (See Acts 2:37-39.) In our nation, there is *little* discernable difference between those declaring themselves to be Christians and those who are not.[1]

Has this "Churchianity" spawned followers, a whole different breed of believers who really don't believe? In our desire to preach God's acceptance, have we been preaching a gospel requiring no criteria for Kingdom entrance but "try Jesus"? Do we want results so badly that we are willing to sell a product that isn't real? No one doubts that Americans have some of the world's best salespeople, but what has the majority of the American church ended up selling?

Now let me assure you, I'm not talking about the legitimate reality and power that comes when the authentic gospel of the Kingdom is preached. I am referring to a brand of Christianity and lifestyle being peddled that is not a true apostolic community of faith, but instead a corporate system dispensing bite-size doses of spiritual relief, creating dependent believers who stay perpetually needy and immature. This brand creates a system that discourages the believer from personally being involved in ministry. Instead, believers are thrown into an endless treadmill of activities, programs, and rehashed ideas that have long ago lost their effectiveness. The emphasis: "Come to our activities and stay busy. Oh yeah, and take *some* responsibility but not too much."

## The Gospel of Churchianity

We now have millions of so-called "believers" who don't believe the gospel of the Kingdom because many of them have never really heard it. Instead, they hear a gospel spawned in one of the many results-oriented, seeker-friendly churches that created this "harvest." These millions of converts have lifestyles that reveal little or no commitment to the gospel of the Kingdom and reflect little desire to grow and mature beyond their minimal commitment to "Churchianity."

This "other brand" of Jesus is identified by these earmarks:

—It is based on bringing the gospel to "seekers" in an inoffensive and understandable way so everything is focused on those who visit and are seeking;

—The message is brought in "bite-sized bits of Jesus" so it doesn't shock or overwhelm the seeker;

—Since the motive is to get people who are seeking to "find," there is an overemphasis on evangelism and it primarily focuses on ministering to the uninitiated and immature;

—The short messages are hip and to the point with drama and the arts used to communicate a story or message. Presentations are aimed at seekers or baby Christians. (I personally feel the use of these many creative ways of presenting the gospel is a positive aspect.)

All of this emphasis on the seeker instead of *God* leaves the seekers with this mind-set:

—Because Christ was shown to me in such a convenient form, Christ is apparently most concerned with my convenience and meeting my needs.

—Because I came to Christ as I am and I've heard that the gospel is free (which it is) I therefore need to do nothing to be included or involved in the Church. Because the gospel costs me nothing, His Kingdom apparently requires nothing of me.

—Since God has been served up to me in a way I can "handle," my God will therefore never force me to think outside of my comfort zone or box.

—Since the only Kingdom I will see is after I die, my life here is mainly taken up with waiting for the end, living the best I can, and asking God to bless me.

—Since all this church stuff is so palatable, easy, and understandable to me, I need little or no supernatural revelation to comprehend God.

—The church exists for *me*.

The following are the obvious problems with this type of defective gospel:

—While Jesus loves us all and is not one to show favoritism, He is little concerned with catering to our convenience or insuring we are comfortable with our arrangement. The Lord requires us first to believe—not fully understand or even feel comfortable with it. Without faith it is impossible to please Him. God's ways are inscrutable and beyond understanding.

—We must actually believe in the supernatural, mysterious aspects of the gospel and relationship with Christ; otherwise the gospel is just a moral lifestyle.

—The gospel is free but it cost God His Son and will cost you all of your natural life in exchange for His. Receiving Christ is not like trying a new flavor of the month or turning over a new leaf. Instead, it is a serious life-altering covenant. It is injurious to promise these seekers that they can just "try Jesus." We don't try Him on for size. We have to learn to die for Him.

—The Kingdom of God is here now, not just in the sweet bye and bye. While many churches won't mention the Kingdom because it requires a much greater accountability, we must tell new Christians about their King and His Kingdom, whether it is comfortable or not.

—A hungering, seeking, knocking heart desirous to find God will find Him. God is looking for diligent seekers, not casual inquirers. Unless the Lord reveals Himself, going to a cool Bible study won't necessarily make any difference.

## Seeker-Friendly or God-Friendly?

The emphasis on seeker-friendly churches was initially born out of a legitimate desire to be relevant to unbelievers. But in the desire to try anything that works and operating in a vacuum of true apostolic leadership, churches in the United States haven't used discernment and have swallowed this emphasis almost as apostolic doctrine. More and more seeker-friendly churches are popping up. Their "lite" worship services are happy sing-a-longs, and their "lite" messages have "dumbed down" the army of God, creating an army of spiritually retarded babies. The majority of these lite believers don't yet believe, but are still seeking. Is this overemphasis on seeker-friendly churches and growth at any cost making the spiritual depth of the church a mile wide, but an inch deep?

Evangelistic strategies and methods like these, while often very creative and attractive, will not produce apostolic churches of mature believers. We have had over 20 years now to see the fruit of this strategy, and it isn't good. They reproduce after their own kind. While there have been many churches and followers of this ideology over the past 20 years, most research suggests that the number of legitimate new converts has decreased and the impact on our society has been unnoticeable or negligible.[2]

Instead of simply doing church another way or creating a new church system, we must first allow reformation to come to each person from the inside out. This will only occur when we begin preaching an authentic Kingdom message like those Jesus and Paul preached that started either revivals or riots.

In addition, we must start using God's Kingdom method, which is discipleship. Jesus taught this way, and it works much better than using seeker-friendly methods. Training and releasing believers is God's method and is the only way the Body will come into their calling and fulfill His purpose for them. God's ways and methods must be used rather than man's clever ideas or marketing gimmicks.

Currently, the Church is in a preliminary phase of a major overhaul orchestrated by the Spirit. This revolution will birth new, more biblical definitions of *church* and *ministry*, and it will radically alter the Church, making her fruitful again. These changes are not unlike the social and economic changes witnessed during the last 20 years as we entered the Information Age. Communication methods, programs, and strategies that were previously effective and innovative are now unable to reach a new harvest. However, just buying a digital projector to replace a transparency machine won't suffice.

What is needed now more than anything is the discovery and complete recovery of the authentic gospel message, uncontaminated with any cessationist bias. When this occurs, it will spawn a fresh biblical view of ministry, the Church, and everything else. An uncontaminated message will lead to all the other great stuff God reveals in His Book!

Remember, *the Body* is supposed to be doing the ministry, not simply a few television evangelists, church leaders, or best-selling authors. Billy Graham, one of Christianity's most beloved leadership models of integrity, said in an interview with Larry King—referring to his autobiography—that if he could do it all again, he'd spend more time with his family and disciple a small group of disciples instead of conducting only large crusades.

George Barna, a pollster who monitors Christian trends, commented about the failure of the church to affect Americans who, after the 9-11 attacks, were looking for spiritual reality. He said:

> After the attack, millions of nominally churched or generally irreligious Americans were desperately seeking something that would restore stability and a sense of meaning to life. Fortunately, many of them turned to the church. Unfortunately, few of them experienced anything that was sufficiently life-changing to capture their attention and their allegiance.
>
> They tended to appreciate the moments of comfort they received, but were unaware of anything sufficiently unique or beneficial as to redesign their lifestyle to integrate a deeper level of spiritual involvement. Our assessment is that churches succeeded at putting on a friendly face but failed at motivating the vast majority of spiritual explorers to connect with Christ in a more intimate or intense manner.

The September 11 tragedy was another amazing opportunity to be the healing and transforming presence of God in people's lives, but that, too, has now come and gone, with little to show for it.[3]

These findings indicate that if we don't seize this moment, we will cease to be effective in this new era. The words of President George W. Bush are prophetic: "This is a new war." Our methods and tactics must change for us to be effective. We must break out of the slumber of our matrix and see!

## They Will Know Us by Our Love

As a result of Christianity's continuing influence in American culture, Christians have become almost obsessed with having someone, anyone attend their largely powerless services each Sunday. With an almost manic desire and attention to be perceived as relevant, loving, and unreligious, many churches have resorted to becoming detached from anything perceived as "churchy" or in any way "fanatical."

While few are aware that this notion is simply the natural consequence of 20 years of preaching a watered-down gospel with an emphasis on drawing an audience rather than glorifying God, the decline of Christian influence in America is profound. While I am not a prophet of doom, I *am* an enlightened thinker who recognizes the bad fruit of pursuing "seekers" and building seeker-friendly churches rather than pursuing the Lord, His gospel, and His Kingdom. In the desire to attract everyone, we have lessened the gospel's power to eternally change people's lives.

While there are highly influential people in leadership in Western Christianity today, few have much Holy Ghost power or even the anointing. And while they may generate untold numbers of followers, they have created their *own* following. It's all about *their* kingdom, not the Lord's Kingdom. Jesus said, *"My kingdom is not of this world..."* (John 18:36).

While not maligning the motives of the majority of these men of God, most of the influential ones are simply stoking the present unworkable system and attracting a following that has a little influence on the ever-shrinking church, and little or no impact on society as a whole. This is due to the fact that many leaders, in a desire to be accepted, have exchanged a desire to achieve acceptability for the anointing. Without the anointing, these large gatherings of "seekers" rarely find, hardly knock, and never ask. Entertained but not freed, they continue to exist in their spiritual Matrix, thinking they are something they are not.

While traditional denominations are shrinking and dying, the remainder of Christianity, with a few bright spots, is in great danger of becoming nothing more than a nuisance to the advance of evil. Also, because the church largely has been unable to attract the young, it is in danger of becoming filled with retirement-age people looking back only to the "good ol' days." Because many baby-boom parents stopped attending church after it fell short of their Woodstock-influenced, Utopian ideal of "peace and love," their kids know about church but are looking for something better. Sadly, many baby boomers have become so cynical that they have not only not passed on a bitter baton of their faith to their kids, but some have actually become stumbling blocks to their children ever finding God! These kids are found sitting on Christianity's sidelines. Even though many of them have a solid Christian history, their parent's attitudes have left them wanting.

We have been told that love is all the world needs for it to believe. *Wrong*. While the Beatles may have sold a million records touting that virtuous-sounding philosophy, it is not founded on the teachings of Jesus, but on the thoughts of John Lennon. Jesus said that the world would see the love of the church.

> By this all will **know** that you are My disciples, if you have love for one another (John 13:35).

> Jesus answered and said to them, "Are you not therefore mistaken, because you do not know the Scriptures or the power of God?" (Mark 12:24).

Here are a few Greek word definitions for the word *know* taken from Strong's Dictionary:

KNOW-1492-eido – from G3708; to gaze (i.e. with wide-open eyes, as at something remarkable; and thus differing from G991, which denotes simply voluntary observation; and from G1492, which expresses merely mechanical, passive or casual vision; while G2300, and still more emphatically its intens. G2334, signifies an earnest but more continued inspection; and G4648 a watching from a distance):—appear, look, see, shew self.

708. horao, hor-ah'-o; prop. To stare at [comp. G3700], i.e. (by impl.) to discern clearly (phys. Or ment); by extens. To attend to; by Hebr. To experience; pass. To appear:—behold, perceive, see, take heed.

Knowing is *not* a passing glance, *not* voluntary observation, *not* mechanical, *not* passive or casual vision.

This same Greek word is used in First Peter 1:8-9 (NKJV): *"whom having not seen, you love; Though now you do not see Him, yet believing, you rejoice with joy inexpressible and full of glory, receiving the end of your faith; the salvation of your souls."*

James 4:4 (NKJV): *"Adulterers and adulteresses! Do you not know that friendship with the world is enmity with God? Whoever therefore wants to be a friend of the world makes himself an enemy of God."*

**Endnotes**

1. George Barna, The Year's Most Intriguing Findings, From Barna Research Studies, 12-17-01, The Barna Group, www.barna.org.

2. Ibid.

3. Ibid.

# CHAPTER 4

# DELUSIONAL CHRISTIANITY

## Our Delightful Delusion

I have already mentioned that the research findings about American Christianity are quite grim. They show that in spite of the proliferation of several mega-churches (in Atlanta alone there are 100), the number of new church buildings, and the proliferation of church programs, our American culture is more influenced by Coke, Mickey Mouse, MTV, Bill Gates, Paul Allen, al Qaeda, and a dozen or more other people or things.

In the last ten years, billions of dollars have been spent by American churches and ministries to preach and communicate the gospel. However, fewer people are now attending church than ten years ago.[1] In addition, the immaturity of those who do attend is quite startling.

Mainstream media newscasters are quick to expose the shortcomings of the church. News about sexual abuse and homosexuality among priests and nuns are shaking the oldest denomination—Catholicism. The high-profile exposure of the head of the National Association of Evangelicals was played out internationally on television; his drug use and homosexual relations serve to illustrate the weak condition of the church. While no truly forgiven Christian can "cast stones" at this sad situation, isn't it obvious we should attempt to do better?

Locally, in my city just a few years ago, nightly media reports chronicled the bitter divorce of a prominent author and pastor of one the city's oldest churches. His son, who had been working with him for years, publicly rejected his father's position and started his own church, now one of the city's most influential. A pastor in another large church in my city was sued for over 25 years of sexual abuse of dozens of women, even offering staff members as sexual objects to guest speakers!

No denomination is immune to this wave of moral and ethical weakness that permeates church leadership at many levels. These and other examples reveal that we are all fallible and make mistakes. That should not take us unaware. However, someday soon the Church must start exercising apostolic church discipline, and in a redemptive way righteously judge and scripturally deal with these messy issues and avoid having them played out on the television news night after night. Instead of allowing the world to expose and deal with our problems, we should address them with apostolic courage, scriptural authority, and biblical integrity.

The Church continues to endorse leaders who reject God's chastening which reveals a profound lack of spiritual discernment in the Body of Christ. It is another example of how giftedness and prestige is more esteemed in our Christian culture rather than character. Christians are now more likely to commit adultery and get divorced than non-Christians and just as likely to steal and cheat as non-Christians. All of these signs point to something foundationally flawed in the way the church is "doing business." We are definitely, delightfully deluded.

### Churchianity Versus Kingdom Christianity

While it's good to join the booming neighborhood church, attend Easter services, go on a marriage weekend, participate in marches, or work at your local Christian School, how effective are these activities in transforming our culture? While all these have a valid purpose and seem good, increasing evidence indicates the majority are ineffective in making a major difference. The church, with all its programs and activities has created an alternate society that is completely unattractive to the lost. It is nearly impotent in providing life for those who are perishing.

Very few care what the church has to say about important matters. Our present church structures are more "American" than Kingdom, based more on skillful business and marketing expertise than supernatural intervention. We have created our own cult of Churchianity (apologies to John G. Lake who first coined this phrase) that does not resemble the Kingdom of God. Our American Churchianity is probably the biggest obstacle to experiencing real Kingdom Christianity.

Part of the reason for this is that for some time now the church has become spiritually dull and proud, and we've succumbed to a state of denial and delusion about our effectiveness and fruitfulness.

The word *delusion* means "to hold to a false belief; a deception that has been disseminated in spite of invalidating evidence."

To be *delusional* means "to hold to that false belief no matter what evidence is brought to the contrary."

> *...They perish because they refused to love the truth and so be saved. For this reason God sends them a powerful delusion so that they will believe the lie and so that all will be condemned who have not believed the truth but have delighted in wickedness*
> (2 Thessalonians 2:11-12 NIV).

The Kingdom of God is expanding worldwide and entrance is not exclusively reserved for church attendees in the United States, but includes believers from all nations who believe in Jesus and accept His Kingdom Lordship. There is a stubborn rebellion in America against accepting this truth. Just a few years ago, several best-selling evangelical American books took issue with the concept of "Lordship Salvation" and "Kingdom Now.". While there are valid points of contention with any teaching emphasis, there still can be no legitimate biblical reason to reject the concepts of the Kingdom of God and Christ's supreme lordship in a believer's life.

While America has heard the truth that "Jesus saves," not all Americans have yet heard that "Jesus reigns"! It's much more pleasant to preach a gospel that an omnipotent being wants to save and bless and protect you, than to be honest and preach that this same God is also your King who is to be totally obeyed and owns everything you have including your time, gifts, and money! This gospel is rarely preached in American churches because it might require radical changes in the way we "do church."

Any honest American Christian should be humbled by an honest look at the church's absolute failure to change our culture or reflect the Kingdom. Currently, the vast majority of the church is preaching a message that lacks God's power and ability to change lives. I believe this is due to the fact that a large segment of the church believes in cessationism, a belief that rejects the truth that God can and still does work through spiritual gifts like tongues, healings, and miracles.

Cessationism continues to be taught in prominent evangelical seminaries that train a significant segment of Protestant ministers in America. Is it possible that our missionary influence around the world will begin to wane because countries will reject a cessationist view?

I have a friend who is one of the key spiritual leaders in South Africa. He commented to me recently how the South African Bible school students were being negatively influenced by the American gimmicks and programs. He said that these students, who were once on fire for the Lord and spent much of their time seeking the Lord in prayer and fasting, stopped after being exposed to American leaders who taught them gimmicks and programs about church growth. Because so many adopted these American methods that don't necessarily work in their culture, they became ineffective in South Africa.

Sometimes programs and activities that appear to work, don't work long term. Jack Taylor made this statement in a conference I attended in Atlanta, *"Whatever is truly of God will ultimately succeed, even though it may look like it has failed. And whatever is not of God will ultimately fail even though it may look as if it is successful on the surface."* I agree. The church's rejection of biblical methods and standards with the resulting fruit has been abandoned in favor of methods that bring supposed church growth and "success." Paul was a successful apostle by God's standards, but by American-church standards, he would be deemed an immense failure.

## Left Behind

According to the Christian media, over 25 million copies of Tim LaHaye's *Left Behind* series have sold in bookstores—both Christian and secular. These fictionalized stories tell about what might happen after the Rapture occurs. While they tell a popular version of end-time events and might be a successful evangelistic tool, I don't believe the Church's greatest victory will simply be to survive until Jesus returns to rescue Her.

*"That He might present to Himself the church in all her glory, having no spot or wrinkle or any such thing; but that she should be holy and blameless"* (Ephesians 5:27).

This passage says Jesus is coming back to present to Himself a spotless, glorious bride, not a cowering band of wimps awaiting rescue!

The immense popularity of these books reveals a longing in the church to "get it all over with." While this view may be popular, it isn't entirely biblical. While this version of the end is popular and even appetizing to many believers, it lacks completeness because the end-time church the Bible describes isn't trying to "get it over with,"—it is beginning to *"take over"*! The last-day displaying and unveiling of God's glory in earthen vessels is described in Song of Songs as being "as awesome as an army with banners." This victorious end-time company of believers will raise the dead, heal the sick, and proclaim a gospel with apostolic authority, unintimidated by the devil or the antichrist!

So much of popular American teaching on the end-times is more concerned with looking for the antichrist than the glory of Christ spoken of as coming forth like the sun! This fatalism and hopelessness is the basis for much of the American churches' end-time teaching. The end of all things is more about the light of God coming to the earth than the devil. After all, Jesus said that *we* would do even greater works than He did!

*Truly, truly, I say to you, he who believes in Me, the works that I do will he do also; and greater works than these will he do; because I go to the Father* (John 14:12).

Since so much of America is all about what's popular now, we must be willing to let go of those things that don't work and deploy the right message, methods, and the ways that Jesus used. The church's infatuation with deploying faddish trends leaves the saints immature and exhausted. We must let go of these ideas and we must relinquish beliefs born of an unbelieving person's experience and reactions. We must embrace the truth of God's Word over our experiences or our biases.

## The Old Group

Every church or ministry over two or three years old has an "old group," those people who love the Lord and have sincere motives, but feel like they must have their say in case anything gets too far out of hand. These saints love the thing they call church, but are unwilling to admit how they must change—or that change is even necessary.

I talk to many pastors and folks who attend traditional denominational, or even charismatic, churches. While they always acknowledge how their pastor really "preaches the truth" and "wants God," they seem to always mention the "old group" who really runs the church. When the pastor starts to preach about miracles or healing, they rise up and straighten him out. And if he goes too far outside their belief box, they stage a walkout while making sure they inform everyone why they had to leave.

Unfortunately, our current church system fosters this behavior because instead of challenging folks, discipling them, and encouraging them to mature, they instead are kept busy and happy doing anything *except* ministry. That way they stay immature and struggle with anything new. A spiritual person is given to constant change, but a natural person is content with keeping "things the way they are."

We make a grave error when we think that those who don't like change or new things are simply being cautious or more conservative. *Just maybe, they are filled with fear and unbelief!* As Christians, we must love change and be willing to keep changing! The Bible tells us a natural man doesn't even understand the "things of the Spirit." It also says that God is a God of new beginnings, and that requires change.

In more ways than one, we have been "left behind" in the things of the Kingdom. Apostolic Christianity born of a Kingdom message and a biblically accurate gospel is erupting in Africa, South America, Asia, and even Russia, but is slow to be received in the American religious system, and occasionally it takes the outside eyes of others to help us see our spiritual deficiencies.

In the 1990s, thousands of missionaries from other nations flocked to America to help prepare us for a spiritual awakening. These missionaries to America came here to preach the gospel of the Kingdom, declaring God's reign and describing His ways and means. While the gospel preaches salvation in Jesus, it also calls us to a higher level of commitment and allegiance to the Lord Jesus.

## The King and the Kingdom

*The Law and the Prophets were proclaimed until John; since that time the gospel of the kingdom of God has been preached, and everyone is forcing his way into it* (Luke 16:16).

*From the days of John the Baptist until now the kingdom of heaven suffers violence, and violent men take it by force* **(Matthew 11:12).**

While certainly the gospel has been preached here, it has been incomplete, and certain aspects that involve a Christian's citizenship in the Kingdom have not been taught. Most preaching is directed at getting people to respond and "be saved," "come to the altar," or "join the church." While these are important aspects, they were just another part of the lifestyle of the church in the Acts era. The gospel is *not only* an invitation, but also a declaration of a Kingdom that is here *today*, not coming "someday" or "in the sweet bye and bye."

Most American preaching and teaching is focused on the church rather than the Kingdom. While the word *church* is found 76 times in the New Testament, the *Kingdom of God* is mentioned 160 times! The Kingdom is the rule and reign of God and not a meeting, program, or activity. It is also not a topic to be taught occasionally. Because of this, many Christians have little real understanding of an alternate way of living or a higher realm of being.

The Church, on the other hand, is the Body of Christ, the group of people who are called out of darkness into His light to demonstrate and declare the light and glory that proceeds out of the activity of His Kingdom. While the local church and ministries can be built, the Kingdom cannot. It can only be recognized, unlocked, and acknowledged. Jesus is Lord whether anyone acknowledges it or not. (See Philippians 2:10-11.) The Bible teaches that earth is filled with the knowledge of the glory of God. Right now it may not be fully acknowledged, but someday soon it will be! Just because people do not see or acknowledge something about God, doesn't make Him or it any less real.

*For the earth will be filled with the knowledge of the glory of the LORD, as the waters cover the sea* (Habakkuk 2:14).

## Fraidy Hole

In parts of Oklahoma and Kansas where tornadoes occur regularly, many rural homeowners dig and build a below-ground shelter that provides safety from a twister. Some call this their "fraidy hole," a place where they can run and hide when twisters come.

In an honest attempt to keep the people of God away from other influences, the American (and much of the Western) church has attempted to create a fraidy hole. It's another society where Christian music, Christian television, Christian writing and art is segregated from the world. While the motive for creating this alternative is a desire to be holy, the church is no longer having a positive effect on the world. Salt can't flavor something hidden in the cupboard, and light doesn't remove darkness from well-lit areas.

Instead of being the salt of the earth and light of the world, the church has become a sub-standard sect of ineffective, immature Christians unaccustomed to persecution and unable to overcome adversity. The church has ended up segregating itself away from the world it has been called to save, convert, and deliver because of the fear of becoming contaminated by it. This "fraidy hole" mentality is pervasive throughout the church.

## False Understanding of Holiness

One of the prime reasons for the Church's retreat from the world is a false and unbiblical view of holiness based on a few passages of Scripture that have been misunderstood:

> *I wrote you in my letter not to associate with immoral people; I did not at all mean with the immoral people of this world, or with the covetous and swindlers, or*

*with idolaters; for then you would have to go out of the world. But actually, I wrote to you not to associate with any so-called brother if he should be an immoral person, or covetous, or an idolater, or a reviler, or a drunkard, or a swindler— not even to eat with such a one. For what have I to do with judging outsiders? Do you not judge those who are within the church? But those who are outside, God judges. Remove the wicked man from among yourselves.* (1 Corinthians 5:9-13).

*Do not be bound together with unbelievers; for what partnership has righteousness and lawlessness, or what fellowship has light with darkness?*
(2 Corinthians 6:14)

While these passages talk about a separation between the Christian and the unbeliever, they are more clearly admonishing believers to use discernment and judgment in the church, to police themselves. In addition they spell out the peril of mixture and the need to keep things clear and unbiased by compromise or wishy-washiness. The first reason the church has lost the capacity to judge itself is because there's such a profound lack of moral authority in leadership. How can we understand true righteous judgment if we don't comprehend the fact that God called the church to judge *itself* and keep itself pure first?

*Therefore, having these promises, beloved, let us cleanse* **ourselves** *from all defilement of flesh and spirit, perfecting holiness in the fear of God*
(2 Corinthians 7:1).

The second reason the church has lost its capacity to judge itself is a fear of making moral judgments based on the present atmosphere of "tolerance" and political correctness in the world. There is a pervading atmosphere in our society that no one has the right to have an opinion about anything. The question, "Who am I to say that is wrong?" rings through our minds. If we hold something up to the standard of the truth of the Word of God we think we are being judgmental or a hypocrite. Peter describes this moral ambiguity as "falling from your own steadfastness."

> *You therefore, beloved, knowing this beforehand, be on your guard so that you are not carried away by the error of unprincipled men and fall from your own steadfastness, but grow in the grace and knowledge of our Lord and Savior Jesus Christ...*
> (2 Peter 3:17-18)

Many Christian leaders abstain from dealing with these unpleasant things by quoting Matthew chapter 7, when Jesus commanded us to "judge not." This can easily become a cop-out to excuse our non-involvement. Also, many are afraid of being persecuted or scrutinized so they don't challenge people or issues, even when they know it is wrong. This passage is about making spiritual calls, not rash judgments based on our own opinions and preferences, or operating in the flesh based on outward appearances.

> *Do not judge according to appearance, but judge with righteous judgment* (John 7:24).
>
> *...for God sees not as man sees, for man looks at the outward appearance, but the Lord looks at the heart*
> (1 Samuel 16:7).

While we are warned not to judge outwardly, we still have a clear responsibility to take an uncompromising stand for the very clear biblical standards concerning integrity, marriage, homosexuality, and purity. Someone must stand up and call these things by the light of clear biblical standards instead of looking the other way. While denominations can separate Christians based on an interpretation of one or two Scripture passages, these things are exceedingly clear. We must call light; *light* and darkness; *darkness*. The first area we must judge is ourselves and the church.

> *Woe to those who call evil good, and good evil; Who substitute darkness for light and light for darkness; Who substitute bitter for sweet, and sweet for bitter!* (Isaiah 5:20)

One of the great end-time battles will require us to stand up for the Truth against a great end-time wave of lawlessness.

**Endnote**
1. George Barna, 5/4/2004 poll, The Barna Group, www.barna.org.

# CHAPTER 5

# LAST DAYS' LAWLESSNESS

It was Sunday, July 4th, Independence Day! We had a powerful, Holy Spirit-energized, morning church service, and many in our congregation brought papers with the names of people who needed prayer for salvation, deliverance, and healing. It was a wonderful time of crying out to God for the lost, the sick, and those in bondage; and so good for all of us to focus our attention on others who needed Jesus. Much power was present and many miracles happened due to the intercession we brought that day.

But on the way home, I was sick at heart. Something was wrong. In my spirit I felt it, knew it, and even tasted it.

Six months before that day, we had experienced some of our most challenging times in our years of ministry. We watched as trusted colleagues and people we'd known for years became hardened, cold, and disinterested in the things of God. It seemed as if the more we upheld the standard of righteousness and integrity found in the Word of God, the more we became targets of attack. At times I wondered how Moses felt as he presided over the trial of Korah. I wondered if I was experiencing what the apostles might have felt as they observed the hearts of Ananias and Sapphira being exposed, leading to their judgment and death.

We knew something seriously wrong was going on beneath the surface. We watched people, who at one time appeared to be spiritually strong and stable, buckle to the prevailing atmosphere and become spiritual children. People with great potential, who were given unparalleled freedom to use their gifts, were now reacting to the idea that they had to be accountable for them. Instead of desiring input and wanting to grow, people abandoned their callings amid complaining, grumbling, slander, and backbiting. Many were convinced I or someone else was their problem, and they had plenty to say about it. Disappointing was not the word for what happened—we were watching a meltdown of our future.

That afternoon I went into my office and stretched out on the carpet in front of my desk. I cried out to God, "What's going on, God? What is this I'm seeing? Why are these people who looked so good falling away?" Then I cried, my heart crushed, thinking of each of them and how they were deceived. I was sobbing uncontrollably when suddenly, instead of being on the floor of my office, I was in the throne room of God. My office carpet became clear gold and what was my desk an instant before became the throne of the Holy One. I didn't look up but I saw His feet of bronze! I was wailing in intercession at His feet, perplexed by the questions I'd been asking Him all afternoon, "What is this, God?" I continued pleading with Him for an answer when suddenly I heard His booming voice welling up in my spirit. I heard the audible voice of God say, "lawlessness."

In an instant, I saw a panoramic view about how lawlessness had already effected me, come into our church and people, and also how insidious and pervasive it was. I also saw how it pervaded the landscape of the American church. I was shocked when the Lord revealed to me how to expose it.

He showed me that a "falling away" of the people we cared about would take place, and it would require every bit of strength we had to handle the shaking that was ahead. Then, just as quickly as the revelation came, it was over and I was back in my office again on the floor crying, tears running down my face. After this experience, I was determined to find out more about this lawlessness and how it had to be dealt with. It was clear to me that lawlessness was one of the key enemies hindering the Kingdom of God.

The following are a few things the Lord showed me while I was before Him that afternoon.

> *Let no one in any way deceive you, for it will not come unless the apostasy [falling away] comes first, and the man of lawlessness is revealed, the son of destruction, who opposes and exalts himself above every so-called god or object of worship, so that he takes his seat in the temple of God, displaying himself as being God. ...For the mystery of lawlessness is already at work; only he who now restrains will do so until he is taken out of the way. And then that lawless one will be revealed whom the Lord will slay with the breath of His mouth and bring to an end by the appearance of His coming; that is, the one whose coming is in accord with the activity of satan, with all power and signs and false wonders, and with all the deception of wickedness for those who perish, because they did not receive the love of the truth so as to be saved* (2 Thessalonians 2:3-4;7-10).

## What Is Lawlessness?

The Greek word used in this passage is *anomia*, which means "lawless deed." Lawlessness is also spoken of in Hebrews 1:9: *"You have loved righteousness and hated lawlessness; Therefore God, your God, has anointed you with the oil of gladness above your companions."*

The Bible teaches lawlessness is:

—A spirit that embodies all that is not righteous; it is unholy and the place where evil is allowed to breed; a demonic atmosphere that pervades the earth; (see 2 Tim. 3:1-5) the last days will be permeated by a climate of lawlessness. The world system, or *Kosmos*, (see 1 John 2:16) is caught up in this spirit. This is similar to that described in Judges 17:6, when *"every man did what was right in his own eyes."*

—An attitude of disobedience. *"for the weapons of our warfare are not of the flesh, but divinely powerful for the destruction of fortresses. We are destroying speculations and every lofty thing raised up against the knowledge of God, and we are taking every thought captive to the obedience of Christ and we are ready to punish all disobedience, whenever your obedience is complete"* (2 Cor. 10:4-6). And, *"Let no one deceive you with empty words, for because of these things the wrath of God comes upon the sons of disobedience"* (Eph. 5:6).

—The essence of the antichrist spirit which is self-will— "I will." *"How you have fallen from heaven, O star of the morning, son of the dawn! You have been cut down to the earth, you who have weakened the nations! But you said in your heart, 'I will ascend to heaven; I will raise my throne above the stars of God and I will sit on the mount of assembly in the recesses of the north. I will ascend above the heights of the clouds; I will make myself like the Most High'"* (Isa. 14:12-14).

— Lawlessness is the opposite of righteousness and a religious counterfeit. It is the antithesis of love and intimacy for the Lord, substituting activity for intimacy, religious duty for devotion, fanatical zeal for passionate fervor for Him. It substitutes a religious act for honest relationship. Saul and David are good examples. The Lord said David was a man who was after

His own heart. King Saul, when he saw that the Word of the Lord thru Samuel was being delayed in coming, that the Philistine armies were massing, and the people scattering, committed a lawless deed of religious duty bringing the sacrifice reserved only for the priest. (See 1 Samuel 15:22-24.) He lost his place as king because of the Lord's anger.

—Lawlessness is not anarchy as we might think or necessarily the lack of rules or government, but lawlessness is described in Scripture as sin, breaking God's ways; violating God's ways, and missing the mark of God's standard. It is better described as iniquity or self-will; governing our lives apart from God, His Word, His ways, and His Spirit. Doing sacrificial religious acts outwardly, yet rebelling inwardly against the heart intent of God's will. It is living out of one's own rules, laws, and ways: doing what seems right in one's own eyes. (See Judges 17:6.) It resists true intimacy and knowledge of God. *"I never knew you"* (see Matt. 24: 12).

## A Manifestation

These last days of lawlessness are the seedbed for the manifestation of the antichrist spirit that ultimately will be revealed in the form of a person, the antichrist or son of lawlessness as the Bible calls him. Just as Jesus Christ is the Son of righteousness, the antichrist is the son of lawlessness.

> *Dear children, this is the last hour; and as you have heard that the antichrist is coming, even now many antichrists have come. This is how we know it is the last hour* (1 John 2:18 NIV).

Fanatical, religious devotion to sacrificial causes born out of self-will is a clear earmark of this spirit. We've all seen news reports about how Osama bin Laden, Al-Zarquawi, and other terrorists in their dark network allow the lawlessness spirit to operate through them to steal, kill, and destroy without serving any logical purpose other than to satisfy their religious zeal. This spirit will stop at nothing, including suicide. It destroys rather than builds, curses rather than blesses.

Revelations 9:11 speaks of this destroying spirit: *"They had as king over them the angel of the Abyss, whose name in Hebrew is Abaddon, and in Greek, Apollyon."* Both *Abaddon* and *Apollyon* mean "a destroyer or destroying angel." Destroying things and destruction makes little sense to a rational person, but the spirit of lawlessness inflames the zeal and fanaticism of religious people, turning them from excited zealots to fanatical martyrs for a cause born out of a judgmental, religious mind-set. Fanatical zeal reasons, "It is better to tear things down that I can't control."

*The thief comes only to steal, and kill, and destroy...*
(John 10:10).

## Spiritual Terrorism

Just as our nation was taken by surprise on 9-11-2001 by those who were living in our neighborhoods, shopping in our stores, and eating in our restaurants, our churches may also be taken by surprise by that same fanatical, terrorist spirit. The spirit of lawlessness is alive and well, and operating in many churches. Lawlessness and religious zeal creates fertile soil for growing "spiritual terrorists." They are rebellious, defiant, and completely committed to their cause and goal. If a church or ministry doesn't conform to their zealous view, they will stop at nothing to prove their point.

## Identifying Lawlessness

Lawlessness is a practice involving action, a pre-intentioned act of self-will. Not just presumptuous acts, but a deliberate activity that may appear godly, yet emanates primarily out of selfishness.

> *"Many will say to Me on that day, 'Lord, Lord, did we not prophesy in Your name, and in Your name cast out demons, and in Your name perform many miracles?' And then I will declare to them, 'I never knew you; depart from me, you who practice lawlessness.'"* (Matthew 7:22-23).

> *The Son of Man will send forth His angels, and they will gather out of His kingdom all stumbling blocks, and those who commit lawlessness* (Matthew 13:41).

It is worked and must be energized by self-will. The delusion that works this kind of deception is so pervasive that normal definitions don't apply. Black is white, up is down, and evil is anything opposing its ideology. Agape love is absent. It is essentially religious and zealous, invoking this behavior as righteousness. Because love is sincere and involves an honest giving of oneself without pretense, true love and lawlessness can't coexist. Jesus said in His description that there appears to be much outward appearance of righteousness, while the inside is full of hypocrisy and lawlessness.

> *So you, too, outwardly appear righteous to men, but inwardly you are full of hypocrisy and lawlessness* (Matthew 23:28).

> *And because lawlessness is increased, the love of many will grow cold* (Matthew 24:12).

> *"Let love be without hypocrisy…* (Romans 12:9).

It is a mystery the way it appears, because in the case with lucifer himself, his lawlessness manifested after countless eons of time, in the most beautiful of all beings who spent all his time ministering to the Lord as the "covering cherub." If this kind of lawlessness can be revealed in him, should we then be shocked when we see it among God's people? No, we shouldn't. While outwardly things might appear right and good in those under the delusion of it, there is inwardly another agenda that violates God's true desires and purpose.

> *...For just as you presented your members as slaves to impurity and to lawlessness, resulting in further lawlessness, so now present your members as slaves to righteousness, resulting in sanctification*
> (Romans 6:19).

It truly is mysterious how outwardly there can be individuals who are pursuing moral and religious purity, but all the while there is an unbroken religious will within them. Isn't this the same fruit we see in the radical Islamic terrorists as well?

## Earmarks of the Lawless Spirit

While we know these end-time strongholds are of a spiritual nature and that we do not battle against flesh and blood, it is important to recognize the manifestations. The following are the earmarks:

—Superspiritual. Patronizing and display a condescending attitude, especially to those in positions of legitimate spiritual authority. Detached and aloof, acting as if they have the "last word" with God. *"He who separates himself seeks his own desire, he quarrels against all sound wisdom"* (Proverbs 18:1).

Like terrorists, they are willing to destroy everything that has been built by another rather than fail to get their own way. They would rather destroy than press into any kind of relationship. *"…for what partnership have righteousness and lawlessness…"* (2 Cor. 6:14). This is the same spirit that causes divorces, divides churches, and destroys relationships—Judas is a good example of self-pity leading to death.

—Sacrificial. This is a perversion of the concept of true sacrifice, like the sacrifice God the Father made through His Son for the purpose of redemption. This is a sharp contrast to the actions of the king of Moab in Second Kings. *"When the king of Moab saw that the battle was too fierce for him, he took with him 700 men who drew swords, to break through to the king of Edom; but they could not. Then he took his oldest son who was to reign in his place, and offered him as a burnt offering on the wall. And there came great wrath against Israel, and they departed from him and returned to their own land"* (2 Kings 3:26-27). The king of Moab was willing to sacrifice everything, even his son, to get revenge and prevent being defeated by Israel. Insincerely acts like a martyr.

—Judgmental and Critical. This spirit can be brought into the church by outsiders who come to spy out the liberty of others. (See Jude 1:11-22.) Paul called them "false brethren" (see Gal. 2:4). These have a mind-set that judges everything out of their personal subjectivity and experience. This can be a danger for legitimate, budding prophetic people who tend to hear God so subjectively.

—Committed. Totally committed to whatever the cause. Many times the cause is a result of being rejected, wounded. Ruled by personal vows, like "I'll never do that again…" or "On a bandwagon." Tend to be focused on one-issue. The spirit insists on having its own way.

—Strife-filled mouth. *"…A perverse man spreads strife and a slanderer separates intimate friends"* (Prov. 16:27-28). (See also

Matthew 12:30.) Lack self-control, so they talk and have opinions about everything.

—Love of money. They clearly have an agenda, and it involves money. Remember, Judas sold out Christ for only 30 pieces of silver. While there might be noble talk about sacrifice and "giving the Lord everything," it's ultimately about money and the pursuit of it. *"between men of depraved mind and deprived of the truth, who suppose that godliness is a means of gain..."* (1 Tim. 6:5)

There is no question that for the present system of Churchianity to be transformed, it will require a major confrontation with lawlessness, and it can only be overcome with truth and humility.

# CHAPTER 6

---

# 9-11

The September 11, 2001, terrorist attacks changed the world as we knew it. Although labeled "The Day that Changed America," did, or does, the church realize the significance of what happened?

I wonder if this devastating attack was allowed by God because God's representative on the earth, the Church, was too busy with Churchianity than with winning the lost and bringing His Kingdom to the earth. Jesus gave the Church a few direct commands before He ascended to Heaven. One was to watch and pray. Another was to preach the gospel and make disciples. The infamous 9-11 terrorist attacks were an inevitable consequence of a nation that has not made God welcome in their churches or their land. *"Those who cling to worthless idols forfeit the grace that could be theirs"* (Job 2:8 NIV).

More often than not, our nation has placed its hope in its enormous financial, political, and military power. In the same way, the church has also put its trust in programs, politics, and religious piety rather than a passionate pursuit of God's presence and power. When we look for protection from the wrong source, we lose the blessing that He promises us. We are enjoying too much the fruit of our American way of life where we live in relative ease, and have been complacent—even oblivious—to what is truly happening in the world. On 9-11-2001 America was jolted awake.

The church should be wide awake now, especially because Israel has been almost daily experiencing this kind of violence, although on a smaller scale, for decades. The predicament we find ourselves in as a nation is indicative of the condition of the church the last several years: asleep and complacent. We slept while great evil crept into our borders and planned heinous acts against us, using our nation's freedoms to cloak their fanatical deeds.

The same way that our nation was caught by surprise, so also the church has allowed the acceptance of and tolerance for anything and everything. This allows God's enemies to work freely within the church. But now we can and must speak the truth in love whenever we see enemies of righteousness within our midst.

## A Sign

> *The Pharisees and Sadducees came up, and testing Jesus, they asked Him to show them a sign from heaven. But He replied to them, "When it is evening, you say, 'It will be fair weather, for the sky is red.' And in the morning, 'There will be a storm today, for the sky is red and threatening.' Do you know how to discern the appearance of the sky, but cannot discern the signs of the times?"* (Matthew 16:1-3).

A *sign* is something that points to something else, or "a motion or gesture by which a thought is expressed or a command or wish made known, something material or external that stands for or signifies something spiritual." The signs of 9-11-01 have both spiritual and national significance for every American.

Religious activity clouds our ability to even hear what God is saying in the obvious. Notice in the passage from

Matthew, it was the lawyers (Pharisees) and those who did believe in the resurrection (Sadducees) who were unable to discern what was going on. We can't afford to be oblivious or complacent—we must see the significance of what is going on around us and around the world.

Read Isaiah 30:23-26. Verses 23 and 24 speak of abundance, increase and blessing, but in verse 25 it says,

> *On every lofty mountain and on every high hill will be streams running with water on the day of the great slaughter, when the towers fall. And the light of the moon will be as the light of the sun, and the light of the sun will be seven times brighter, like the light of seven days, on the day the Lord binds up the fracture of His people and heals the bruise He has inflicted.*

Does this passage tie to the other well-known passage in Isaiah 60?

> *Arise, shine; for your light has come, and the glory of the Lord has risen upon you. For behold, darkness covers the earth and deep darkness the peoples; But the Lord will rise upon you, and His glory will appear upon you.*

The World Trade Center towers and their vulnerability were a prophetic symbol and message to an arrogant, worldly-minded church. The towers are like the dual natures of the double-minded church in the United States of America—vulnerable but still trusting in man-made riches; powerful but unmindful of the enemy. Without God as our protector and the source of our power and guidance, we will fall. Every man-made structure burns and falls when subjected to the fire of God's testing. The only construction that can endure the attacks of the enemy will be one "patterned" after God's ways.

)f 9-11-01 were far more than a great human

acks were a virtual reality picture of the

he verge of a new reformation, one in which

-made authority, and worldly systems will be

Apostolic authority and the five-fold ministry will be reestablished in their place. It is significant to note that five years after the World Trade Center towers were destroyed, the site remains empty. In the same way, it has taken the church many years to figure out what to do differently.

## The Significance of 11

The number 11 in Scripture has much prophetic significance. It is obviously closely associated with key historical events in the Scriptures and often (if not always) is associated with the birthing of apostolic and governmental events as a sort of precursor or "forerunner." In Scripture, the number 11 means "removal" (Judas), "disorganization and chaos" (Genesis 11, Babel), and even "double" (1+1).

But its most significant meaning is "transition." Eleven is the number transitioning between 10 and 12, the numbers signifying "being complete" (10) and "government" (12). The number 12 is the numerical symbol of God's ordained government. Scripture tells us about the 12 tribes of Israel, 12 spies sent into Canaan, 12 stones on the ephod of the Levitical priest, 12 lions on each side of Solomon's throne, 12 brazen oxen under the brazen sea, and so on. Then 12 disciples are tested and become the 11—an apostolic remnant or seed.

In the life of Elisha there is the double anointing. The number 11 is representative of this and is part of the September 11 message as well. There were two United Airlines aircrafts and two American Airlines aircrafts; also a flight #11 and a flight #77. Flight #93 carried 44 passengers.

The "double" United-American is a strong signal to the American church to unify. This will not happen given the current level of political and doctrinal separatism found in the church today. But the rise of the apostolic will change that. Only the manifestation of this true apostolic ministry can lead the church to its God-ordained victory; and it is coming!

## Additional Biblical References to 11 and Transition

Genesis 32:22—Transition from bondage (Laban) to freedom (Isaac).

Genesis 37:9—Transition from least (youngest) to leader (in Egypt).

Exodus 26:9—Transition in worship (carrying God's presence).

Deuteronomy 1:1-3—Transition from wandering to rest.

2 Kings 24:1-2—Transition from God's protection to God's discipline.

2 Kings 24:1-2—Transition from blessing (Israel) to exile (Babylon).

Luke 24:9—Transition from hiding (death) to hoping (resurrection).

Acts 1:25-26—Transition from fearful remnant to a faithful whole.

Acts 2:14—Transition from denial to declaration.

## A Muslim Revival?

More than occasionally, my wife, Linda, would glance at the alarm clock, drive by a bank sign, notice our computer clock, or see the time on our microwave and she see saw "11:11." As she told me about it each time, I began noticing it as well. We asked the Lord several times what it meant, and as we searched for the meaning, we found scriptures like Isaiah 11:11 which says, *"Then it will happen on that day that the Lord will again recover the second time with His hand the remnant of His people, who will remain from Assyria, Egypt, Pathros* [Northern Egypt], *Cush, Elam, Shinar* [present-day Iraq], *Hamath, and from the islands of the sea."*

This passage denotes a significant, sudden change—"on that day." It signifies a new era or time. This passage even appears to speak of a revival among those whose nations are presently Muslim. In addition, a large number of these people groups live in the United States and Western Europe. Could this passage be a prophecy concerning a Muslim awakening? While this passage definitely could identify those who moved back from these lands to create the new nation of Israel in 1948, it also appears to speak of an ingathering to the Kingdom of His people from other lands. It encompasses more people coming to Jesus Christ and His church that or are part of these people groups.

I believe it strongly points to a latter-day revival among the Islamic people. If I had been told 25 years ago that 38,000 Chinese would be coming to Christ every day and that China would become a superpower with the world's fastest growing capitalistic economy, I probably wouldn't have believed it. And if I would have been told 30 years ago that the Soviet Union would be dismantled and would be becoming a democratic society, I probably wouldn't believe it—but it happened! Right now Islam looks to be a major obstacle to spreading the gospel, but nothing is impossible with God. *"Is anything too difficult for the Lord?"* (Genesis 18:14).

Nothing is impossible for Him—things that used to seem impossible are becoming realities! It's God's heart to bring all His children back to Himself.

## A Time for War

*"The best defense is a good offense."* Vince Lombardi

> *There is an appointed time for everything. There is a time for every event under heaven—a time to give birth, and a time to die; a time to plant, and a time to uproot what is planted. A time to kill, and a time to heal; a time to tear down, and a time to build up. A time to weep, and a time to laugh; a time to mourn, and a time to dance. A time to throw stones, and a time to gather stones; a time to embrace, and a time to shun embracing. A time to search, and a time to give up as lost; a time to keep, and a time to throw away. A time to tear apart, and a time to sew together; a time to be silent, and a time to speak. A time to love and a time to hate; a time for war and a time for peace* (Ecclesiastes 3:1-8).

We have now entered into a time of all-out spiritual war. While this is not what most of us would desire, at this moment in history we have little choice but to accept this fact and engage so as to win. This is a major shock to the way we have formerly perceived our environment and surroundings, yet we as Christians must shift our mentality to keep pace in this new and precarious season. *"If you have run with footmen and they have tired you out, Then how can you compete with horses? If you fall down in a land of peace, How will you do in the thicket of the Jordan?"* (Jeremiah 12:5).

We have become so accustomed to an atmosphere of comfort and safety, that many now find themselves uncomfortable and even anxious with the fact that we are at war. The Bible teaches that we live in a constant state of spiritual conflict, so none of us should be completely surprised that we entered an entirely new era on September 11, 2001.

In addition, many times natural things are simply a mirror of what is actually occurring spiritually. (See Ephesians 6:10-18 and 1 Corinthians 15:46.) We must face the realities of these new times. In the past we spent much of our time and energy devoting resources to our own comfort, prosperity, and ease; now we must change our priorities to defeat evil in these new, unpredictable days. We must make this crucial shift and channel our time, energy, and resources to developing our spiritual weapons, training soldiers, and acquiring all the necessary equipment and instruction to fight and win. Finally, we all must start using the weapons God has already given us to win this war.

### War Is Hell

William T. Sherman, the Union general who torched Atlanta during the Civil War, said, "War is hell." It's true, because the evil we see in war is a reflection of all of the wages and consequences of sin. For the Christian, it's part of our daily struggle between opposing kingdoms—the Kingdom of God and light versus the kingdom of darkness.

> *Finally, be strong in the Lord, and in the strength of His might. Put on the full armor of God, that you may*

*be able to stand firm against the schemes of the devil.
For our struggle is not against flesh and blood, but
against the rulers, against the powers, against the
world forces of this darkness, against the spiritual
forces of wickedness in the heavenly places. Therefore,
take up the full armor of God, so that you may be able
to resist in the evil day, and having done everything,
to stand firm. Stand firm therefore, having* **girded
your loins with truth,** *and having put on the*
**breastplate of righteousness,** *and having* **shod your
feet with the preparation of the gospel of peace;** *in
addition to all, taking up the shield of faith with which
you will be able to extinguish all the flaming missiles
of the evil one. And take the helmet of salvation, and
the sword of the Spirit, which is the word of God. With
all prayer and petition pray at all times in the Spirit,
and with this in view, be on the alert with all perseverance and petition for all the saints*
(Ephesians 6:10-18, emphasis added).

We are participants in an ongoing intense spiritual conflict, with battles that rage at us any time and any place. Our
only guarantee of peace is abiding in the Lord and hanging close
to Him. He is the Prince of Peace. He is our shield, hope, and
protection, and only in Him do we have true peace and safety.

## Our Weapons

Second Corinthians 6:6-7 says: *"...in purity, in knowledge,
in patience, in kindness, in the Holy Spirit, in genuine love, in the
word of truth, in the power of God; by the weapons of righteousness for
the right hand and the left."* These weapons are real and powerful. They are *grace, truth,* and *humility.* It's all a "fight of faith,"
but this faith releases grace (see Eph. 2:8-9) while it is sustained
by humility (see James 4:6). These weapons are not fleshly or

carnal, but weapons of faith and power that bring the Kingdom into being.

## Our Enemy

Even while we are in the midst of a war, there are many of us who are still ignorant about the true nature and intent of our enemy. Without having a realistic understanding of the evil we're dealing with, we tend to think that we're safe and sound and that it is someone else's problem. The church in the United States has been in a state of slumber for a very long time. After 9-11 most realized that war was waged against us; the possibility of danger and threat of attack shook us from our slumber—for a while. It's unfortunate that we had to experience such tragedy and difficulty before we realized the gravity of the conflict.

Our enemy then and now is the oldest enemy of God, His people, and purposes; and he has been successfully waging war since the dawn of time. *"For we do not wrestle against flesh and blood, but against principalities, against powers, against the rulers of the darkness of this age, against spiritual hosts of wickedness in the heavenly places"* (Eph. 6:12 NKJV). Pride and presumption is our Achilles heel and in this battle, humility, confidence in the Lord, and the knowledge of God and His ways are our most powerful assets.

## Denial

*The Day After*, a made-for-television movie, aired in 1983. It depicted the horrific effects of a nuclear exchange between America and the Soviet Union. This "anti-nuke" movie was made at the same time the Reagan Administration had begun a massive buildup of America's military after many years of neglect and low morale after the Vietnam War. One aspect of this buildup was the bold and even daring decision by President Ronald Reagan to station Pershing nuclear-tipped missiles in West Germany, just minutes in the air from Communist East Germany and Russia. His action was called a reckless and dangerous act by some who thought it could lead to nuclear war.

One scene in the movie shows a Kansas family getting ready for their daughter's wedding, while at the same time the Minutemen missiles lift off from silos just a few miles away. The father, knowing that retaliation is imminent, tells his family to take cover in their underground shelter. After the father gets his family into the shelter, he discovers that his wife isn't with them. He goes upstairs and finds her putting new sheets on the bed, determined to press through with the wedding plans. He finally drags her into the shelter and within minutes there are explosions. She was in denial.

While those who saw the movie were shocked by it's depiction of nuclear war and caused many to get on the antinuclear bandwagon, President Reagan stood firm against an increasingly belligerent Soviet Union government. By placing nuclear-tipped missiles in West Germany, he showed the world that he wasn't a leader to be trifled with and that he was serious about defending Europe from a Soviet attack.

Ultimately, the American military buildup and Reagan's constant pressure on the Soviet Union led to the collapse of the Soviet Union six years later. At the time, Reagan's decision was perceived as reckless and dangerous and the Western media portrayed him as a renegade cowboy. But the Soviets took him seriously. No one knows what might have happened if America would have unilaterally disarmed as many were screaming for at the time. That course of action may have led to nuclear war because as history has taught us, perceived weakness invites aggression.

Someone once said, "Evil triumphs when good men do nothing." Denial of evil and the war it brings unfortunately has no effect on stopping it other than to move us to ignore it or hope it will go away—which it won't. One of the enemy's greatest victories has been to convince believers that we are not in a spiritual war.

## His Strategy

It is absolutely imperative that we quickly discover how our enemy, the devil, operates against us.

> *Now the serpent was more cunning than any beast of the field which the Lord God had made. And he said to the woman, "Has God indeed said, 'You shall not eat of every tree of the garden'?" And the woman said to the serpent, "We may eat the fruit of the trees of the garden; but of the fruit of the tree which is in the midst of the garden, God has said, 'You shall not eat it, nor shall you touch it, lest you die.'" Then the serpent said to the woman, "You will not surely die. For God knows that in the day you eat of it your eyes will be opened, and you will be like God, knowing good and evil." So when the woman saw that the tree was good for food, that it was pleasant to the eyes, and a tree desirable to make one wise, she took of its fruit and ate. She also gave to her husband with her, and he ate. Then the eyes of both of them were opened, and they knew that they were naked; and they sewed fig leaves together and made themselves coverings*
> (Genesis 3:1-7 NKJV).

This passage is mandatory learning for believers so we can know the enemy's strategy and tactics. Take a look at just a few insights gleaned from this passage:

—The enemy is cunning. *Cunning* means "skillful in deception, sly, or crafty." We can surmise that our enemy is much more experienced at this than we are and will use any and all manner of deception to beguile us. Without the Lord's help, we can't outwit him.

—He tries to make us question what God said to us. *"Did God really say…?"* He doesn't attack God directly, but questions us in such a way that we begin to wonder.

—He then challenges the truth of what God said. *"You will not surely die."* And even attempts to make us question God's good intentions toward us! *"For God knows that in the day you eat of it your eyes will be opened, and you will be like God, knowing good and evil."*

Do you see the brilliance of this strategy? Without directly accusing God and only asking a few questions, the enemy takes us from wondering about what we *thought* God said, to questioning the integrity of God's word, questioning why God said it, and then attempts to make us suspicious of God Himself! No, with our own natural wits and strength we don't stand a chance against our cruel foe. For example, think about the words of Martin Luther in his hymn, "A Mighty Fortress Is Our God."

"For still our ancient foe doth seek to work us woe;

His craft and power are great and armed with cruel hate,

on earth is not his equal."

## The Battleground

In the same way, we are all born into a world system that tells us we are something much less than what God says we are. The Greek word for this world system is *cosmos*. While we've all heard teachings that say our mind is the main battleground in this spiritual war, we must open up our thinking to see the true scope of the war and its focus. If the battle is only in our minds, then why did Jesus instruct us to have "faith on the earth"? While it is true the spiritual battle begins in our minds, it is manifest on the earth and ultimately it is for the earth and the souls of all people. The world system that captivates our minds is like *The Matrix* we are content to live in, all the while being led to the slaughter house.

We must see that the enemy's primary and strategic target is God's covenant people and our inheritance, which includes the salvation of the lost. If the enemy can remove the people of God and what they possess, he removes his opposition and controls the ability of the church to wage war and win.

In other words, the front in this current war is not against the lost but against the Church and what God has promised to them. If the Church is neutralized, the lost will not be won, there will be no forward advancement or resistance, and the war is over!

## Keeping in Step with His Voice

It takes knowing the Holy Spirit to know what the Spirit has for us. Pastor and Christian author, Mike Bickle, said, "It takes God to love God."

> Now we have received, not the spirit of the world, but the Spirit who is from God, that we may know the

*things freely given to us by God, which things we also speak, not in words taught by human wisdom, but in those taught by the Spirit, combining spiritual thoughts with spiritual words. But a natural man does not accept the things of the Spirit of God; for they are foolishness to him, and he cannot understand them, because they are spiritually appraised*
(1 Corinthians 2:12-14).

Bishop Joseph Garlington said, "We are not human beings having a temporary spiritual experience, but spiritual beings having a temporary human experience."

To move forward in our walk in the Spirit, we have to change our ways and the limits we place on hearing His voice. We have to stretch more than just a little. We have to open our closed minds and hear God in ways we've yet to experience. To soar to these heights of faith and peace that we've never experienced before will require a new understanding of walking after the Spirit.

Galatians 5:16 in the New King James Version says: *"I say then: Walk in the Spirit, and you shall not fulfill the lust of the flesh."* Then verse 25 says: *"If we live in the Spirit, let us also walk in the Spirit."* The Greek word for "walk" in verse 16 is *peripateo*, and it implies "to tread all around and down a circuit of territory." In verse 25 it is a different word, *stoicheo*, which means "to march in rank, to walk in an orderly way." A good way of saying: to follow after the Spirit as in a military fashion; as if the Holy Spirit was our drill sergeant and we're following his specific and direct commands, whether we understand their ultimate outcome or not! Not enough understand this aspect about the Holy Spirit being our Teacher.

During military basic training, new recruits rarely comprehend why their drill sergeant insists on 10-mile hikes, standing at attention for hours, and the constant instruction about understanding their weapon, taking it apart, putting it back together, and cleaning it. But all these disciplines will serve them well and may *save their lives* during a combat situation.

With this in mind, Christians need some basic training that includes more than just trying to fit Bible reading and a little prayer into busy days. It means a whole new lifestyle of waiting on the Lord throughout each day and being willing to follow after and listen to His voice attentively. In addition, it means placing a much greater value on what His voice means in our lives—allowing Him access to every area.

## By Force

> *And from the days of John the Baptist until now the kingdom of heaven suffers* **violence,** *and* **violent** *men take it by force. For all the prophets and the Law prophesied until John* (Matthew 11:12-13 NKJV).

This passage says that the violent take it by force, by a violent snatching away of those things that have been withheld. It also implies that the Kingdom (the rule and reign of God) only comes this way. Those two Greek words in this passage are:

G971. biazw, from G970; to force:— forcing a way(1), suffers violence(m)(1) and:

G726. harpazw, from a prim. root arp; to seize, catch up, snatch away:— carry off(1), caught up(4), snatch(2), snatched away(1), snatches(1), snatches away(1), snatching(1), take by force(1), take by force(2). [1]

Since 9-11-01 in both the natural and in the spiritual realm, we have been thrust into a new season where whatever we are to receive from God won't be gained without a fight. Unless we have the resolve and determination to win and possess that which we have been promised, we will not receive it. Yes, we are sons and daughters of the King, but we are now in the midst of a violent fight of faith for our inheritance. What we previously took for granted, we now have to spiritually fight for.

We have to fight to possess these things because of the lawlessness in the world and how it affects us. We are surprised at the brutality of the evil that we see, but it is a fact and a part of life. The only way evil can triumph is when good people do nothing, so we can no longer do nothing and "hope it all works out." We can no longer afford to merely muster ourselves against the enemy, but instead we must now engage him.

*Fight the good fight of faith; take hold of the eternal life to which you were called, and you made the good confession in the presence of many witnesses* (1 Timothy 6:12).

Jesus said it was necessary for us to have a violent spirit to possess the Kingdom. It *is* warfare. It *is* a battle. Our politically correct climate says that violence begets more violence. While there is a little truth in that statement, the *whole* truth is that evil and violence when unanswered and not resisted will sooner or later lead to tyranny and slavery. We must see the value in the following terms because they relate to our very survival: freedom, force, and resolve.

*Freedom* is not free because it did and will cost somebody, somewhere, something—and maybe everything. We take for granted the benefits others provided for us without fully appreciating the sacrifices they made to secure them. Every victory was secured by someone. Thankfulness and gratefulness must be part of our lifestyle so we can understand what awesome blessings we live under.

*Force.* The application of force takes willpower and determination to be successful. *It is appropriate to use force to possess the Kingdom.* Justifiable force must be used at times to wrest away from the enemy that which is ours.

*Resolve.* Most people do not have the resolve to deal with the things that need to be dealt with and do all that is necessary to defeat evil. Determination is important, but resolve is even more important. To be able to press through obstacles, we have to take back what has been stolen from us. Which is a better story? The person who ultimately wins the battle, or the one who instantly wins the lottery? The instant winner of course! While we all love the fantastic idea of something for nothing, reality is that it takes tenacity and determination to possess something. I regularly tell our church, "You are guaranteed the victory if you will engage and not quit!" Quitters never win and winners never quit! *Our victory is assured if we have resolve.*

From the familiar song:

Did we in our own strength confide, our striving would be losing; were not the right Man on our side, the Man of God's own choosing... Dost ask who that may be? Christ Jesus, it is He; Lord Sabaoth His name, from age to age the same, and *He must win the battle.*[2]

Hallelujah! In Him and working together with Him, we cannot lose! By trusting in and relying on the Spirit we have the victory.

*Now thanks be to God who always leads us in triumph in Christ, and through us diffuses the fragrance of His knowledge in every place* (2 Corinthians 2:14 NKJV).

God will always lead us to victory as we face every battle, test, and trial. While God will never tempt us, He regularly allows us to be tested. Why are students required to take tests? To insure that the student has learned enough to advance to the next level.

Pastor and Christian author Francis Frangipane says, "With God, we never fail a test, we just take it over—till we get it." God only tests us so we will grow up into mature believers who the enemy fears. Our ultimate weapon is the same weapon David, Joshua, and Paul had: the knowledge of God and trust in the Lord of Hosts. After all, *"If God is for us, who can be against us?"*

**Endnotes**

1. Strong's Exhaustive Concordance; Copyright 1980 and 1986 assigned to World Bible Publisher's,Inc.
2. "A Mighty Fortress Is Our God" by Martin Luther- Public Domain.

# CHAPTER 7

# THE "TITLE" WAVE

One of the most drastic changes of new revelation of the Kingdom is how we will begin to see ourselves as part of a living organism that is bringing a new form of government to the earth. We are part of a family whose Father is God, called to live an overcoming supernatural life. Simply "going through the motions" of our current church lives will no longer satisfy. Programs and activities that might have been encouraging will seem lifeless. Instead, a desire and hunger for the things we see in the Book of Acts—and much more—will invade our spirit and vision.

However, this vision for more must first be declared and then lived by church leadership. *"Without vision, the people perish..."* (Prov. 29:18 KJV). Leaders must be willing to break free of old mind-sets and move forward. We must have leaders who will see the vision God is bringing and who are unafraid to step out of the boat in faith, especially if the boat represents an old wineskin that needs to be changed.

We must also get a new revelation of what leadership should look like and how it should operate. Jesus said in Matthew 20:25-28 *"But Jesus called them to Himself, and said, 'You know that the rulers of the Gentiles lord it over them, and their great men exercise authority over them.' It is not so among you, but whoever wishes to become great among you shall be your servant, and whoever wishes to be first among you shall be your slave; just as the Son of Man did not come to be served, but to serve, and to give His life a ransom for many."*

Jesus made a clear distinction between those who lead to be recognized (and/or get a paycheck) versus those who lead humbly as a servant, unconcerned with their reputation or the approval of others. As representatives of the Lord, we must take a humble, broken approach to leading. Leaders must confidently and unapologetically exercise spiritual authority but with an attitude of servanthood. This new paradigm shift in church leadership will dramatically bring about the demise of the old form of church, but not without cost.

Several within our ministry have had dreams about tidal waves. Because we live 400 miles inland, we didn't think the dreams were about a natural event, so we began to pray for understanding. Then someone showed me a short article written by John Paul Jackson titled, "Dangers of Riding the Title Wave."[1]

The article exposes the dangers of church leadership, especially those who have prophetic gifts, deriving their identity or value from their title. John Paul Jackson writes, "By giving ourselves the title of 'prophet,' we are yearning for distinction and recognition. But we need to beware; doing so is giving in to the subtle, religiously acceptable means of calling attention to our gift."

## Function or Office?

For Churchianity to decrease and the Kingdom to increase, we must be willing to overhaul the hierarchical structure of current church leadership. Before that can be done however, we must understand the simple truth that every gift mentioned in Ephesians chapter 4—apostle, prophet, pastor, evangelist, and teacher—are for the edification of the church, *not* the glorification of those who exercise them. These descriptions

are more functional than official. While much teaching has glorified the offices of these gifts, we must examine the reality of
how they truly operated in the New Testament.

For example, the word *pastor* is only used one time in the
New Testament, but the entire Western church uses this title for
their local church leadership. Paul only used the word *apostle* to
describe what he did, but there are dozens of books about
"Apostle Paul." In the Bible, however, it reads: "Paul, an apostle." Before Jesus came on the scene, the word *apostle* was never
used as a term to describe a religious office; it was a nautical and
military term to describe an emissary sent to colonize distant
lands. Jesus, not the Pope, first used it to refer to His disciples.

Calling someone a prophet or apostle doesn't make them
one and doesn't somehow magically release them to operate in
that gift. The prophetic and apostolic gifts must be seen as the
functions they serve and be de-mystified! (I will discuss this
regarding the apostolic later in this book.) The use of a title is
not in itself a problem, and we must have a healthy respect for
those who serve. However, it is dangerous to give someone a
title or office unless they have first proved themselves worthy.
Too many congregations currently give unflagging allegiance to
leadership to the point of obeisance.

## The Untouchables

There are several denominations that sooner or later will
have to look at the titles they are using and ask the Lord, "Do
we really need this hierarchy to do what we are called to do?"
Many churches and movements give their leaders titles that
refer to legitimate biblical functions, yet their leaders are little
more than extremely talented, gifted managers and CEOs.
There are even some churches that reverence the titles they give

their leaders so powerfully that they would never challenge them, which places them in an untouchable position with zero accountability.

Because of the great giftedness and success of many of these leaders, when they are given a title in place of a first name, some of the congregations tend to elevate them to a celebrity status rather than a servant of God. God never intended His servants to have this kind of elevation, and the temptation for these leaders to feel they are somebody special is overpowering. It is then when they do things that violate the criteria we see in the New Testament for church leadership, as well as for a Christian. Pride truly does come before a fall.

## The Political Spirit

The Book of Revelation refers to an unholy trinity that will surface to rule the world in the last days just before Christ's return. Revelation refers to this person as the beast.

> *And I saw coming out of the mouth of the dragon and out of the mouth of the beast and out of the mouth of the false prophet, three unclean spirits like frogs; for they are spirits of demons, performing signs, which go out to the kings of the whole world, to gather them together for the war of the great day of God, the Almighty* (Revelation 16:13-14).

The beast will be a real man and will wield unlimited power over every nation and every economy on the earth. The beast will be supernaturally empowered by the devil himself, the dragon. He will be a "spiritual" political ruler who has at his side a false prophet who energizes his regime and does signs and wonders that convince people he is God.

The political spirit is a huge part of the antichrist system and is to be fully unveiled in all its ugliness in the last days. This spirit is already operating in church leadership and will always raise its head to counteract the anointing operating through God's chosen leaders. The true government of God is released through the anointing flowing through leaders who allow the Spirit to move in the Body. This political spirit will use anything at its disposal to come against the manifestation of the true government of God.

Many church leadership boards and teams have this spirit lurking among them, ready to manifest at the appropriate time to stop or at least compromise the Word of the Lord and moving in the prophetic dimension.

There are clear distinctions between the political spirit and the anointing. Because the political spirit seeks to impersonate the power that comes with God's placement of an individual into a place of authority, it is important to look with discernment at the contrast. To operate in ministry based on one's own resources, gifting, and capabilities not only excludes the need for God, it also misrepresents Him.

*The anointing:*

—breaks the yoke of oppression.

—represents the Anointed One's rule.

—confronts darkness allowing the Kingdom in.

—releases liberty without compromise.

*The political spirit:*

—brings a yoke of oppression by "tying up heavy loads and laying them on men's shoulders." (Matthew 23:4 NIV)

—represents the covering from man.

—confronts anything threatening the status quo and "the way we've always done it here."

—can do nothing but compromise, leading to bondage.

The political spirit must be repented of and removed from God's leaders. The days of "I'll scratch your back if you'll scratch mine" must end. This is no longer tolerable for God's called. I believe that just as we saw through dreams, a *tidal* wave of the Spirit is coming that will be so powerful it will overturn the *title* wave entrenched in the church that has politicized leaders and sapped the power of God from the church.

## Denominational Deliverance

While denominations have been used of God over the years to focus on gains made by real moves of the Spirit and consolidate them, they were never intended to remain as such. Instead, I believe that the apostolic model we see in Scripture will become more and more prevalent. Instead of denominational headquarters and councils of leaders, we will see more apostolic streams based around apostolic leaders and their teams. There will be many differences between these teams and the present denominational paradigm. Here are a few major ones:

The power and authority of the apostolic teams will come from the anointing that rests on the apostolic leaders and their teams and their adherence to the Word of God rather than political or denominational methods.

The teams will be more concerned about the advancement of the Kingdom than their own church or ministry. The apostolic teams will focus first on chronicling and testifying about the many wonders and mighty deeds the Lord has done rather than parochial business only. They will have a childlike quality, and yet they will be in awe of God's power. They will first be given to the Word of God and prayer rather than administration and management techniques. Prayer will receive more attention than budget meetings.

## The Best Is Yet To Come

The other day an old Tony Bennett song, "The Best Is Yet to Come," kept coming to my mind as I was contemplating the contents of this book. I heard it several times over the next few days on the radio, in my car, and while watching television. I realized I was having a prophetic experience, and the Lord was speaking. He was revealing things to me through the song. I searched and found the lyrics on the Internet:

"The Best Is Yet To Come"
Words by Carolyn Leigh, Music by Cy Coleman

Out of the tree of life I just picked a plum.
You came along and everything's startin to hum.
Still, it's a real good bet the best is yet to come.

The best is yet to come and, babe, won't it be fine?

You think you've seen the sun, but you ain't seen it shine.
Wait till the warm-up's underway, wait till our lips have met,
Wait till you see that sunshine day,
You ain't seen nothin' yet!

The best is yet to come and, babe, won't it be fine?
The best is yet to come, come the day you're mine.

Come the day you're mine, I'm gonna teach you to fly.
We're gonna taste of the wine; we're gonna drain the cup dry.

Wait till your charms are right for these arms to surround.

You think you've flown before but you ain't left the ground.

Wait till you're locked in my embrace, wait till I draw you near

Wait till you see the sunshine place—ain't nothing like it here!

The best is yet to come and, babe, won't it be fine

The best is come, come the day you're mine.

While today the church isn't where it should be and is still inundated with this Churchianity, what God is about to do could be appropriately titled, "The Best Is Yet To Come"! This is foretold in Isaiah 60:1-7: *"Arise, shine; for your light has come and the glory of the Lord has risen upon you. For behold, darkness will cover the earth, and deep darkness the peoples; But the Lord will rise upon you, And His glory will appear upon you. And nations will come to your light, and kings to the brightness of your rising. Lift up your eyes round about, and see; they all gather together, they come to you. Your sons will come from afar, and your daughters will be carried in the arms. Then you will see and be radiant, and your heart will thrill and rejoice; because the abundance of the sea will be turned to you, the wealth of the nations will come to you. A multitude of camels will cover you, the young camels of Midian and Ephah; all those from Sheba will come; they will bring gold and frankincense, And will bear good news of the praises of the Lord. All the flocks of Kedar will be gathered together to you, the rams of Nebaioth will minister to you; they will go up with acceptance on My altar, and I shall glorify My glorious house."*

God is about to turn the church upside down, inside out, and any which way He can! Why? By this shaking off of the old and the realigning to Him, the church will gleam with the light and glory of the Lord! God will remove those things that man in his own reasoning and ways brought into the church that has removed the *life*!

## "Out of the tree of life..."

For too many years, God has received a bad rap because of church representatives. Many in our society look to the church to find God, and instead they see congregations with no life. In fact, they see death. As the world looks around, most of what they see in the church is religion, rules, and death. This is because the church is primarily no longer ministering life, but only the "knowledge of good."

> *And the Lord God commanded the man, saying, "From any tree of the garden you may eat freely; but from the tree of the knowledge of good and evil you shall not eat, for in the day that you eat from it you shall surely die"* (Genesis 2:16-17).

*Good* can be the greatest enemy of the *best*. The church has fallen for this trap of telling people how to be good instead of how to *live*! The knowledge of good is just as bad for us as the knowledge of evil—both prevent us from coming to Him.

> *When Christ, who is our life, is revealed, then you also will be revealed with Him in glory* (Colossians 3:4).

## "You think you've seen the sun but you ain't seen it shine...You ain't seen nothin' yet!"

We have yet to see the glory of the Lord revealed through His Church! In this new era, healings, miracles, and signs and wonders working through love will spring forth from the corporate Body. But it will only happen as we begin to grasp the revelation that only *He* is our life, and that religion, activity, and dead works impede the release of the glorious life within us. Jesus said that this Kingdom is within.

> *Jesus replied, "The kingdom of God does not come with your careful observation, nor will people say, 'Here it is,' or 'There it is,' because the kingdom of God is within you"* (Luke 17:20-21 NIV).

> *Now to Him who is able to do exceeding abundantly beyond all that we ask or think, according to the power that works within us* (Ephesians 3:20).

## "I'm gonna teach you to fly..."

> *Yet those who wait for the Lord will gain new strength; they will mount up with wings like eagles, they will run and not get tired, they will walk and not become weary* (Isaiah 40:31).

God wants His Church to do the things only a supernatural people who know their God can do! We are to do exploits and adventures in God!

> *Beloved, now we are children of God, and it has not appeared as yet what we will be. We know that, when He appears, we will be like Him, because we will see Him just as He is. ...By this, love is perfected with us, that we may have confidence in the day of judgment; because as He is, so also are we in this world* (1 John 3:2;4:17).

The Bible declares a day when God's people will begin to see Jesus for who He really is, and when that happens they will begin to move into that supernatural realm of living that accompanies the revelation that we are children of God. The Bible even says all creation is longing to see that day! *"For the anxious longing of the creation waits eagerly for the revealing of the sons of God"* (Romans 8:19).

That Greek word for *revealing* is the same root word as for revelation, meaning "to unveil, uncover or to reveal something that is hidden." *"For nothing is hidden, except to be revealed; nor has anything been secret, but that it would come to light. If anyone has ears to hear, let him hear"* (Matt. 4:22-23).

That same word is also found in Colossians 3:4, which makes a correlation between a believer who receives a full revelation of who Christ is, and how He is actually working in that believer to unveil the glory of God within! *"When Christ, who is our life, is revealed, then you also will be revealed with Him in glory"* (Col. 3:4). We see that *when* Christ is fully revealed, *then* the glory of God comes out in that person.

Jesus even said those who believe could and would do greater works than the ones He did. *"Truly, truly, I say to you, he who believes in Me, the works that I do he will do also; and greater works than these he will do; because I go to the Father. Whatever you ask in My name, that will I do, so that the Father may be glorified in the Son"* (John 14:12-13).

For example, Jesus raised four people from the dead in His 3? years on the earth. But there have already been several men and women of God on earth who have far surpassed that number. Smith Wigglesworth, who lived during the early 20th century, raised at least 11 people from death. David Hogan, along with his team of 18 who have been working in remote areas of Mexico for over 25 years, have seen more 300 raised from the dead through their prayers of faith!

Many preachers and theologians in the United States who were taught cessationism twist the meaning of these and other Scriptures to suggest that miracles will take place only after the believer enters Heaven. But Jesus didn't say that, and He had much to say about what awaits the believer in Heaven. Their unbelief is obvious by their attempt to change the meaning of the passage, but the bottom line: Jesus said we would cast out demons, heal the sick, raise the dead, and preach to the poor, *period*. There are many passages that make this clear that to argue any other way only exposes that person's dogged unbelief.

## "We're gonna taste of the wine; we're gonna drain the cup dry..."

The new wine that Jesus spoke of is coming and that new wine will be drunk in full measure by those in this generation who desire it. He also told a parable: "*...No one puts a piece from a new garment on an old one; otherwise the new makes a tear, and also the piece that was taken out of the new does not match the old. And no one puts new wine into old wineskins; or else the new wine will burst the wineskins and be spilled, and the wineskins will be ruined. But new wine must be put into new wineskins, and both are preserved. And no one, having drunk old wine, immediately desires new; for he says, 'The old is better'*" (Luke 5:36-38 NKJV).

The big danger is when the new wine cannot be stored or held in the old wineskin. Jesus said both would be lost. The old wineskin would be damaged, and the new wine poured out.

This addresses the principle involving the attempt of those with a *new* revelation attempting to fit it into an *old* structure, method, or form. It's not simply the structure we need to change, but also the mind-set about the form through which Jesus is revealed to them.

Luke 16:12 tells us Jesus appeared in a different form to the two men on the road to Emmaus, and the two could not see that it was Him until near the end of their journey. Then he revealed Himself in a form they were familiar with. The Greek word *form* comes from the same Latin word as *morph*, meaning "to change appearances like a chameleon, to morph to a different shape."

In each generation, the Lord reveals Himself in a form that they can relate to and understand. The way God chose to come and reveal Himself to the Woodstock generation would not necessarily be the same as how God reveals Himself to today's generation. What worked in the 1970s will not work on today's youth. Most churches today resemble the youth ministries of 20-25 years ago. Jesus said it is futile to put the new thing God is doing in an old form or way. By doing so, both the new and old are damaged—the new wine is even lost.

**"Wait till you're locked in my embrace; wait till I draw you near,**

**Wait till you see the sunshine place, ain't nothing like it here!"**

Wow! This is truly the best part. God's people are about to enter into a realm of rest and intimacy with God that will surpass anything experienced before. While mystics through the centuries have had awesome encounters with God, their beliefs about God hindered them from truly experiencing the incredible riches of the knowledge of God. False understandings about God limited their ability to grasp all they could have. The best is truly yet to come as God will reveal Himself to hungry seekers. As we return to the simplicity, purity, and devotion to Christ, we will enter into a level of intimacy with God few have ever understood or experienced.

> *But for you who fear My name the sun of righteousness will rise with healing in its wings; and you will go forth and skip about like calves from the stall. And you will tread down the wicked, for they shall be ashes under the soles of your feet on the day which I am preparing," says the Lord of hosts* (Malachi 4:2-3).

Many teachers and preachers have implied that the sun mentioned in Malachi is really the Son of God. While that is a cool play on words, it can diminish the ramifications of what the verse is actually declaring. This passage is speaking of a new day dawning when righteousness is the light that brightens everything and exposes all wickedness, even as the sun now gives us natural light.

It also speaks of healing and the defeat of the wicked being part of this generation's inheritance. When it says, *"the sun of righteousness will rise with healing in its wings..."* it is good to know what is implied by the term *"in its wings."* The word *kanaph* means "edge or extremity" and is easier to understand in the context of a bird's wingspan. It is describing this sun rising as a picture of a giant eagle spreading its wings; and within the breadth of the enormous wingspan, healing goes out even to the corners and edges! Even at the very edges of the sunlight that is dawning, healing and the defeat of the wicked will be found. This new day is dawning and is upon us even now.

## Endnote

1. John Paul Jackson, Streams Ministry Blog, posted June 9, 2005, 9:54 p.m., found at http://www.streamsministries.com/blogger/2005_06_01_streamsministries_archive.html.

# CHAPTER 8

# NORMALIZATION OF THE APOSTOLIC

## Then...and now

Just 30 years ago the term *prophetic* was only used to describe those things foretold in the Books of Revelation and Daniel or the events leading up to Armageddon. There were a few prophetic conferences but nearly all of them were about end-time events and emphasized the rapture or mark of the beast.

At that time the concept that "you may all prophesy" was gaining acceptance but only in a few small group settings. Public prophecy was relegated to a few bold enough to blurt out something (usually loudly) between songs during worship, and mainly it was of the "my children, my children" variety. Every Charismatic church had one. Prophets were seen, based on the Old Testament model, as odd, eccentric, mystical types, and the prophetic ministry was limited to only a few.

In Charismatic churches then, the idea that somebody would be called a prophet or use the term prophetic to describe his or her ministry, was considered far-fetched. Prophetic people were primarily those attending Revelation conferences; and while most Bible prophecy teachers were considered prophetic, most rarely prophesied. The prophetic ministry was considered legitimate but because there were few authentic models, it was not widespread. Today that is no longer the case, as prophetic books, ministries, and conferences proliferate in the church with the greatest increase of involvement coming from denominational Christians and leaders who are hungry for more of God than they've previously experienced.

## Progressive Restoration

As Martin Luther's revelation about justification transformed the status quo of his time and began the Reformation, successive generations have also seen a progressive restoration of God's pattern for His Church. Revelation and enlightenment concerning key truths about salvation and sanctification have been and are being restored. Now foundational gifts and ministries are being recognized to accelerate the restoration.

*And God has appointed in the church, first apostles, second prophets, third teachers, then miracles, then gifts of healings, helps, administrations, various kinds of tongues* (1 Corinthians 12:28).

This passage reveals God's priority placement concerning eight different gifts in the church.

If we look back to the beginning of the last century, we see an accelerated restoration of each of these gifts in reverse order with the last one on the list being restored first. *"Thus the last shall be first, and the first last"* (Matt. 20:16).

## Tongues

On New Year's Day 1901, Charles Parham and over half the class at his Topeka Bible College spoke in tongues for three days. Then in 1904, William Seymour and others ushered in the modern Pentecostal movement with the Azusa Street revival in Los Angeles, California, which was characterized with believers speaking in tongues. Today the Pentecostal segment is the fastest growing of all others in Christianity.

## Administrations and Helps

While there is less interest in chronicling the restoration of these gifts, there is no question that these two gifts have enabled churches and ministries to grow exponentially due to their activation.

## Healings

In the 1940s and '50s the healing movement paralleled the prolific spread of Pentecostalism. Healing preachers like A.A. Allen, F.F. Bosworth, Jack Coe, Gordon Lindsay, and Oral Roberts are credited with bringing legitimacy to healing while William Branham is the one most credited with initiating the huge post-war healing movement.

## Signs, Wonders, and Miracles

With the advent of the Charismatic movement in the '60s came a rise in reports of miracles. Missionaries like T.L. Osborn and Rheinhard Bonnke experienced extraordinary signs, wonders, and miracles in their African crusades. African churches had amazing reports of people who were raised from the dead and other restorative miracles. Deliverances of demons occurred regularly in Charismatic and Pentecostal churches. With the renewal sparked by the Toronto and Brownsville Revivals in the 1990s, it became more common to hear of extraordinary miracles, such as diseased organs restored and deformed limbs growing back perfectly. Bizarre signs such as gold fillings, gold dust, and even feathers appeared in church meetings all over the United States and Canada beginning just prior to the turn of the century—the year 2000.

## Teachers

The 1970s saw a proliferation of teaching on faith, spiritual gifts, deliverance, and prayer. To realize restoration in any given area, the Church must, in addition to teaching about the truth, also be taught insights into God's purpose and timing for each truth. Teachers began to flourish and brought historical understanding and biblical context to what was occurring.

## Prophets

The restoration of prophetic ministry in the church has taken giant strides forward since the early 1980s. Leaders like Mike Bickle, Bill Hamon, John Paul Jackson, Rick Joyner, Graham Cooke, and others, introduced the notion that all believers can hear the voice of God and exercise prophetic gifts. By training prophetic people, these ministries demystified the spooky and seemingly unattainable aspects of the prophetic. By their teaching and example, these and others took abstract concepts and made them understandable, practical, and accessible.

## Apostles

From the very beginning, Pentecostal leaders such as Charles Parham, William Seymour, and John G. Lake described themselves as "apostolic" because thousands of their followers were being sent around the globe with the Pentecostal message. Since the Pentecostal movement had a clear identification with end-time revival and the "restoration of all things" described in Acts 3:19-21, it was not a big stretch for them to embrace the restoration of the prophetic and the apostolic.

The Center of World Missions announced that more people have come to Christ worldwide since 1980 than have been saved since the beginning of the church! We have seen global advances the last few years in prayer, evangelism, Tabernacle worship, and the prophetic—the restoration of the apostolic ministry is next on God's list. It will be the last to be fully restored, but is the first in the order of God's appointing in the Church. The last day apostolic ministry is placed last, as the final capstone of God's Church building (see Eph. 2:21).

## The Role of Apostle

The term *apostle* was first used by Jesus. *"It was at this time that He went off to the mountain to pray, and He spent the whole night in prayer to God. And when day came, He called His disciples to Him; and chose twelve of them, whom He also named as apostles"* (Luke 6:13).

As I said, the word *apostle* was well-known as a military or nautical term, not a spiritual one. The Greek word in its verb form simply means "to send," and could be applied generally to anyone or anything that was sent. However, in its noun form, an apostle was a specific title that referred to a specific function.

Bill Scheidler, in his excellent book, *Apostles*, writes: "The word "apostle" was originally a seafaring term that was most specifically applied to military expeditions. It at times referred to a fleet of ships and the officer that commanded the fleet. As time went on, it came to be applied to a man or group of men who were sent out on an official expedition that was authorized by the government for a particular purpose. It carried with it the idea of authorization and commissioning by the higher power to act on behalf of that power. Its meaning grew even more specific over time as the Greeks, and later the

Romans, sought to spread their cultural influence into all of the regions that had been conquered by their armies. In order to bring Greek or Roman rule to alien cultures, apostles would be authorized by the state and sent on expedition with a fleet of ships filled with colonists. These colonists would then set up a model city or colony with a model culture in the newly conquered lands. These colonies became regional centers from which Greek or Roman culture could be spread to the smaller cities and regions round about. In this way those nations that had been conquered militarily could be conquered ideologically and culturally as well."[1]

Later, an apostle was an official ambassador or emissary for a higher authority. As such, he was the embodiment and true representation of the sender. The "sent one" was to be absolutely faithful to the purposes and intentions of the sender. In the church realm, being named an apostle was a significant designation because it meant being sent to represent and further the advancement of the King and His Kingdom.

> *And He called the twelve together, and gave them power and authority over all the demons, and to heal diseases. And He sent them out [Greek word-apostello] to proclaim the kingdom of God, and to perform healing. And He said to them, "Take nothing for your journey, neither a staff, nor a bag, nor bread, nor money; and do not even have two tunics apiece. Whatever houses you enter, stay there until you leave that city." And as for those who do not receive you, as you go out from that city, shake off the dust from your feet as a testimony against them* (Luke 9:1-5).

## The Term Apostle

What other term could be better used that is so profoundly practical but also serves to describe the military and ambassadorial aspects of this gift? Our old view of what an apostle is must be adjusted to accommodate a more practical, biblical view rather than old, inaccurate concepts. The apostolic must be demystified and accepted as a normal part of church life.

To accept the apostolic we must demystify the concept of the apostolic through teaching and example, the same way the role of the prophetic has been changed. Since the Greek word for apostle as a verb could apply to anyone sent anywhere, it describes the kind of people we ought to be—those who "do exploits." Therefore our people and churches could *all* be characterized as apostolic if we acted that way.

We must begin to shift the complexion and vision of churches from a pastoral mind-set to an apostolic one. Instead of being maintenance-driven and primarily concerned about accommodating the flock and their needs, churches must exist to glorify God and expand His Kingdom. The historic pastoral mind-set has been little concerned with advancing God's purposes, instead wanting to maintain the status quo and care for the flock, which has helped create a condition I call "progressive immaturity." Rather than allow Christians to remain in this state of progressive immaturity, I suggest that apostles will broaden and sharpen the pastoral role alongside the other equipping ministries.

## Widespread and Reality-Based

There has been widespread popularity of reality-based television programming. "Cops," "Survivor," and others all tell tales of real people responding to real situations that are dangerous and sometimes life threatening. If something is not worth dying for, it's not worth living for either. Most Christians don't live a reality-based life of faith worth dying for, let alone living for. Part of the reason is the message hasn't been complete. The apostolic will help complete the church's message and restore the gospel of the Kingdom to the church.

The restoration and normalization of the apostolic will bring excitement, adventure, and danger back to the church's lifestyle. It will also scare those living on the fence, playing around with holy things. What was "normal" in the Book of Acts will no longer seem remote and distant. Look out! Apostles and prophets are being restored—what an exciting day awaits; the church is about to be "normal" again.

## The Corporate Anointing

*The hand of the Lord was upon me, and He brought me out by the Spirit of the Lord and set me down in the middle of the valley; and it was full of bones. He caused me to pass among them round about, and behold, there were very many on the surface of the valley; and lo, they were very dry. And He said to me, "Son of man, can these bones live?" And I answered, "O Lord God, You know." Again He said to me, "Prophesy over these bones, and say to them, 'O dry bones, hear the word of the Lord.' "Thus says the Lord God to these bones, 'Behold, I will cause breath to enter you that you may come to life.' I will put sinews on you, make flesh grow back on you, cover you with skin, and put breath in you that you may come alive; and you will know that I am the Lord.'"*

*So I prophesied as I was commanded; and as I prophesied, there was a noise, and behold, a rattling; and the bones came together, bone to its bone. And I looked, and behold, sinews were on them, and flesh grew, and skin covered them; but there was no breath in them. Then He said to me, "Prophesy to the breath, prophesy, son of man, and say to the breath, 'Thus says the Lord God, "Come from the four winds, O breath, and breathe on these slain, that they come to life."'" So I prophesied as He commanded me, and the breath came into them, and they came to life, and stood on their feet, an exceedingly great army.*

*Then He said to me, "Son of man, these bones are the whole house of Israel; behold, they say, 'Our bones are dried up, and our hope has perished. We are completely cut off.' "Therefore prophesy, and say to them, 'Thus says the Lord God, "Behold, I will open your graves and cause you to come up out of your graves, My people; and I will bring you into the land of Israel. Then you will know that I am the Lord, when I have opened your graves and caused you to come up out of your graves, My people. I will put My Spirit within you, and you will come to life, and I will place you on your own land. Then you will know that I, the Lord, have spoken and done it," declares the Lord'"* (Ezekiel 37:1-14).

While a few Bible scholars say this passage in Ezekiel was fulfilled in 1948 when Israel became a nation, I believe we have only partially seen the fulfillment. First of all, the prophetic ministry must be at a greater level of operation in the church at large for the works in the Scripture to be completed.

I believe the spirit of Elijah is a release of a new level of prophetic ministry coming to the earth through the church that will bear many earmarks to the ministry Elijah had. Jesus spoke of this coming ministry and the many things it would fulfill.

The power and authority seen in this type of ministry will be revealed with several different, clear signs:

## Fathering

> *Behold, I am going to send you Elijah the prophet before the coming of the great and terrible day of the Lord. He will restore the hearts of the fathers to their children, and the hearts of the children to their fathers, so that I will not come and smite the land with a curse* (Malachi 4:5-6).

This implies the restoration of the family. It also signifies the restoration of the whole concept of fathering and passing along a spiritual heritage and inheritance to the next generation. Elisha, with whom Elijah had no blood relationship, was the one the Lord told Elijah to transfer his mantle and anointing to when he disqualified himself by running away from his calling into the desert. Elisha called Elijah father.

> *When they had crossed over, Elijah said to Elisha, "Ask what I shall do for you before I am taken from you." And Elisha said, "Please, let a double portion of your spirit be upon me." And he said, "You have asked a hard thing. Nevertheless, if you see me when I am taken from you, it shall be so for you; but if not, it shall not be so."*
>
> *Then it came about as they were going along and talking, that behold, there appeared a chariot of fire and horses of fire which separated the two of them. And*

*Elijah went up by a whirlwind to heaven. And Elisha saw it and cried out, "My father, my father, the chariots of Israel and its horsemen!" And he saw him no more...(2 Kings 2:9-12).*

## Prophetic Signs and Apostolic Wonders

Acts 2:17-21 refers to the prophesy of Joel: *"'and it shall be in the last days,' God says, 'that I will pour fourth of my spirit upon all mankind; and your sons and your daughters shall prophesy, and your young men shall see visions, and your old men shall dream dreams; even upon my bondslaves, both and men and women, I will in those days pour forth of my spirit and they shall prophesy and I will grant wonders in the sky above, and signs on the earth beneath, blood, and fire, and vapor of smoke. The sun shall be turned into darkness, and the moon into blood, before the great and glorious day of the Lord shall come. And it shall be that everyone who calls on the name of the Lord shall be saved."*

Acts 2:43 speaks of this as well: *"Everyone kept feeling a sense of awe; and many wonders and signs were taking place through the apostles."*

## The Prophetic Confrontation

Elijah had the release and mandate from God to change the weather, the government, and the entire spiritual climate of Israel through his prophetic intervention. Can you imagine the upheaval that would come today if men and women of God would confront the brazen spiritual forces wrestling over cities and regions? Apostolic evangelists like Carlos Anacondia of Argentina have been doing this for over 20 years.

## Release of the Corporate Anointing

The passage in Ezekiel chapter 37 speaks of an "exceedingly great army" of God's people filled with His Spirit breathed into the bones by the prophetic ministry. As God's breath enters them, they become a wholly formed being, then a fully operating body, then an army. This reveals how crucial the prophetic ministry will be in forming the great end-time army. The prophesying over and to the body the very "breath of God," will bring about life.

This great army is not just a few gifted people and their followers; or simply a highly disciplined and aligned unit; it is the new move of God that is coming upon the earth, the corporate anointing! This describes a church that is fully formed, fully dressed, and ready for combat against the schemes of the enemy. This army of dread champions will no longer be intimidated by the taunts of the devil or back down when a battle arises; this army will not lose the war for the souls of men. In the Old Testament we see Moses, the man of God, followed by a great multitude that looked to him for everything. They expect Moses to hear from God for them, to defeat their enemies for them, and to daily provide for their needs.

The corporate anointing will not operate that way.

## The Anointing

The main distinction of this corporate anointing is that the churches and the Body of believers will work and move as one, much like the tribes in Israel when they gathered and coordinated their efforts for war. This will require a united company that realizes the need to work together, focusing their talents, energies, and resources on accomplishing one task. In addition, each member is equipped and ready to do whatever is necessary to get the job done.

The New Testament is clear that the church is to operate as a body, where each part is dependent on the other to function and succeed.

> *If the whole body were an eye, where would the hearing be? If the whole were hearing, where would the sense of smell be? But now God has placed the members, each one of them, in the body, just as He desired. And if they were all one member, where would the body be? But now there are many members, but one body. And the eye cannot say to the hand, "I have no need of you"; or again the head to the feet, "I have no need of you." On the contrary, it is much truer that the members of the body which seem to be weaker are necessary; and those members of the body, which we deem less honorable, on these we bestow more abundant honor, and our unseemly members come to have more abundant seemliness, whereas our seemly members have no need of it. But God has so composed the body, giving more abundant honor to that member which lacked, that there should be no division in the body, but that the members should have the same care for one another. And if one member suffers, all the members suffer with it; if one member is honored, all the members rejoice with it. Now you are Christ's body, and individually members of it* (1 Corinthians 12:17-27).

While we will maintain our individual callings, anointings, and functions, we must begin to join and work together to make the greatest impact. When all of us not only desire to see a large metro region, such as Atlanta won for Christ, but also take personal responsibility for it, then it will come to pass. That is what the Bible means when it says, "being of the same purpose". If we could just start to grasp the vision of the unleashed power of the Spirit through the church operating as a corporate entity cities will begin to fall to the Spirit's influence.

## "God's Gym"

Before I share the following vision, I must mention a few things about the word *gymnasium*. It is a European term for a secondary school that young people attend in preparation to attend a university. It comes from the Greek word *gymnasion* which means "place for exercising"; and the German word *gymnazein* which means "to train naked." The gym was a place to train and exercise openly and without shame. I find this was very true of what I saw in my vision.

After a near "intervention" by my older kids who were concerned about my health, I joined our neighborhood Gold's Gym. I go 2 or 3 times a week and have become familiar with the gym's people and operation. During one of my workouts, the Lord told me, "Look around— this is the church of the future." Instantly, my eyes were opened to see things about this gym I'd never seen before.

## 24/7 Church

The first thing I noticed was although the building was new and well equipped, it could never hold all of its 1,000+ members at the same time. Members have the option of dropping in between 5 A.M. and 10 P.M.—whenever it suits their schedules. Young moms stop in after their children are in school, businesspeople work out before or after going to the office, etc. All of a sudden, the concept of the 24/7 church went through my spirit, a place where every "member" is a participant, and all members are "working out" their gifts throughout the night and day.

## The Way It Is

In the vision I was then taken to a 1000+ seat auditorium that was filled with the gym's members who were quietly sitting and watching an experienced body builder ("...*for the equipping of the saints for the work of service, to the building up of the body,*" Eph. 4:12) work out on stage. While he did some bench presses, rode a bike, and used an "abs" machine, admirers watched from their seats. I thought, "How silly—all these people are all dressed up to work out, but they are sitting there watching someone else do it."

The only equipment was on the stage, and there was no place for anyone else to work out. The entire auditorium was designed so all could observe someone else do what they were dressed and ready to do—work out. I knew that the Lord was using this example to show me how the church was currently operating—99 percent of the members watch the other 1 percent use their gifts.

Then this Scripture came to me "...*continue to work out your salvation with fear and trembling, for it is God who works in you to will and to act according to his good purpose.*" (Philippians 2:12-13 NIV).

Imagine a church where the members are functioning and participating rather than the entertainment-driven, spectator-oriented churches we see today! What if the church had full employment? Remember that Scripture about the landowner?

*For the kingdom of heaven is like a landowner who went out early in the morning to hire laborers for his vineyard. And when he had agreed with the laborers for a denarius for the day, he sent them into his vineyard.*

*And he went out about the third hour and saw others standing idle in the market place; and to those he said, 'You too go into the vineyard, and whatever is right I will give you.' And so they went.*

*Again he went out about the sixth and the ninth hour, and did the same thing. And about the eleventh hour he went out, and found others standing; and he said to them, "Why have you been standing here idle all day long?" They said to him, "Because no one hired us." He said to them, "You too go into the vineyard."*

*And when evening had come, the owner of the vineyard said to his foreman, "Call the laborers and pay them their wages, beginning with the last group to the first."*

*And when those hired about the eleventh hour came, each one received a denarius. And when those hired first came, they thought that they would receive more; and they also received each one a denarius. And when they received it, they grumbled at the landowner, saying, "These last men have worked only one hour, and you have made them equal to us who have borne the burden and the scorching heat of the day."*

*But he answered and said to one of them, "Friend, I am doing you no wrong; did you not agree with me for a denarius? Take what is yours and go your way, but I wish to give to this last man the same as to you. Is it not lawful for me to do what I wish with what is my own? Or is your eye envious because I am generous?"*

*Thus the last shall be first, and the first last* (Matthew 20:1-16).

While this Scripture seems only to be teaching us about having a good attitude toward people God blesses, if we look closely, we see it is primarily about employment, not enjoyment. It shows us Father's desire to get all His children employed in ministry. While the landowner went out five times to attempt to employ people for work, his rate of pay was great especially for those employed late in the day.

## Every Member Functioning

The next thing I was shown about this gym was that everybody who came in had a different area where they "worked out," each had a part in one aspect of the whole—whether it was waiting...(*Wait for the Lord; be strong, and let your heart take courage*, Ps. 27:14); or running...(*Do you not know that those who run in a race all **run**, but only one receives the prize? **Run** in such a way that you may win*, 1 Cor. 9:24); or the bench press (*Not that I have already obtained it, or have already become perfect, but I **press** on in order that I may lay hold of that for which also I was laid hold of by Christ Jesus*, Phil. 3:12).

## "Working out"

I was shown one last but significant thing—people were coming to the gym because they could work out and exercise their gifts. They came to "do" and "be" something, not just hear talk or theory. They came to be equipped, not entertained. It was clear to me then that this "God's Gym" was His desire for

His Church, where every member is a participant rather than a spectator; where the body is equipped rather than entertained; where the five-fold ministry—apostles, prophets, pastors, teachers, and evangelists—no longer do the majority or all of the ministry; but instead, the body is "working out" and doing the ministry.

## Ex-or-cising

Finally, I was shown that in the immediate future there will be a lot of exorcising (casting out of demons) among God's people. The Lord spoke to me in August 2002. He said: "My church is out of shape, and it needs to exorcise." I felt this meant that without deliverance and cleansing, the church will be unable to arise to her God-given destiny. I believe we will see a much more powerful manifestation of the deliverance anointing poured out on the church, causing deliverances in the saved and unsaved!

## Authority and Responsibility

*And He called the twelve together, and gave them power and authority over all the demons, and to heal diseases."* (Luke 9:1).

*And having summoned His twelve disciples, He gave them authority over unclean spirits, to cast them out, and to heal every kind of disease and every kind of sickness* (Matthew 10:1).

The Greek word for authority used here is *exousia* meaning "power to act, authority": It is translated authorities (7 times), authority (65 times), control (1 time), domain (2 times), dominion (1 times), in charge (1 time), jurisdiction (1time), liberty (1 time), power (11 times), powers (1 time), right (11 times).

It's interesting to note that in Luke chapter 9 Jesus calls the disciples together and gives them this authority. The progression: called, gave, sent. We read in Luke 9:6: *"Departing, they began going throughout the villages, preaching the gospel, and healing everywhere."*

By Luke 10:1, Jesus sees how well this is working so He sends 70 more!

*Now after this the Lord appointed seventy others, and sent them two and two ahead of Him to every city and place where He Himself was going to come. And He was saying to them, "The harvest is plentiful, but the laborers are few; therefore beseech the Lord of the harvest to send out laborers into His harvest. Go your ways; behold, I send you out as lambs in the midst of wolves. Carry no purse, no bag, no shoes; and greet no one on the way. And whatever house you enter, first say, "Peace be to this house." And if a man of peace is there, your peace will rest upon him; but if not, it will return to you. And stay in that house, eating and drinking what they give you; for the laborer is worthy of his wages. Do not keep moving from house to house. And whatever city you enter, and they receive you, eat what is set before you; and heal those in it who are sick, and say to them, "The kingdom of God has come near to you." But whatever city you enter and they do not receive you, go out into its streets and say, "Even the dust of your city which clings to our feet, we wipe off in protest against you; yet be sure of this, that the kingdom of God has come near."*

*I say to you, it will be more tolerable in that day for Sodom, than for that city. Woe to you, Chorazin! Woe to you, Bethsaida! For if the miracles had been performed in Tyre and Sidon which occurred in you, they*

*would have repented long ago, sitting in sackcloth and ashes. "But it will be more tolerable for Tyre and Sidon in the judgment, than for you. And you, Capernaum, will not be exalted to heaven, will you? You will be brought down to Hades! The one who listens to you listens to Me, and the one who rejects you rejects Me; and he who rejects Me rejects the One who sent Me. And the seventy returned with joy, saying, "Lord, even the demons are subject to us in Your name"*
(Luke 10:1-17).

Just look at this. In Luke chapter 9, Jesus called, gave, and sent. In Luke chapter 10, things are going so well that He even sent 70 more; by verse 17 they say "even the demons are subject to us in Your name." Then look at Luke 11:1: *"It happened that while He was praying in a certain place, after He had finished, one of His disciples said to Him, 'Lord, teach us to pray just as John also taught his disciples.'"*

Steve Thompson, vice president of Morningstar Ministries and a good friend of mine, was the first to help me notice this: Jesus' order of releasing people to do ministry begins with Him calling and sending them with His authority. They are first called, then sent. They didn't even know how to pray yet, and He still sent them and trusted them with His authority. *Wow!*

God's calling and giving them His authority is what qualifies them. They are so inexperienced; they don't know how to pray, but they do know how to trust and believe and then do what they saw Jesus doing just as Jesus did what He saw the Father doing! There is also a clear correlation between receiving authority from the Lord to do the things mentioned in Scripture, and also being willing to bear the responsibility that comes with using that authority.

For example, we could all say we desire more spiritual authority to heal sicknesses like cancer or cast out strongholds with a word. But how willing are we to take on the responsibility that comes with the job? Are we willing to endure the drought so we may prophesy, like Elijah? Are we willing to nurse and care for the visions we prophetically birth?

In His wisdom and plan, God has amazingly entrusted us (believers) with the ability to exercise His authority to deal with sickness, demons, and death. Jesus never told us to pray for the sick, but Jesus said, "heal the sick," assuming we would.

Shirking responsibility is one of the reasons there is a "great divide" between the clergy and laity in the church, between those who do the ministry and those who watch others do it. While much has been written and said about the "control spirit" operating in most churches by the leaders, more needs to be presented about the Body's responsibility to do the works of the ministry.

When push comes to shove, there seems to be reluctance on the part of many Christians to do what it takes to do the job. Currently the majority of believers are content to sit, watch, and go home, unfazed with any personal responsibility. The adage, "Everybody's responsibility is no one's" is true. While leadership hasn't led the way in releasing the saints as they should, the Body at large hasn't taken steps to assume responsibility. While the typical pastor would love his congregation to begin to shoulder responsibility for aspects of ministry, many either back off or "drop the ball" when given the opportunity.

## Why?

Christians in the United States have been reluctant to take responsibility and use the authority that God has given us.

The attitude is, "The pastor gets paid to do that, so let him do it."

Most of us would be shocked to know that the New Testament only mentions the gift of pastor one time, teacher three times, evangelist two times, prophet or prophets (in New Testament context) over 60 times, and apostle or apostles over 50 times. Since the preponderance of biblical evidence suggests that the current church system has little resemblance to New Testament Christianity, we ought to reconsider the way we are doing church, if it appears to be successful.

*"Thus says the Lord of hosts, 'This people says, "The time has not come, even the time for the house of the Lord to be rebuilt."'" Then the word of the Lord came by Haggai the prophet saying, "Is it time for you yourselves to dwell in your paneled houses while this house lies desolate?"*

*Now therefore, thus says the Lord of hosts, "Consider your ways! You have sown much, but harvest little; you eat, but there is not enough to be satisfied; you drink, but there is not enough to become drunk; you put on clothing, but no one is warm enough; and he who earns, earns wages to put into a purse with holes."*

*Thus says the Lord of hosts, "Consider your ways! Go up to the mountains, bring wood and rebuild the temple, that I may be pleased with it and be glorified," says the Lord. "You look for much, but behold, it comes to little; when you bring it home, I blow it away. Why?" declares the Lord of hosts, "Because of My house which lies desolate, while each of you runs to his own house. Therefore, because of you the sky has withheld its dew, and the earth has withheld its produce. I called for a drought on the land, on the mountains, on the grain, on the new wine, on the oil, on what the ground produces, on men, on cattle, and on all the labor of your hands"* (Haggai 1:2-11).

The passage says, *"consider your ways."* I believe that we need to consider the ways we keep doing church. We need to equip the saints and release them into their own ministries rather than corralling them into serving someone else's. The whole "superstar-one man show" thing needs to be toned down. People need to be emancipated with grace rather than driven by laws.

Fear is holding people back from fulfilling their destinies, and holds leaders back from breaking out of their "business as usual" so they can release the saints into their ministries. Fear of tweaking the present system holds leaders back, while fear of failure holds back church members. Fear of political backlash is a major stumbling block within the church.

Considering other ways requires faith and the willingness to take a risk. It will take faith on the part of leaders to develop the new wineskin, and it will take faith for the masses to choose to be functioning members of the Body. Those in leadership risk their security and success. Those in the Body may think, "What if I miss it and they are not healed?" or "what if I fail?"

## Superstar Ministries

The Superstar Syndrome is alive and well as super-gifted leaders amass large ministries around themselves. While the vast majority love God and have pure motives, I believe they are perpetuating a "welfare system" of Christianity where the people stay unemployed (not functioning in their gifts) and receive "food stamps" every Sunday.

Since Dr. Cho of Korea proved it was possible for a pastor to have a church of a million people, the epitome of success for most pastors is to have a 2,000-5,000-member church. These ministries are thought to have a powerful anointing from the Lord on the leader, the main one using their gifting in the ministry while the others use theirs to serve his. Jack Coe, William Branham, Oral Roberts, and others all operated this way, as well as many do today. I have studied and admired the lives and ministries of great men and women of God, and have noticed that the great majority of them have either fell or failed.

As I questioned why, I came up with at least one answer. All of these leaders operated their ministries under the assumption that they were God's anointed *one*, God's chosen vessel, God's anointed. This helped spawn a group of followers who emulated their tremendous ministry. Rather than helping their followers find their own unique gifts and callings, they enjoyed the idea of being supported and watched as they did their ministry. Many godly people have been willing to follow someone like this because they have no need for the spotlight or the things associated with that type of recognition.

While it is true that many in the Body operate in the ministry of helps (which exists to help others), what about everyone else? The Scripture is clear that New Testament ministry is plural, corporate, and humble. While the majority of the leaders of these great ministries were gracious and released many around them into their callings and destinies, the masses they ministered to were only blessed and not in the least bit equipped. A few started schools of healing and such, but the model was still the same—the one-man show where people came to see one person function in their gifting.

Most of these great leaders did not have the revelation that the Body is more than one organ or one part. Most didn't understand that we all have the mind of Christ. The whole concept of team leadership, corporate anointing, and the need we all have for one another, is something they didn't understand.

## Nameless and Faceless

I have prayed and worked with ministers in our city for the last 10 years pursuing unity and citywide revival. During that time several popular national leaders moved here to start churches or base their ministries. Figuring we could use their help, my wife and I asked the Lord about their involvement with us in the area of city leadership. While all had significant ministries, they were more concerned about building their own ministry rather than working with city outreach. I asked several to "take the ball" of leadership in efforts to reach the city, but they declined or seemed uninterested. I simply assumed my approach was wrong or I was too idealistic in approaching them. After asking the Lord about this, He startled us with His quick response to our inquiry. He said, "They are neither nameless nor faceless."

We understood what this meant because prophets had given words years before that God was going to raise up a nameless, faceless company that would shake the world and redefine how Christianity is understood by the world. It was obvious that while these significant and influential ministries could have helped, they would not because they had a name to uphold and a reputation to protect.

The lesson I learned from this experience was that the church must change the old concepts to allow the new to come. The old wineskin of the superstar ministry and the one-man show must be relinquished; and leadership hanging onto the old will impede the way for the new. The new wineskin of a nameless, faceless company can only be led by God's servants who truly have no desire for their own name to be recognized. In the old wineskin's place will come the new wineskin where the corporate anointing is priority, and a substantial and subsequent release of saints operating in their ministries will be seen.

## The Church Welfare System

In the 1980s and '90s, American politics recognized the failure of the social welfare state put in place in the 1960s to bring help to the unemployed. This welfare system gave families food stamps and a monthly check to assist them while looking for work. While the idea behind this was a noble and generous attempt to help those less fortunate, it proved a failure in getting people employed and instead created a system that an entire generation depended on for support. The poor stayed poor and the rich got richer.

The failed government welfare system is eerily similar to what the church has experienced in the last generation. A small caste of people, government bureaucrats (pastors), do nearly all the ministry and the rest exist to serve their ministries and remain unemployed, not using their gifts. They receive a check (blessing) as well as food stamps (Sunday message) regularly.

The problem: as long as this system is in place, the masses will continue to stay chronically unemployed with little self-esteem and knowledge of God. Just as those in government realized the spectacular failure of this program, leadership must consider the ways and change the failed system.

Nowhere in Scripture do you find this kind of spiritual welfare state except when Israel demanded to have a king like all the other nations. What they got for that request was Saul, who proved to be quite a problem. God's intent was never to have a superman or star-based ministry but a Body or company of saints representing Him on the earth—their legacy and destiny God wants to be glorious! In my Bible I find the plural word *saints* 68 times. Just look at a few of the promises they have been given:

—Psalms 16:3 *"As for the saints who are in the earth, they are the majestic ones in whom is all my delight."*

—Daniel 7:18 *"But the saints of the Highest One will receive the kingdom and possess the kingdom forever, for all ages to come."*

—Daniel 7:22 *"until the Ancient of Days came, and judgment was passed in favor of the saints of the Highest One, and the time arrived when the saints took possession of the kingdom."*

—Daniel 7:27 *"Then the sovereignty, the dominion, and the greatness of all the kingdoms under the whole heaven will be given to the people of the saints of the Highest One; His kingdom will be an everlasting kingdom, and all the dominions will serve and obey Him."*

—Ephesians 1:18-23 *"I pray that the eyes of your heart may be enlightened, so that you may know what is the hope of His calling, what are the riches of the glory of His inheritance in the saints, and what is the surpassing greatness of His power toward us who believe. These are in accordance with the working of the strength of His might which He brought about in Christ, when He raised Him from the dead, and seated Him at His right hand in the heavenly places, far above all rule and authority and power and dominion, and every name that is named, not only in this age, but also in the one to come. And He put all things in subjection under His feet, and gave Him as head over all things to the church, which is His body, the fullness of Him who fills all in all."*

—Colossians 1:25-27 *"Of this church I was made a minister according to the stewardship from God bestowed on me for your benefit, that I might fully carry out the preaching of the word of God, that is, the mystery which has been hidden from the past ages and generations; but has now been manifested to His saints, to whom God willed to make known what is the riches of the glory of this mystery among the Gentiles, which is Christ in you, the hope of glory."*

All of these Scriptures and prophecies point to today, when the saints, the corporate Body of Christ, will awaken and possess the inheritance they have in Christ—no longer intimidated by the enemy. The prophetic have already declared it, the apostolic will do it, the army of God will arise, and His glory will truly be seen!

**Endnote**

1. Bill Scheidler, *Apostles: The Fathering Servant: A Fresh Biblical Perspective on Their Role Today* (Portland, Oregon: City Christian Publishing, 2004).

CHAPTER 9

# THE LAND RUSH

The Land Rush of 1889 in the Oklahoma territories generated zeal, excitement, and shear energy. Folks were to get their land, to possess their future! Over 50,000 participated in this government-sponsored race for land!

As you read earlier, I had a series of three dreams over a five-week period that shook and even frightened me. I know that the Lord intended for me to include them in this book and realized that their timing was significant.

Right after we moved into our new home, I had a vision of this Oklahoma Land Rush of 1889, highlighted in the movies, *Far and Away*, *Cimarron*, and *Oklahoma*. I saw all the wagons and horsemen lined up heading off toward the Oklahoma territory in a cloud of dust to "stake a claim" on the land that they found and would settle on. The federal law driving the surge westward was the "Homestead Act" which specified that each family or person could have up to 160 acres of land free and clear if they would work and develop the land for five years. The act also stipulated that the property was immune from any person attempting to use it as a lien on a debt they might have. Bottom line: the land was free and unable to be seized by anyone as long as they were willing to work it.

I felt the Lord was saying that an edict was released from Heaven allowing us to grab our "land in the Spirit" *now*, and that we should "stake our claim" in this land race in the spirit realm and possess our callings and destinies. *Now* is the time, not tomorrow, but today!

Like the uncharted territory of Oklahoma represents uncharted spiritual places, believers need to take advantage of the opportunity to claim the land. But there is one condition— we must work our land. I am not in any way implying that these callings and gifting are not free, they are. But God rewards stewardship, and faith has to be exercised and worked for it to grow and flourish. It is free and clear of any obligation; *however*, we have to do the work to make it fully ours.

There is a difference between work ,which we can enjoy  and toiling by the sweat of our brow. In Genesis chapter 3, Adam was cursed to toil and work the land to produce fruit.

*Then to Adam He said, "Because you have listened to the voice of your wife, and have eaten from the tree about which I commanded you, saying, 'You shall not eat from it'; cursed is the ground because of you; in toil you shall eat of it all the days of your life"* (Genesis 3:17).

Before this Adamic curse was placed on this planet, things grew without any human effort or help. But after Adam sinned by eating of the tree of good, hard work became necessary for us to live, eat, and prosper.

While all of us would love not to labor for a living, having something to do in the garden is essential for our well-being. Nothing is more rewarding than to see the fruit of productive labor or to bring in a good crop. On the other hand, nothing can be more discouraging than for us to slave away at something for months or years and then see no fruit or even bad fruit from such toil. One of the results of the Fall is man toiling in vain without seeing a crop harvested and realizing that sweat was the only result of his labor.

Solomon spoke of the reward of fruitful labor, marriage, and a blessed life even when it comes to an end:

*Enjoy life with the woman whom you love all the days of your fleeting life which He has given to you under the sun; for this is your reward in life, and in your toil in which you have labored under the sun. Whatever your hand finds to do, verily, do it with all your might;...* (Ecclesiastes 9:9-10).

We must "work the land" of our callings and destinies to fully possess them. They require our commitment to be willing to "pay the price" to clear the time in our schedules, reprioritize our lives, and deal with the many excuses we have not to work out these things. All our callings are gifts, but they all require stewardship.

Just as in the beginning Adam was given authority over this planet that required stewardship, so we too have to step up, quit making excuses, and enter into using our gifts and working our calling. The Lord won't do this for us. He won't hand us a fully worked out calling; we have to do it in His power and strength. *"And working together with Him..."* (2 Cor. 6:1). He won't do it for us, and we can't do it without Him.

*Now may the God of peace who brought up our Lord Jesus from the dead, that great Shepherd of the sheep, through the blood of the everlasting covenant, make you complete in every good work to do His will, working in you what is well pleasing in His sight, through Jesus Christ, to whom be glory forever and ever* (Hebrews 13:20-21 NKJV).

Because our present church system accommodates chronic spiritual unemployment, as we move over to "full employment" and all begin to function (however imperfectly), it will be quite a shock to the system. But the world has little problem with having a relationship with Jesus if we present Him as

He really is. Many people in the world have nothing good to say about the church, but they really haven't seen the church except in a distorted form.

A pastor friend of mine from South Carolina said that he was asked to present a school commencement service. He said that he walked up on stage and was getting ready to pray from the well-known passage in Isaiah 64:1: *"Oh, that Thou wouldst rend the heavens and come down;..."* But all of a sudden the Lord spoke to him and said: "Instead why don't you pray, 'Oh that you would rend the flesh so I might come out!'" The pastor was shocked.

Ever since the ark, people have been trying to put God in manmade boxes! God wants to arise out of us so He can touch and affect others. If we could get out of God's way just enough so people could see Jesus in us, they would love Him! But instead we show them us, religion, church, and all kinds of other stuff that aren't too attractive. It is time to go get our land and work it.

Caution: there is a danger for those choosing to sit on the sidelines during this time. Because we are all called to fulfill our ministries and work out our salvation, those who won't or don't will feel condemned and may become critical and judgmental of those who do. We must not allow this judgmental spirit to deter the ones who are finding their callings.

> *For we hear that there are some who walk among you in a disorderly manner, not working at all, but are busybodies. Now those who are such we command and exhort through our Lord Jesus Christ that they work in quietness and eat their own bread*
> (2 Thessalonians 3:11-12 NKJV).

Busybodies are really not those busy with the work of the Kingdom; they are busy maligning those who are through gossip and judgment. The only thing a busybody is busy doing is giving into a jealous, critical spirit. Because these folks won't work their land, they spend all their time tearing down those who do. After being in ministry for more than 25 years, I am absolutely convinced that most church splits and schisms occur not as a result of differences or a lack of unity, but as a result of discontented, fussy, unproductive people becoming jealous and critical while watching happy, productive people.

Those who are clear about their callings and are pursuing them do not criticize others who are doing the same. In other words fruitful believers do not those cause problems. Winners won't cause problems, but whiners will. Those who are lazy, disobedient, fruitless, and failures *love* blaming others for their ineffectiveness and lack of power. Bitter jealousy, worldliness, and laziness are the reasons behind most church splits, *not* a need for some kind of gushy unity.

> *What is the source of quarrels and conflicts among you? Is not the source your pleasures that wage war in your members? You lust and do not have; so you commit murder. And you are envious and cannot obtain; so you fight and quarrel. You do not have because you do not ask. You ask and do not receive, because you ask with wrong motives, so that you may spend it on your pleasures. You adulteresses, do you not know that friendship with the world is hostility toward God? Therefore whoever wishes to be a friend of the world makes himself an enemy of God* (James 4:1-4).

Get hold of your land, stake your claim, and work what the Lord is giving you! God's inheritance is free for the taking. If you're still not clear what it is, God can make that clear to you if you are willing and able. It will take courage to possess and defend our inheritance! Joshua received the following marching orders before he went to war to possess his inheritance:

*Now it came about after the death of Moses the servant of the Lord that the Lord spoke to Joshua the son of Nun, Moses' servant, saying, "Moses My servant is dead; now therefore arise, cross this Jordan, you and all this people, to the land which I am giving to them, to the sons of Israel.*

*Every place on which the sole of your foot treads, I have given it to you, just as I spoke to Moses. From the wilderness and this Lebanon, even as far as the great river, the river Euphrates, all the land of the Hittites, and as far as the Great Sea toward the setting of the sun, will be your territory.*

*No man will be able to stand before you all the days of your life. Just as I have been with Moses, I will be with you; I will not fail you or forsake you. Be strong and courageous, for you shall give this people possession of the land which I swore to their fathers to give them. Be strong and very courageous; be careful to do according to all the law which Moses My servant commanded you; do not turn from it to the right or to the left, so that you may have success wherever you go.*

*"This book of the law shall not depart from your mouth, but you shall meditate on it day and night, so that you may be careful to do according to all that is written in it; for then you will make your way prosperous, and then you will have success. Have I not commanded you? Be strong and courageous! Do not tremble or be dismayed, for the Lord your God is with you wherever you go."*

*Then Joshua commanded the officers of the people, saying, "Pass through the midst of the camp and command the people, saying, 'Prepare provisions for yourselves, for within three days you are to cross this Jordan, to go in to possess the land which the Lord your God is giving you, to possess it.'"*

*And to the Reubenites and to the Gadites and to the half-tribe of Manasseh, Joshua said, "Remember the word which Moses the servant of the Lord commanded you, saying, 'The Lord your God gives you rest, and will give you this land.' Your wives, your little ones, and your cattle shall remain in the land which Moses gave you beyond the Jordan, but you shall cross before your brothers in battle array, all your valiant warriors, and shall help them, until the Lord gives your brothers rest, as He gives you, and they also possess the land which the Lord your God is giving them. Then you shall return to your own land, and possess that which Moses the servant of the Lord gave you beyond the Jordan toward the sunrise."*

*They answered Joshua, saying, "All that you have commanded us we will do, and wherever you send us we will go. Just as we obeyed Moses in all things, so we will obey you; only may the Lord your God be with you, as He was with Moses. Anyone who rebels against your command and does not obey your words in all that you command him, shall be put to death; only be strong and courageous* (Joshua 1:1-18).

Look at the things the Lord focused Joshua on before he went into battle:

1. Acknowledgment of the old leadership and the anointing of the new one—Joshua. New leadership must be recognized and released to bring the people into the new land!

2. Assurance that God would be with Joshua (the new) even as He was with the old (Moses) and even more so, as well as a charge to the Body to obey, submit, and follow Joshua as much as or more than they followed Moses.

3. A command to be *strong* and *courageous* four times. This clearly reveals the dangerous and threatening situations that they would be facing. However, the Lord assures that He will be with them and they *will* possess the land, if they don't wilt or faint.

I have recently seen numbers of believers just...quit! They quit their walk with the Lord, quit their marriages, quit church, quit their jobs, and abandon their callings all because they ended up in situations that required courage, and they couldn't handle the pressure of battle. The thing we all fear most is losing our life, but that was the first thing that Jesus said we had to lose to follow Him! The word "life" is the Greek word *psuche* and means our "natural, organic life" here on earth. Jesus promised if we followed Him and lost our *psuche*, we would gain eternal life which is the Greek word *zoe*. God give us *zoe* as we lose our love for our *psuche*.

## The Rodan/Rodin Dream

The Lord can use movies, songs, and other means to speak to us. He uses many unique and personalized ways to speak to His people so they will hear Him and believe. While some people think that any use of secular media cannot be God speaking, I disagree. The Bible is clear that God uses *all* creation and even things created by humans to draw us to Him. Most Christians would view Michelangelo's painting of the Sistine chapel as divinely inspired—there are many manmade things that absolutely reveal the Creator operating through His created ones.

> *For I am not ashamed of the gospel, for it is the power of God for salvation to everyone who believes, to the Jew first and also to the Greek. For in it the righteousness of God is revealed from faith to faith; as it is written, "but the righteous man shall live by faith."*
>
> *For the wrath of God is revealed from heaven against all ungodliness and unrighteousness of men, who suppress the truth in unrighteousness, **because that which is known about God is evident within them; for God made it evident to them.***
>
> ***For since the creation of the world His invisible attributes, His eternal power and divine nature, have been clearly seen, being understood through what has been made, so that they are without excuse.** For even though they knew God, they did not honor Him as God, or give thanks; but they became futile in their speculations, and their foolish heart was darkened* (Romans 1:16-21).

This passage says that God's nature is evident everywhere. This include beings created in His image who have divine sparks of genius and intellect, who solve immense problems, invent miraculous cures, write brilliant music, or create inspired works of art. All of these things cry out telling about our Creator. Even the unbelieving  preach the attributes of God. There are no secular and sacred divisions of life. Everything good ultimately proceeds from a good God.

> *Every good thing given and every perfect gift is from above, coming down from the Father of lights, with whom there is no variation or shifting shadow* (James 1:17).

*Just as you do not know the path of the wind and how bones are formed in the womb of the pregnant woman, so you do not know the activity of God who makes all things* (Ecclesiastes 11:5).

While it is less complicated to lump every person, action, and activity on earth into either a secular or spiritual box, it is entirely inaccurate to do so based on Scripture and life. I believe that the idea that certain forms of music are from the devil or certain genres of writing are reserved for satan, is laughable and severely limits God. It takes little faith to limit God. God is not a "mob boss" competing with satan for territory.

God can and does speak through whatever medium we allow Him to. He speaks through His Word in a primary way, but He will use any and all means to communicate to us. It is interesting to note that if God uses only the Scripture to speak to us, then why did Jesus tell parables about farming, fishing, building, and life to teach His disciples? God cannot be forced into a limiting and confined space just because that is the only way our minds can comprehend Him.

Scripture is the primary way He communicates with man, but He also can use dreams, visions and many other ways. These "other ways" need to pass through the scrutiny of Scripture. The Bible is filled with bizarre stories of God coming in supernatural experiences to get through to His people.

Scripture tells us we receive the good we have faith for, and that unbelief hinders us from seeing things purely.

*To the pure all things are pure, but to those who are defiled and unbelieving nothing is pure; but even their mind and conscience are defiled* (Titus 1:15 NKJV).

We all have a different set of impressions, visual and auditory, as a result of our life experiences. God will use these images for His glory and our edification and admonishment. For example, if you are an avid hunter, God might use pictures or analogies that an experienced sportsman can relate to such as a tree stand, shotgun, etc. To someone who is a disciplined musician, it wouldn't be especially effective or meaningful for God to use hunting. The Lord uses what you are familiar with to speak to you.

The MTV generation was raised on video and music imagery, not books or images of their parent's generation. Many of today's young people are more versed in visual images than English literature, so God speaks to them in familiar, relatable ways. Bottom line: God is speaking in many ways, and we need to be listening.

## The Third Dream

Before I relate to you my third and strangest dream, let me caution you if you are unfamiliar with the prophetic. The typology of individual dreams is not the same for everyone. It has taken me many years to receive the level of understanding I have now, which is still limited and imperfect. I believe that most supernatural communication from God comes in the form of dreams, yet the church knows very little about them.

> *In a dream, in a vision of the night, when deep sleep falls upon men, While slumbering on their beds, then He opens the ears of men, and seals their instruction. In order to turn man from his deed, and conceal pride from man, he keeps back his soul from the Pit, And his life from perishing by the sword*
> (Job 33:15-18 NKJV).

All prophetic dreams and visions seem to have three different ingredients. Sometimes without getting the other ingredients, the revelations are incomplete and difficult to understand. The three ingredients:

1. Revelation (what is seen or perceived);
2. Interpretation (the meaning);
3. Application (how it is applied).

I will relate this dream in these three different pieces.

## Revelation

A familiar, local leader in Atlanta was leading a group of young people on some kind of trip, and my 16-year-old son, Jordan, was invited by the leader to go along. They were not flying on an airplane, but the passengers were in a compartment strapped to the back of what seemed to be a huge prehistoric pterodactyl—similar to the one featured in the 1960s Japanese sci-fi movie *Rodan*. The compartment was similar to the four-passenger seats with a roof that they strap on an elephant's back to transport royalty in India and Thailand. The group was lifting off over a nearby lake, and they went down right on the edge of the water. It appeared that no one was hurt, and the passengers who fell into the water swam out, most not even getting wet. I don't know what happened to the big, prehistoric bird.

I woke up, and I have to admit I was a little upset and wondering what it meant for my son, Jordan. But after just praying for a few minutes the Lord began to speak to me the interpretation, and I was assured that Jordan was only in my dream for what he represents. It took me about three days to receive enough understanding about it to have a rudimentary interpretation and application.

## Interpretation

The leader represented a local but also national leader who at one time was very radical and on the cutting edge of what God was doing with young people. However, today that leader is mired in old beliefs and failed systems that severely limit his effectiveness. Jordan and the other youth going on the trip represent the new breed of young people who are very prophetic and on fire for God. They haven't bought in to my generation's failures enough for him to be tainted with religion. *Jordan* also means "inheritance of worship." This new breed of youth are totally committed, on fire, and already active in signs and wonders ministries to the lost. Church to them is defined as any two in His name. They will make no excuses if they have a lack of power; instead they expect to operate with it.

The meaning of *Rodan* was the most intriguing. While airplanes sometimes represent ministry vehicles, this was an imaginary, prehistoric bird with little semblance to today's birds. No one has ever seen one except through fossils. This method of transportation represented a desire to lead young people on an idealistic and archaic quest to discover aspects of early Christianity that don't exist or may have never existed. Just the idea that it crashed so quickly was a sign of the mercy of God. It also symbolized the danger of letting leaders like that lead our young. They could have all been killed.

In addition, they were all being carried by Rodan (the bird). I felt the Lord showed me a double-meaning for it was *Rodin*, the French sculptor, whose crowning work was a colossal sculpture called "The Thinker." Most know about this classic work. I sensed those attempting to minister or fly by relying on "The Thinker" would crash and fail. The crash of this bird/flight represents the old leadership attempting to take the young on "a flight of fancy" that wouldn't work and has never worked. It is with the heart that people believe, and that is how all is accomplished in the Kingdom. It will not be done by intellect or strategic thinking, but faith operating through the Spirit.

## Application

This dream was a warning about older leaders who attempt to take the young or the next generation on flights of fancy that don't work and are even dangerous, born out of deep thought (The Thinker). Older leaders can only lead where they have actually been in the Spirit. In addition, each generation needs its own crop of young leaders to lead. A combination of both young and old leaders is necessary.

**Endnote**

1. Rodan is a trademark of Sony Pictures©

# CHAPTER 10

# GOD RELEASED

Ever since the Fall in the Garden of Eden, God has wanted to restore His personal relationship with His creation and walk in close proximity with them even though they were tarnished by sin.

> *Then I will dwell among the Israelites and be their God. They will know that I am the Lord their God, who brought them out of Egypt so that I might dwell among them. I am the Lord their God* (Exodus 29:45-46).

There is something inherent in the fallen nature of humankind which fears intimacy and relationship with God the Father. A relationship will cost us something, so to keep our distance, we tend to indulge in religious activity which on the surface may look moral, benevolent, and even noble. However, it is more or less a smokescreen to evade an inevitable encounter with his Creator that demands accountability for the way we live our lives and spend our time.

From Moses' day when God seemed to be only "up on that mountain," to King David's reign when God was viewed to exist in the Ark of the Covenant box, to today, people have consistently tried to avoid any relationship with God that might become "too personal." Even though Jesus Christ has accomplished through the Cross all that was required to remove all barriers to a vital and personal relationship with God, we still attempt to hold on tightly to our "personal space."

The tendency to evade this intimacy is nothing new or even surprising. Many wives can relate to this "avoidance of intimacy" at which some men have become experts.

*And they heard the sound of the Lord God walking in the garden in the cool of the day, and the man and his wife hid themselves from the presence of the Lord God among the trees of the garden* (Genesis 3:8).

## Avoidance Anxiety

Avoiding a personal relationship with God has created a tolerance for a distant sort of Christian "gentleman's agreement" with God. And while this without any strings attached Christianity is very popular in our land right now, God would never consider it successful. Every church leader wants to make an impact for the Kingdom and attempting to be relevant to the unchurched is essential to accomplishing that goal. That is one of the prime reasons "seeker-friendly" churches and "emergent" ministries have infiltrated the spiritual landscape. They are proliferating at a rapid pace as an antidote to religious traditionalism, and because spiritual leaders, searching for success, have endorsed these types of ministries. Outwardly these ministries appear to be taking ground, but under the surface this brand of "easy believism" is keeping many new believers spiritual infants, making dependents instead of disciples.

Jesus judged by using the criteria of: *"What kind of fruit is it producing?"* What kind of spiritual fruit is this new phenomenon producing? How do we evaluate its spiritual fruit, and then what does that tell us?

## The Blind Leads the Blind

*But He answered and said, "Every plant which My heavenly Father did not plant shall be rooted up. Let them alone; they are blind guides of the blind. And if a blind man guides a blind man, both will fall into a pit* (Matthew 15:13-14).

If we look at the fruit of most ministries today, as Jesus told us to, we might evaluate how we are doing a little differently. Paul exhorted believers to examine themselves: *"Test yourselves to see if you are in the faith; examine yourselves"* (2 Cor. 13:5).

Most ministries now use topical, self-help sermons on Sunday mornings in a quest to be practical; while preaching the Cross, the gospel of the Kingdom, and anything pertaining to supernatural power is rarely discussed. There are few miracles or demonstrations of God's power, and the Holy Spirit is not welcomed. This is what mainstream Christianity has become—well-marketed meetings and programs advertised with creatively written brochures, catchy titles, and elaborate Websites.

Instead of healing the sick, delivering the oppressed, and preaching to the poor, there are support groups for all manner of diseases and psychological problems. One large ministry has 200 support groups for people afflicted with all manner of diseases, such as fibermyalgia, cancer, and the like. Instead of healing them, their sickness and bondage is now "supported"!

Social programs and activities are promoted rather than training people to discover and deploy their spiritual gifts. There is little evidence of supernatural activity, signs and wonders, or miraculous intervention. We are not seeing what we read about in Matthew 4:24 being fulfilled: *The news about Him spread throughout all Syria; and they brought to Him all who were ill, taken with various diseases and pains, demoniacs, epileptics, paralytics; and He healed them.*

Instead of repenting of sins, now it's called "dealing with our issues." Instead of casting out demons, we are persuaded to go through 12-step programs to "recover from our addictions." And instead of healing the sick, we can "celebrate wholeness." While I am sure nearly all of these things were initiated with the lofty goal of helping people and come from some big-hearted folks, they still fall short of anything closely resembling Jesus' gospel ministry where the lame walk, the blind see, and the oppressed are freed!

In a desperate attempt to be relevant and unreligious, the church has forgotten its primary mission—to liberate captives from sin, sickness, and bondage! Any quick glance at Jesus' work reveals that His ministry was liberating, not convalescing. Jesus healed rather than consoled. The way Jesus comforted and expressed the Father's love is a far cry from our current understanding. Jesus set emotional and spiritual captives free rather than feeling pity for their sorry place in life. He knew He had the ability to change their circumstances and He did! The ministry of Christ always comes with hope, life, liberation, and power!

## Supercarnal or supernatural?

The supernatural atmosphere and lifestyle of the early church is rarely visible in the typical American church expression today. The supernatural power and awe of God that pervaded the Acts church has been displaced with extraordinary marketing. Awestruck disciples have today given way to yawning, bored congregants; and signs and wonders have been replaced with eye-catching wonderful neon signs.

One church in a major metro area is known for its 100-foot neon sign with an updated weather report and stock ticker.

(I'm not kidding!) While all of these things are not harmful in themselves and maybe excellent tools to facilitate ministry, they are no substitute for the lifestyle of the early church.

Instead of Jesus' manifest presence captivating men's hearts with passion and purpose, successful ministries are now well-run corporations that strive for great customer service. A lot like an excellently produced Hollywood movie, the service is very entertaining, with exciting stories and wonderful technical effects that stir the soul and emotions. However, like going home after a cinematic feast from Hollywood, there is no real or fundamental change in the person who watched it. Within a few days, everything is back to normal. Consequently the Body stays oppressed, and in fact gets worse. It's the fulfillment of Jeremiah 5:31: *The prophets prophesy falsely and the priests rule on their own authority; and My people love it so!* And also: Revelations 3:17-18: *Because you say, "I am rich, and have become wealthy, and have need of nothing," and you do not know that you are wretched and miserable and poor and blind and naked, I advise you to buy from Me gold refined by fire, that you may become rich, and white garments, that you may clothe yourself, and that the shame of your nakedness may not be revealed; and eye salve to anoint your eyes, that you may see.*

The one main problem is that the product and the message have "no power to deliver." Fashionably dressed ministers with colorful PowerPoint presentations have no power to heal or deliver the people without God's anointing. The best that software, hardware, and technology offers us is still no match for the presence of God! While technology is a great benefit and an excellent tool which we all must utilize, it is still no replacement for the move of God's Spirit. Reliance on the anointing and the power of the Spirit is mandatory if we aspire to accurately represent Jesus to our culture.

## Formulaic Churches

When I addressed this issue at the beginning of this book, I mentioned then that the problem isn't the church itself, it is the forms that the church has taken and the formulas it is using to communicate Christ to the masses that we should look at. Peter Wagner has observed that even with administrators and teachers leading most Western churches, the church has successfully reached all but a billion and a half people on the planet.

Largely concocted by a leadership composed of pragmatic administrators, teachers, pastors, and a few very gifted evangelists, the church is in danger of becoming so weak and infantile that her people are now easy prey for a shrewd and experienced enemy. The church services and ministry have been reduced to a formula that can be packaged and franchised but hardly works to even save, let alone deliver, and disciple new believers.

Because the church is the primary vehicle God has established to bring the Kingdom to the earth, one way or another God will see to it that it will be transformed to accomplish what the Spirit desires to do in this generation. Change is coming to the church to facilitate God's designs on this generation.

## An Extraordinary Bypass

*"For My thoughts are not your thoughts, neither are your ways My ways," declares the Lord. "For as the heavens are higher than the earth, so are My ways higher than your ways, and My thoughts than your thoughts"* (Isaiah 55:8-9).

The Lord spoke to me recently and He said that because the church in the United States has largely not heeded His voice (except missions) and scarcely even desires His ways, He was going to begin to bypass mainstream and traditional church structures and raise up a new breed of leaders faithful to His Word and His ways who will listen to and obey His Spirit without fear or hesitation. New ways of doing the business of the Kingdom are coming to the church to facilitate this massive harvest of souls that God desires for this generation.

Without the Holy Spirit bypassing the present system and doing this major "workaround," we might not be able to see this accomplished because many ministries have become stumbling blocks to His purpose. God will not allow this new harvest of babies to be cared for by shepherds who are more married to a hopelessly flawed structure than to Him.

When the Lord began to speak to me about this dilemma, He led me to these Scriptures:

> *Then Jesus said to his host, "When you give a luncheon or dinner, do not invite your friends, your brothers or relatives, or your rich neighbors; if you do, they may invite you back and so you will be repaid. But when you give a banquet, invite the poor, the crippled, the lame, the blind, and you will be blessed. Although they cannot repay you, you will be repaid at the resurrection of the righteous." When one of those at the table with him heard this, he said to Jesus, "Blessed is the man who will eat at the feast in the kingdom of God."*
>
> *Jesus replied: "A certain man was preparing a great banquet and invited many guests. At the time of the banquet he sent his servant to tell those who had been invited, 'Come, for everything is now ready.' But they all alike began to make excuses. The first said, 'I have just bought a field, and I must go and see it. Please excuse me.' Another said, 'I have just bought five yoke*

*of oxen, and I'm on my way to try them out. Please excuse me.' Still another said, 'I just got married, so I can't come.'*

*The servant came back and reported this to his master. Then the owner of the house became angry and ordered his servant, 'Go out quickly into the streets and alleys of the town and bring in the poor, the crippled, the blind and the lame.'*

*'Sir,' the servant said, 'what you ordered has been done, but there is still room.' Then the master told his servant, 'Go out to the roads and country lanes and make them come in, so that my house will be full. I tell you, not one of those men who were invited will get a taste of my banquet'"* (Luke 14:12-24 NIV).

While some say "change takes time," we are now at a point when we can no longer hope that the system will fix itself. The system is broken and needs a massive overhaul, even a rebuild. It is high time for the church to break out of her antique boxes of fruitless religious tradition and formalism, and to leave the vain pursuit of the "latest oxcart" and humbly begin to do those simple things Jesus told us to do.

This book only reveals part of the answer, but it is a step. We need to release God into our church meetings, programs, schedules, and service times—bring Him with us to Wal-Mart, the grocery store, mall, the dentist's office, the workplace, and wherever we are! He lives within us, let's take Him with us wherever we go.

Most of us don't realize just how desirous the Lord is to be among those who need Him, wherever that may be. The Lord desires to be among His creation more than we can understand, and He is releasing much grace to get to His creation through His people.

> For I am not ashamed of the gospel, for it is the power
> of God for salvation to everyone who believes, to the
> Jew first and also to the Greek. For in it [the gospel]
> the righteousness of God is revealed from faith to faith;
> as it is written, "But the righteous man shall live by
> faith" (Romans 1:16-17).

## An Impaired Message

Right now in the Western church at large, a faulty, incomplete message is being declared that props up and even enables a carnal people and does little to fundamentally bring change. While this seems a blunt statement, it is true. Just look at the fruit! While this is a strong indictment on the church, I am not necessarily faulting any minister or ministry as it is all we have known for a long time. The church in the United States has primarily preached the gospel of salvation rather than the gospel of the Kingdom, and is being led by administrators and teachers rather than the first-ranked gifts of apostles and then prophets that we see in First Corinthians 12:28: *"And God has appointed in the church, first apostles, second prophets, third teachers, then miracles, then gifts of healings, helps, administrations, various kinds of tongues."*

Peter Wagner has observed that even with this flawed model where pastors and administrators run most ministries, the world is being rapidly converted.[1] Just imagine what might happen if we got things right! Many only reluctantly mention and rarely demonstrate the power of God; that which relates to salvation, the theology of the Kingdom, and our dominion are rarely discussed. Without preaching the Kingdom, the spiritual progress we could have and the spiritual ground we should have taken, still eludes us.

> *And God blessed them; and God said to them, "Be fruitful and multiply, and fill the earth, and subdue it; and rule over the fish of the sea and over the birds of the sky, and over every living thing that moves on the earth"* (Genesis 1:28).

By neglecting to declare the ramifications of this message of the Kingdom that Jesus taught, demonstrated, and preached, we hand out a drastically impaired message. And this impaired message produces retarded and incomplete believers with little understanding of the power of the Cross and the resurrected life, and even less of an understanding about how to vanquish demons or heal the sick.

While the Gospels reveal how Jesus specifically described what the Kingdom of God looks like, it is still rarely mentioned. Maybe that's because many leaders would rather avoid it. The gospel Jesus preached involves declaring and demonstrating God's Kingdom power to break the bondage of sin, sickness, poverty, and ignorance. Unfortunately, the church has by and large dumbed down the gospel so much now that one can communicate without God's help! For many, it has become just a series of vignettes and cute stories, like motivational "talks." Christians sit in auditoriums every week and hear good sermons or great preaching. But for all the many words given and heard through these great sermons and messages, the lifestyle-altering response of God's peoples is just not evident.

With the proliferation of church Websites and streaming sermons online, there is no end to the American church's new-found reliance on modern science and technology. But in all this, have we lost sight of our need for a Healer, Savior, and Deliverer? Instead of crying out for the Deliverer, our society has 12-step support groups. Instead of crying out for the Healer, we grab our medical insurance cards and rush to our nearest PPO or HMO to see our MD or GP. Instead of crying out for the Savior, we are sent to therapy sessions to be "affirmed" about our self-image.

We have issues or diseases rather than sin or demons. We need to define these bondages by what the Word—not the world—tells us they are. Christian ministries have made a practice of prescribing ongoing counseling sessions that even after years of "talking it out" people are still in bondage. Again, we must all humbly look at the fruit of this way of doing things. If after years of counseling, a person is still not well emotionally or spiritually, they are worse off than they were in the beginning.

Maybe that is because the Bible is clear that if we behold the flesh and focus on our problems or weaknesses, it ultimately leads to death. (See Romans 8:6.) While psychology can be helpful in diagnosing problems, it is largely unfruitful in removing them. Didn't Jesus tell us that He left us the Holy Spirit as our Helper and Counselor? You can't counsel demons. They can only be cast out. Is "working through issues" just a way to avoid personal responsibility? Our culture wants to blame someone else for all our problems—the government, our parents, our employers, the kids. But until we lay the responsibility for our condition squarely where it belongs—at our own feet—we will never change.

## Self-improvement for the Old Self

The recent self-improvement movement in our country is fanatical, hopeless, and ultimately motivated by human pride. Churches have jumped on the bandwagon, making an art form of creating ways to keep the old-self alive, when in reality it needs to be killed! When Paul wrote, *"I die daily,"* he was referring to his old, carnal nature (1 Cor. 15:31). The power of the gospel message is not in God blessing our natural self, but about how skilled God is at using things for His glory that were once dead. Unless something is dead, the Lord can't resurrect it.

God doesn't just sprinkle blessing on our gifts or our natural self, we have to die to what we think, feel, and want, only then is He able to resurrect a whole new being operating through us. Rick Joyner has said, "There are two powerful supernatural beings trying to kill you—God and the devil." So go ahead and let God have His way.

A resurrected me is what God wants to work with, not a gifted, carnal me. Much of what passes as teaching in churches today is more about sin management than deliverance from self, sin, and demons. If we would just get out of the way and allow the Greater One to work in and through us, all things will become possible! It is not about a better me or self-improvement, but a crucifixion. It is not about more religious activity fixing up the old me, but entering into the new creation I have become in Him. It is all about letting go of our former ways of beholding, thinking, and acting to work together with Him!

> *Therefore if anyone is in Christ, he is a new creature; the old things passed away; behold, new things have come* (2 Corinthians 5:17).

## We Need Power!

*And my message and my preaching [proclamation] were not in persuasive words of wisdom, but in demonstration of the Spirit and of power, so that your faith should not rest on the wisdom of men, but on the power of God* (1 Corinthians 2:4-5).

The Bible is clear that our faith is to rest on the supernatural power and abilities of God. Yet many of us are letting our faith rest on many things other than His power. The wisdom of people, worldly wisdom, our experiences, and even what looks like common sense can all be things we are tempted to set or rest our faith on, especially when we are afraid. During a test of our faith, we tend to go back to those base things we leaned on in the past instead of our minds being set on Him resting in Him. This is a dilemma especially for Christians in the United States whose lives are rich and full. One missionary recently told us that if we have a change of clothes and a meal a day we are considered wealthy by the standards of the other six billion people on our planet.

As Americans we especially have this conflict when our faith is tested as we have so many other things we can rest our faith on and trust in rather than the power of God. Mark 4:19 speaks of these other things: *"but the worries of the world, and the deceitfulness of riches, and the desires for other things enter in and choke the word, and it becomes unfruitful."*

We must learn to rest our faith on and put our trust in God's miraculous power when we are being tested by our circumstances. A huge breakthrough would come to all believers if they began to live on every word that proceeds out of the mouth of God rather than being moved by their daily circumstances.

Most Christians live their daily lives based on these pressing cir-cumstances or whether doors open or close rather than doing the word of the Lord.

Much of this way of living stems from the wrong doc-trine that bases its teaching on the premise that because God knows everything about us; that must mean He is allowing all things that happen to us—good or bad. The Lord isn't always the author. For example, some believers strongly think that if their 70-year-old Aunt Bessie gets cancer, then, "the Lord gave her cancer to test her." This is utter foolishness because God is not the Lord of death and sickness, but the Lord of Life. Jesus said, *"I came that you may have life and have it more abundantly"* (John 10:10). He did not say, "I came to give you cancer, boils, and sickness."

The whole purpose of God sending His son was not to judge the world but to save and deliver it. Until believers are convinced of the goodness of God as well as the evil present in the world, they will live in an unbelieving state of ambiguous faith.

> *And Jesus cried out and said, "He who believes in Me, does not believe in Me but in Him who sent Me. He who sees Me sees the One who sent Me. I have come as Light into the world, so that everyone who believes in Me will not remain in darkness. If anyone hears My sayings and does not keep them, I do not judge him; for I did not come to judge the world, but to save the world* (John 12:44-47).

We all know the story in Mark chapter 4 where Jesus loaded up His disciples and declared, *"we are going to the other side"* (of the lake). He was tired and went down below to sleep. During this time a terrible storm rose up, and they all thought that they were going to die. So they woke Him up and said, "We are all going to die!" What did He do? He rebuked them for their unbelief and for not believing Him when He said, *"we are going to the other side."* By His answer it seems as if He wanted *them* to rebuke the storm and let Him sleep! He wanted them to learn to walk in faith and trust in Him and not lean on their own understanding. We have got to learn that we can trust in everything the Lord says more than anything else. His power accompanies and backs up His Word each and every time.

## Real Power or Just Talk?

Just look at the incredible results we see when Jesus preaches his Kingdom message rather than the impotent message we typically hear in today's churches. Jesus preached and the lame walk, the blind see, the deaf hear! Typical church messages include some jokes, a little motivational prodding mixed in with a few personal stories, then topped off with an out-of-context Scripture, and there is a Sunday morning message! Unfortunately, these messages rarely have any power accompanying them. It is only in the power of the Spirit that people are set free and high-tech lighting and catchy message titles won't do that. Take a look at Jesus' teaching and His results:

> *...and they were amazed at His teaching, for His message was with authority.... And amazement came upon them all, and they began discussing with one another saying, "What is this message? For with authority and power He commands the unclean spirits, and they come out"* (Luke 4:32,36).

Jesus' teaching was with such authority that demons were easily cast out as a result of His message! Many might say,

"Jesus is God, so of course He can get those kinds of results with that message." But look at the results even double-minded Peter and some of His other disciples got: *"Even Simon himself believed; and after being baptized, he continued on with Philip; and as he observed signs and great miracles taking place, he was constantly amazed"* (Acts 8:13).

Wow, even the early deacons had this kind of authority! While some would suggest this kind of power only rested on the first apostle or apostles, what about these deacons? It wasn't just on Stephen, but also Phillip. These deacons had such power on them that they shook regions and changed lives! So much for the "early apostles only" argument.

> *God was performing extraordinary miracles by the hands of Paul, so that handkerchiefs or aprons were even carried from his body to the sick, and the diseases left them and the evil spirits went out* (Acts 19:11-12).

All those who preached this same message got the same results. They proclaimed and demonstrated that the Kingdom message works, and God is no respecter of persons. While God understands and respects authorities, even evil ones, He can use anyone who will listen and obey His voice.

> *And Jesus knowing their thoughts said, "Why are you thinking evil in your hearts? For which is easier, to say, 'Your sins are forgiven,' or to say, 'Rise, and walk'? "But in order that you may know that the Son of Man has authority on earth to forgive sins"— then He said to the paralytic—"Rise, take up your bed, and go home." And he rose, and went home. But when the multitudes saw this, they were filled with awe, and glorified God, who had given such authority to men* (Matthew 9:4-8).

Here's the secret. The Kingdom isn't accomplished by talk. I love the New International Version of First Corinthians 4:20: *"For the kingdom of God is not a matter of talk but of power."* It isn't by reciting volumes of Scripture or flowery words or loud screaming that heals the sick, the lame, or the blind; it is only by the power of the Holy Spirit released through faith in Him. Though words are used, it isn't by their repetition or the volume or a particular incantation, but the release of authority in the declaration of the King and His Kingdom. The good news of the Kingdom is this: Jesus is King, and I come with His name and His backing!

## Fruitful

The purpose of God from the beginning was that the Creator could have fellowship with His created beings so that humans could be like God on the earth.

God's command to Adam was, *"Be fruitful and increase in number; fill the earth and subdue it. Rule over the fish of the sea and the birds of the air and over every living creature that moves on the ground"* (Genesis 1:28-29). This command is still active today.

The Bible says that, *"The highest heavens belong to the Lord, but the earth he has given to man"* (Ps. 115:16 NIV). God designed the earth and all His creation to submit and be subservient to God and His ultimate creation—humankind. We were always supposed to take dominion and govern the earth rather than sin and the devil.

Our ultimate purpose as Christians is to be like God on the earth. We are called to exercise dominion over the earth and subdue it for God. We must embrace our destiny which is one of warfare and conquest! The Christian life is not just sitting around drinking coffee, eating cookies, and singing our favorite worship songs. We can't even enjoy many of the benefits of God's peace and love without taking dominion and subduing our enemies. As long as we are fighting an enemy, we can't look the other way.

Because I was part of the "Woodstock generation," those born between 1948 and 1964, I am well aware that our generation didn't want war of any kind and looked for a utopia of peace and love. Of course, no one desires conflict or war, but in some situations it is forced on us and without going into battle we will end up in tyranny! War doesn't make sense until we see the grim consequences of not fighting.

The Woodstock, hippy mind-set still operates in many members of today's church. The war spiritual believers engage in now actually began a long time ago, and hoping and wishing that the enemy of our soul is somehow going to go away if we change what we believe is just not true! Any notion that the devil will leave us alone if we only leave him alone is a lie. We must take the fight to the enemy, or he will bring it to us. *"The Son of God appeared for this purpose, that He might destroy the works of the devil"* (1 John 3:8).

There has been a new awareness of the intimacy we are to experience and enjoy with the Lord, and this is important and needful, especially for those who were brought up in a religious system of dead works. Without an understanding of relationship, we only have a hollow religious experience. A love relationship with our Father God is essential. Yet the purpose of intimacy is not only receiving pleasure and personal affirmation and satisfaction, but also reproduction and bearing fruit.

With all of the emphasis in the church on intimacy, prayer, and intercession, why do we still see so little fruit? Is it possible we have made prayer and intimacy the end to our quest rather than the means? Why do we have so little success in winning the lost, healing the sick, or winning a city? We are still waiting to hear of an account of a city or town in our country where the influence of the gospel has such a profound effect on the atmosphere and lifestyles of a region that the Kingdom of God has preeminence. Although we have heard of great revivals in churches, and even accounts of this kind of activity in other nations like Argentina and Africa, it is not a common occurrence here in the United States.

It's as if we want to avoid warfare and the dominion mandates that the Lord has given us and go back to the Garden without throwing out the serpent! But to get back to that state of dominion we had in the Garden, we have to evict the serpent! We have to embrace our call as warriors for God and not just as lovers of God. We can do both—David did! Mike Bickle said, "We're worshipers of God and deliverers of men."

For 15 years, I have participated in many local, regional, and national prayer initiatives, prophetic declarations, and racial reconciliation meetings; yet so far not one city in our nation has been truly taken and transformed by the gospel. Why? While prayer is valuable, necessary, and important, without the corresponding preaching of the gospel of the Kingdom there is little to pray about. While I believe whole cities are going to be taken in our nation for the Lord, we have to change our methods, or rather add to them with the rest of our mandate. Prayer changes things only when obedience is fastened to it!

Albert Einstein said that the definition of insanity was "doing the same things over and over again and again the same way and somehow expecting a different result." What we have done before has been wonderful and glorious at times, but we must move beyond the past for the new wave God is sending to the church. The corporate anointing is when the Body of Christ does the works of ministry rather than only an elite paid staff. We see some prophetic glimpses of this soon coming move of corporate anointing in the Old Testament:

> *How could one man chase a thousand, or two put ten thousand to flight, unless their Rock had sold them, unless the Lord had given them up? For their rock is not like our Rock, as even our enemies concede. Their vine comes from the vine of Sodom and from the fields of Gomorrah. Their grapes are filled with poison, and their clusters with bitterness. Their wine is the venom of serpents, the deadly poison of cobras. Have I not kept this in reserve and sealed it in my vaults? It is mine to avenge; I will repay. In due time their foot will slip; their day of disaster is near and their doom rushes upon them. The Lord will judge his people and have compassion on his servants when he sees their strength is gone and no one is left, slave or free. He will say: "Now where are their gods, the rock they took refuge in, the gods who ate the fat of their sacrifices and drank the wine of their drink offerings? Let them rise up to help you! Let them give you shelter! See now that I myself am He! There is no god besides me. I put to death and I bring to life, I have wounded and I will heal, and no one can deliver out of my hand. I lift my hand to heaven and declare: As surely as I live forever, when I sharpen my flashing sword and my hand grasps it in judgment, I will take vengeance on my adver-*

*saries and repay those who hate me. I will make my
arrows drunk with blood, while my sword devours
flesh: the blood of the slain and the captives, the heads
of the enemy leaders"*
(Deuteronomy 32:30-42 NIV).

## Multiplied Power

In American church culture, we are currently in the
reign of the superstar leader, where one can put a thousand to
flight. While it is wonderful to hear and see great champions of
faith exercise their gifts, until others are trained and released to
do theirs, we will not be fulfilling our biblical mandate to "equip
the saints."

It's exciting to think about what will happen when everyday church people began to chuck their fear and step out in faith
and power to preach the authentic gospel message of the
Kingdom. Preaching the gospel and demonstrations of power
are inseparable! So the quantum effect of every person in the
Body of Christ doing and exercising their supernatural gifts
would shake entire cities and regions! Jesus said we *would* do,
not *could* do, the same works and even greater works than He!

*Truly, truly, I say to you, he who believes in Me, the
works that I do shall he do also; and greater works
than these shall he do; because I go to the Father*
(John 14:12).

*Most assuredly, I say to you, he who believes in Me, the
works that I do he will do also; and greater works than
these he will do, because I go to My Father*
(John 14:12 NKJV).

## Supernatural Works

*Now He could do no mighty work there, except that He laid His hands on a few sick people and healed them. And He marveled because of their unbelief. Then He went about the villages in a circuit, teaching. And He called the twelve to Himself, and began to send them out two by two, and gave them power over unclean spirits* (Mark 6:5-7 NKJV).

It is also interesting that Jesus equated "works," not with handing out bags of food or giving away hot dogs or bags of clothes, but with healing sick people, delivering oppressed people, and other supernatural works only a supernatural God could do! When Jesus said *work* or *works* He wasn't referring to how we primarily think in terms of either: dead works which are those we might do to elicit or get the Lord's favor; or good works such as providing clothes to the needy or giving food to the hungry.

James speaks of a hypocritical faith that needs works to back it up. He uses the example of a Christian who sees a man in need of food and rather than helping him instead says, "Be warm and filled." Showing compassion and expressing kindness and mercy is a given for a Christian, but it's not preaching the gospel.

For instance, if a man with a full stomach is in need of healing, to only say to him, "receive Jesus as Savior" without at least offering God's healing power to him is as much defrauding him as ignoring him would be. While these works of believers may be naturally and readily doable, the works of God are supernatural and demand a response. We must not be afraid to "put God on the spot." Jesus regularly put His Father's reputation on the line each time He did a miracle!

*For I will not presume to speak of anything except what Christ has accomplished through me, resulting in the obedience of the Gentiles by word and deed, in the power of signs and wonders, in the power of the Spirit; so that from Jerusalem and round about as far as Illyricum I have fully preached the gospel of Christ* (Romans 15:18-19).

*And when He had called His twelve disciples to Him, He gave them power over unclean spirits, to cast them out, and to heal all kinds of sickness and all kinds of disease* (Matthew 10:1 NKJV).

## The Joshua Generation

I like to think of this last season the church has been in as similar to the time of Moses. Whenever God spoke, He spoke to the man of God, Moses. Whenever God did anything, He did it through His servant Moses. Whenever the people of God fought an enemy, God did all the fighting through His servant Moses. Moses heard from God for the people. Moses led the way for the people. Moses alone did the signs and wonders. Moses alone led them, kept them, and dealt with them. When they grumbled at God, they grumbled at Moses. When there was a victory, it was all because of Moses, the man of God, God's anointed.

But Moses himself never made it into the Promised Land, and I think a main reason why is because he wasn't meant to do everything. He was never meant to shoulder all the burdens and communication between God and the people. That kind of pressure and burden was just too much to bear, and he became frustrated and even angry at God's people. When Moses became too "people conscious," he got caught up in the cycle of either attempting to make them happy or being regularly angry with them. Either way, God pulled the plug on his leadership, and Moses never crossed over into the land.

What God is doing today is taking us into a season more like the reign of Joshua. Although Joshua led the people, it was their own responsibility to enter into their inheritance. When they entered the land, it was not just Joshua, but the entire nation marching in lock step as a disciplined army that caused the defeat of Jericho. And when there was a defeat such as that at Ai, it was because the people did not obey the Lord. Joshua showed Israel how they could go into the land and possess it themselves. This is the day and season the church is now entering into, when the people of God take responsibility for their callings and destinies being fulfilled.

We can walk in and demonstrate the freedom and power of the Kingdom of God, not just in church but 24/7. Hebrews 4:3 says, *"For we who have believed enter that rest."* This passage implies a correlation between believing and resting—causing us to enter into that place of divine rest from striving then entering into God's best for each of us without limitation!

**Endnote**

Apostles Conference, Atlanta, GA; 6-19-2001, Session 1, Peter Wagner.

# CHAPTER 11

# OUR AMERICAN GOSPEL

*And without faith it is impossible to please God, because anyone who comes to Him must believe that He exists and that He rewards those who earnestly seek Him* (Hebrews 11:6 NIV).

## Faith in God Is Key

Many people today have much more faith in science, technology, politics, and medicine than God. More and more Christians are taught by their church leaders that God is good, real, and powerful. However, He is far too preoccupied with other, more pressing matters than to take the time to heal your body, pay your bills, or deliver your children from drugs. Although God performs an occasional miracle here and there, if you are sick you're told to, "be realistic and get to a doctor." God helps those who help themselves, etc., etc., blah, blah, blah.

Well-meaning or not, this kind of counsel filled with rampant unbelief won't elicit God's attention, because God doesn't primarily respond to mercy, but faith. God doesn't respond to the casual inquirer, but the diligent seeker! We have to expend faith toward Him to receive from Him. I have heard from people who needed something desperately from God, but they were so disillusioned or tired that they say things like, "If God wants to heal me, He knows my address." While it is true He *does* know their address, we are required to move toward Him to receive what He has for us. He has already done all that is necessary to bring about our deliverance.

*"Therefore, in the resurrection, whose wife of the seven will she be? For they all had her." Jesus answered and said to them, "You are mistaken, not knowing the Scriptures nor the power of God"*
(Matthew 22:28-29 NKJV).

*Jesus answered and said to them, "Are you not therefore mistaken, because you do not know the Scriptures nor the power of God?"* (Mark 12:24 NKJV).

Jesus said that knowing the Scriptures and the power of God was essential to understanding the things of the Kingdom. He also said it would take childlike faith to even see it!

## Discerning the Real

United States Treasury agents who track down and apprehend counterfeiters are taught to distinguish counterfeit money by first and most importantly learning by sight and by feel what the authentic American currency in all of the denominations looks and feels like. Their fundamental training is to learn how to discern and identify the real as the way to best distinguish the fake. While counterfeiters might take many different approaches to copying money and be experts in some aspects of the printing or the artwork of paper money, a person who is thoroughly familiar and intimately knowledgeable about the real can always spot the phony. So it is with God's power and healing touch. Train yourself through the Word of God, and you will not be fooled.

## Unprepared for Power

So why don't we see the power we say we are longing for? Maybe because we aren't well-acquainted enough with the power of God, so when it comes many times we are surprised and usually afraid of it. Many leaders, even Charismatic or Pentecostal ones, do not know how to respond when the Lord is present in a meeting or gathering.

Our intellectual mind-sets limit the way we think, which affects how we believe. In America and the Western world, we are largely conditioned and programmed by the ancient Greco-Roman mind-set that was based on logic and science, which ignores the supernatural world and bases truth only on what can be seen, calibrated, and evaluated. Faith is not a factor in this view of things.

On the other hand, Christian believers should be governed more out of the Hebraic mentality and mind-set which historically was directed out of spiritual vision followed by action taken in response to the vision. What was seen with the eyes of the spirit was given much greater weight than what was discerned by the sensory realm in the Hebraic mentality. This why Paul said, *"For indeed Jews ask for signs, and Greeks search for wisdom;"* (1 Corinthian 1:22).

To walk in this supernatural realm, our minds must be governed by our spirits and not the other way around. Man is a three-part being having a spirit, soul, and body. Our spirit must direct and tell our minds, wills, and emotions what to do as well as our bodies. Faith to act on what we have heard or seen from the Spirit should be given much greater weight in directing our lives rather than feelings or circumstances.

To experience revival and the miraculous realms of God, we have to learn to walk in this supernatural power instead of regularly letting ourselves off the spiritual hook by making excuses for our lack of it. Believers all too often make excuses and even defend the lack of power they have in their lives by changing the subject. Why is it that Christians tend to proclaim some "either/or" example when it comes to discussing these things we lack according to the Word of God? When these issues come up, many times there is a tendency to change the subject.

For example, if someone speaks out about the need for the church to walk in the miraculous power like we see in the Book of Acts, someone invariably says: "Well, yes, it is important that we need the power of God but first we need the fruit"...or..."Of course we need the power, but we must first demonstrate His love."

## A Change of Mind

This is a vivid example of what the majority of Christians, including those in Charismatic and Pentecostal churches, are being taught today. There is a tendency to change the subject when we don't measure up; or emphasize another aspect to evade the topic of the supernatural. Instead of admitting that we all have a profound need, and even lack of God, we change the subject and move the discussion to a subject over which we think we have control.

> *Why can't we just admit we are woefully lacking and ask for help from God? Because most of us would rather change our doctrine than change our minds! Jesus said that unless we repent or change our minds and become like little children we can not enter the Kingdom of God. The disciples didn't tell the Lord He was wrong or must have meant something else, but instead they simply asked for help when they needed faith. "And the apostles said to the Lord, 'Increase our faith!'"* (Luke 17:5).

*From that time Jesus began to preach and say, "Repent, for the kingdom of heaven is at hand"* (Matthew 4:17).

What the word *repent* means here means to "change your mind *and* purpose; and change your plans and positions."

*And He called a child to Himself and set him before them, and said, "Truly I say to you, unless you are converted and become like children, you shall not enter the kingdom of heaven"* (Matthew 18:2-3).

When we think we have something naturally or easily attainable, like the fruit of the Spirit, why do some say, "I don't want the gifts, but I want the fruit?" Let's face it—isn't it because of our unbelief? We can rationalize away our utter lack of power with these kinds of arguments. There is a temptation to talk about attaining moralistic goals motivated by religious flesh without humbly admitting we are powerless and need God. When power becomes a measuring stick of spiritual intimacy, it's easy to see this is something we can get only from God Himself!

While fruit comes by abiding in Him, power only comes through exercising faith in Him and doing as He did. Power comes by embracing our natural weakness and receiving the abundance of grace that comes in Him. If we live a life like Christ, this doesn't mean we would necessarily wear a robe, talk of peace, and wear sandals. But we are given the great privilege by His command to bring the Kingdom of light into any situation where there is darkness. This involves a demonstration of the Kingdom through the power of God dislodging the old dark dungeons and kingdoms that captivate people's souls. So how did Jesus describe the effect of proclaiming this gospel message?

*Now when John, while imprisoned, heard of the works of Christ, he sent word by his disciples and said to Him, "Are You the Expected One, or shall we look for someone else?" Jesus answered and said to them, "Go and report to John what you hear and see: the blind receive sight and the lame walk, the lepers are cleansed and the deaf hear, the dead are raised up, and the poor have the gospel preached to them. And blessed is he who does not take offense at Me"* (Matthew 11:2-6).

And this blessing only comes when one spends time with Him and receives His Word that releases faith. (See Romans 10:17.) For all the emphasis on intimacy and relationship with the Lord believers may profess, whenever folks spend real quality time in communion with Him they most assuredly feel and sense His heart and burden for the rest of creation; the lost, the crippled, the blind, the deaf, and those dead in their sins. Those closest to His heart will sooner or later sense the stirrings of the Spirit to get out of the royal bed chamber and go after those in the street and marketplace who are in bondage and who they would never see by only going to church meetings.

When we hang out with God we pick up His nature, and that is a huge aspect of acquiring the heart of God—and a real love and burden for the rest of humanity. To walk in love means we carry His Love with us. It means we can't look the other way when the bound ones are standing in line right in front of us; we have to *do* something, and He will show us what to do.

Why do we so easily attempt to rationalize and explain away why no one we pray for gets healed? And why we have no love for the lost, and why there is little power in our life? To explain away our unbelief and lack of fruit, some try to justify their disobedience to the gospel with Scripture proofs and questionable doctrines. Shouldn't preaching and demonstrating the gospel with signs, wonders, and miracles be the by-product of all that personal intimacy? If folks really know the Lord, shouldn't they look like Him and do what He did? If we really love the Lord shouldn't we do what He says, rather than what we desire?

> *The one who says he abides in Him ought himself to walk in the same manner as He walked* (1 John 2:6).

## But What About...

There is a passage of Scripture and an argument that the religious spirit continually brings up to accuse and shut down folks from moving in Kingdom power. It goes something like this: "What about the passage in Matthew chapter 7? I really want to know the Lord, not just do miracles." OK, let's look at it:

> *So then, you will know them by their fruits. Not everyone who says to Me, 'Lord, Lord,' will enter the kingdom of heaven; but he who does the will of My Father who is in heaven will enter. Many will say to Me on that day, 'Lord, Lord, did we not prophesy in Your name, and in Your name cast out demons, and in Your name perform many miracles?' And then I will declare to them, 'I never knew you; depart from me, you who practice lawlessness'* (Matthew 7:20-23).

To believe that this Scripture passage suggests that miracles are elementary and only for the immature is ridiculous. The miraculous isn't for babies, it's for all believers! That is like saying, "doing miracles is unnecessary if I really know Him" or "That's for baby Christians. I am beyond that. I don't have to have miracles to believe."

The purpose of this line of reasoning is to make people feel immature for desiring God's power and is really a smoke-screen for their own lack of it. Please don't ever buy into this pious line of reasoning. And because this is the only instance in the New Testament where someone was even called into question for performing miracles, you can't build a theology around it. In fact, performing miracles wasn't the problem, it was a heart condition.

When the New Testament is filled with believers having dreams, trances, and visions, miracles, healings, and experiencing signs and wonders, how can we question their validity? Instead why don't we look at a breakdown of this same passage through the eyes of faith rather than doubt and unbelief? Let's look at it with an open mind rather than an excuse for our powerlessness.

Let's check it out with eyes open:

1. Jesus is confident. The verse says, *"you will know them by their fruits."* The Greek word for *know* means to "discern or to ascertain, to judge" if those things really happen through their ministry. Jesus is confident when He declares *"you will know them."* There is no warning like, "beware," "you might not see it," or "you need to watch out."

2. Jesus says check out *their fruit.* He doesn't say to look for His fruit on them, but to see what proceeds from them—is it visible and undeniable? In addition, is it authentic and does it represent and glorify the Father? He is not implying that these miracles and healings are of the wrong source, but are happening in a person detached from a vital relationship with God.

3. Jesus never impugns the motives of this person. It isn't about their motives or why they are doing the miracles; but instead, what's coming forth from them? Is it a love of position or a love of money or rather a passion to set people free? I personally believe the person Jesus was describing in Matthew chapter 7 is similar to what Peter saw in Simon in Acts chapter 8 who was pursuing supernatural power for personal gain. His heart was exposed by his offer to pay for these gifts that freely come by the Holy Spirit. Also, think of this: why would Peter tell Simon of his wickedness if what he was asking for wasn't precious and valuable to the believer? Simon was chastised for imparting the ability for people to speak in tongues. This reveals how special these Holy Spirit gifts of impartation are!

4. Jesus equates real intimacy and love for Him with the obedient faithful exercise and release of this miraculous power flowing out of a relationship with the Father. Jesus doesn't applaud powerlessness or the lack of miracles, instead He rebukes them for their unbelief!

The religious spirit boxes God in and equates any miracle with the occult or something false. But stop and think logically—why would the devil want to heal, free, or deliver people he hates? While in the last days it says there will be deceiving signs and wonders, there have always been false signs and wonders! Moses encountered magicians in Pharaoh's court, and Daniel encountered diviners hanging around Nebuchadnezzar, and Paul encountered them everywhere he went. Instead of looking for the false, shouldn't we instead be busy discovering and knowing the real as I mentioned before? The true knowledge of God is the most effective spiritual weapon we could ever have. You and God are an absolute majority!

## Releasing God

It's not time for living and doing the same old thing. We have got to step out in faith, put ourselves at risk, and let God work outside of our old worn-out boxes of unbelief, failing structures, methods, and forms of ministry that have become unfruitful and unproductive. Just because God blessed something in the past doesn't mean He is still blessing it now. God is not tired, boring, or uncreative! A move of God implies that God wants us to move with Him!

> *For I am not ashamed of the gospel, for it is the power of God for salvation to everyone who believes, to the Jew first and also to the Greek. For in it [the gospel] the righteousness of God is revealed from faith to faith; as it is written, "But the righteous man shall live by faith"* (Romans 1:16-17).

The English word *revealed* is the Greek word *apokaluptw* meaning "to uncover, reveal: *kaluptw* from a prim. word *kalub* (hut, cabin); to cover."[1] The gospel *reveals* the righteousness of God (which we are to possess), and as we let that light of the gospel come out of us, it is taken out of its little cabin of hiding and brought out into the light. The lights are turned on and God's glory in us will be seen as we release Him by exercising faith when preaching the Kingdom message of power! We can do no less than all the believers throughout history who stepped up to the plate and went for it! I greatly honor those champions of the faith who believed in the Word of God and exercised the power of God, then took incredible persecution for it—people like John Wimber, who paid a great personal price to blaze a trail for the church.

> *That is, the mystery which has been hidden from the past ages and generations; but has now been manifested to His saints, to whom God willed to make known what is the riches of the glory of this mystery among the Gentiles, which is Christ in you, the hope of glory* (Colossians 1:26-27).

> *That their hearts may be encouraged, having been knit together in love, and attaining to all the wealth that comes from the full assurance of understanding, resulting in a true knowledge of God's mystery, that is, Christ Himself, in whom are hidden all the treasures of wisdom and knowledge* (Colossians 2:2-3).

Many churches in the United States have been declaring a partial and incomplete message. The message of the Kingdom that Jesus declared during His tenure on earth was described by Him as "spirit and life." But what is largely proclaimed from American pulpits is "gospel-ultralite." The American gospel by and large is accurate in only one regard—communicating the message of salvation. I believe that other aspects of sharing the gospel are woefully inadequate, especially communicating the Kingdom of God, which is His rule, His reign, right here, right now!

> *For the time will come when men will not put up with sound doctrine. Instead, to suit their own desires, they will gather around them a great number of teachers to say what their itching ears want to hear. They will turn their ears away from the truth and turn aside to myths* (2 Timothy 4:3-4 NIV).

The Word of God is clear that days are coming, or are already here, when people will not want to hear the truth of the gospel but instead will create an alternative gospel. Instead of having a love for and desiring the truth, immature believers will want to hear only what makes them feel good and does not confront their carnal nature—"Christian happy talk" is what one leader calls it.

More than 20 years ago, Vance Havner, in his book *Playing Marbles with Diamonds*, offered the following insight that prophetically describes the present church message:

The devil is not fighting religion; he is too smart for that. He is producing a counterfeit Christianity so much like the real one that good Christians are afraid to speak out against it. ...We are plainly told in the Scriptures that in the last days men will not endure sound doctrine and will depart from the truth and heap to themselves teachers to tickle their ears. We live in an epidemic of this itch, and popular preachers have developed ear-tickling to a fine art. Today, the angle is to avoid "negative" preaching and accentuate only the positive.[2]

I agree. In thousands of American churches, it is now no longer acceptable to preach the indisputable fact that Jesus is King and has a Kingdom. It is now considered "negative" to preach or mention sin. Instead, these areas are called "issues." It is in "bad taste" to mention money because that is what they (seekers) would expect. It is just "too depressing" and supposedly, the "wrong place" to mention the reality of hell in church. And of course to mention or speak of the presence and power of the Holy Spirit is just "way over everybody's head."

## Gospel Ultra-lite

I recently was told by a friend of mine, who is a traveling minister, that during a leadership meeting in a large Charismatic denomination, the ministers were told that they were forbidden to mention the words "Holy Spirit" on the platform. This was supposedly done to "avoid confusing people" or "creating controversy." While all pastors like peace and order, not referencing the Holy Spirit is definitely going too far. This is just an example of how far churches have fallen. When leadership attempts to keep references to God the Holy Spirit hidden from "their" people because it is controversial and uncomfortable and might force the leaders to explain who the Holy Spirit is, the God-restricting atmosphere of spiritual political correctness has gone too far.

Too many real matters concerning the Trinity are now considered taboo as they might scare people away from the seeker-sensitive, mile-wide, inch-deep churches that are springing up throughout our country. Self-help practitioners serve up this ultra-lite gospel slop each week. People come to these churches in droves, and many are legitimately hungry, and some even desperate, to find God. But instead of getting the real deal, they get a weak caricature of a God who is powerless and elusive.

Woe to the kind of leaders who lead the flock away from Him and into their own sanitized form of church where the Lord is rarely visible. The cowardice of leadership to help bring the Lord and His presence to those legitimately seeking Him is a serious concern. It is terrifying to think that leaders are "protecting" God's people from God Himself. While the Bible is clear that being a teacher has a double reward, I can only imagine that being a false (or incomplete) teacher has double in reverse.

> *Woe to you experts in the law, because you have taken away the key to knowledge. You yourselves have not entered, and you have hindered those who were entering* (Luke 11:52 NIV).

Look at some of the differences between what many of us have been taught versus what the Word of God teaches:

| American Gospel | Gospel of the Kingdom |
| --- | --- |
| Many choices/options | One choice: obey the Spirit |
| God plus ME | Follow Me (Mark 8:34) |
| Comfortable | Uncomfortable to our flesh (Matt. 26:41) |
| Inoffensive | Offends the mind/reveals the heart (Rom. 9;33) |
| Looks back | Moves forward (Luke 9:62) |
| Convenience is all-important | Covenant is all-important (2 Tim. 2:11-13) |
| Ministry determined by need | Ministry determined by Spirit's leading |
| People rule | Word of God is final authority (Rev. 3:14-16) |
| Avoids conflict | Creates conflict (Col. 1:13-14) |
| People-pleasing | God-pleasing (Heb. 13:21) |
| Seeker-friendly | Holy Spirit friendly (Gal. 5:13) |

| American Gospel | Gospel of the Kingdom |
|---|---|
| Attempts to save people | Makes disciples (Matt. 28:18) |
| Makes converts to the church | Makes believers of God |
| Ministry by an elite few | Ministry by the Body of Christ (1 Cor. 12:12-20) |
| Program-oriented | Bible-oriented (Acts 2:42) |
| Inch deep and mile wide | Rooted and grounded (Col. 2:7) |
| Breeds spiritual babies | Brings maturity (Heb. 5:14) |
| Attendees easily offended | Disciples become immune to offense (Ps. 119:165) |
| Go 'round the mountain | Takes spiritual territory (Deut. 9:4) |
| Proud and puffed up | Humble and meek (Zech. 3:12) |
| Foolishness flourishes | People love wisdom more than being right (Prov. 4:5,6) |
| No fruit or bad fruit | Much good fruit (Matt. 7:16) |

## Another Gospel

This American gospel is uniquely ours in that it is more focused on instant and apparent success and results, rather than on the spiritual fruit, miracles, signs and wonders and the making of disciples that Jesus taught. When John the Baptist sent a messenger to Jesus to inquire if He was the Messiah or not, Jesus responded by describing His ministry. Now ask yourself if this is what is going on in the vast majority of most American churches.

*Now when John, while imprisoned, heard of the works of Christ, he sent word by his disciples and said to Him, "Are You the Expected One, or shall we look for someone else?" Jesus answered and said to them, "Go and report to John what you hear and see: the blind receive sight and the lame walk, the lepers are cleansed and the deaf hear, the dead are raised up, and the poor have the gospel preached to them. And blessed is he who does not take offense at Me"* (Matthew 11:2-6).

Jesus also said that we can do the same things that He did. *"Truly, truly, I say to you, he who believes in Me, the works that I do he will do also; and greater works than these he will do; because I go to the Father"* (John 14:12-12).

## Lowering the Bar...Beneath the Floor!

Apostle Paul spoke of a day when there would be another spirit which proclaimed another Jesus and even another gospel. This fake or counterfeit gospel message will be complicated because it bypasses the simplicity and purity we have in our love for Jesus.

*But I am afraid, lest as the serpent deceived Eve by his craftiness, your minds should be led astray from the simplicity and purity of devotion to Christ. For if one comes and preaches another Jesus whom we have not preached, or you receive a different spirit which you have not received, or a different gospel which you have not accepted, you bear this beautifully* (2 Corinthians 11:3-4 NASB).

We can no longer smile, look the other way, and tolerate this other gospel. It has removed the spiritual gifts from operating in the Lord's church. It is preached out of fear that it will "run people off from church." The bar has been so lowered that the Christian's and the non-Christian's lifestyle and behaviors are indistinguishable.

*Great fear seized the whole church and all who heard about these events. The apostles performed many miraculous signs and wonders among the people. And all the believers used to meet together in Solomon's Colonnade. No one else dared join them, even though they were highly regarded by the people. Nevertheless, more and more men and women believed in the Lord and were added to their number* (Acts 5:11-14 NIV).

In this passage Lord's strategy for the proliferation of the gospel is totally the opposite of modern church growth practitioners. The passage begins shortly after Ananias and Saphira were both struck dead in the church meeting place because they lied to the Holy Spirit about their finances. (See Acts 5:1-10.) The result of this powerful encounter with the Holy Spirit was a tremendous surge of growth of the church, and helped remove and run off those who were merely posing and playing games with God. The imperfect, but honest, believers hung around while the phony and the fake bolted.

Notice the following:

- A great fear of the Lord came on the church.
- The apostles performed many miraculous signs and wonders.
- All the believers were meeting together.
- No one dare join them; but,
- They were highly regarded among the people of the community!

That is the way the Holy Spirit runs a church. There is no question in anybody's mind whether God is there or not!

What the church is *not* supposed to look like:

1. A club of "secret" believers living a clandestine Christian life.

2. A gathering place for isolated individual believers on a "journey of faith."

3. A nursery for spiritual babies or an entertainment complex to cater to the uncommitted.

4. A spiritual hospital that perpetually cares for people while never actually curing them.

5. A clique for gossipers or a town hall for whiners making excuses about why God is so impotent and ineffective.

6. A retirement home for "burnt-out Christian veterans" who're really cynical believers; a haven where the obstinate and rebellious dodge accountability.

7. A place where unbroken believers come to vent their failures and find solace among other believers of the same mind-set.

8. A place where homosexuality is permitted, adultery is accepted, and the worship of mammon is promoted.

While this list is unflattering, it describes what is tolerated in a wide segment of mainstream churches today. Our challenge: how can we move forward for Christ if we know this kind of stuff is going on? The first change must occur in us. Our tolerance level for that which is clearly not scriptural, accompanied by a fervent desire for the authentic and real, is what will bring on the transformation. We also need to begin to change the church from within.

An Australian pastor taking a sabbatical in the Atlanta area for six months had the opportunity to frequent several local churches. I asked him about his observations. His response, "American churches are run more like businesses than Spirit-led ministries." He also commented that one church, in the pursuit of being seeker-friendly, had removed from the service anything and everything that could be construed as offensive, such as receiving the offering, exercising spiritual gifts, and using Christian "language" such as references to "the blood" or "atonement."

Church leaders are overreacting to our culture's political and spiritual "correctness" and are rejecting and eliminating the biblical foundation of our beliefs. Of course, ultimately that won't succeed. One person can make a difference, but it will take a great amount of patience, grace, and love to bring transformation.

**Endnotes**

1. Strong's Concordance.

2. Vance Havner, *Playing Marbles with Diamonds and Other Messages for America* (Grand Rapids, MI: Baker Publishing Group, 1985).

# CHAPTER 12

# WHAT WOULD JESUS DO?

The following is a stark example of a trend that has permeated American church culture which must be confronted if we desire to see an authentic move of God.

Most of us know about the popularity of the bracelets labeled "WWJD" found in most Christian book stores. This whole "What Would Jesus Do" phenomenon is based on a book by Charles Sheldon, *In His Steps*, written at the end of the 19th century advocating the "social gospel." By social gospel, I mean feeding the poor, giving blankets to the cold, finding shelter for those in need, and things like this. The author suggests that Jesus would pass out canned food, bring blankets to the homeless, and help the poor with natural things first, rather than spiritual things. The author's view is that doing these good works is what Jesus meant when He said that His followers would do "greater works."

Charles Sheldon's legacy is that people can do works of kindness and niceness instead of preaching the gospel. He began this trend accepting and promoting a substitute of social works for authentic gospel preaching. He can be credited with creating an alternative for Christians to do kind deeds without preaching or confronting the lost with the gospel. He equated social service with gospel preaching, and to this day, many believers have taken this mentality as a way out of their biblical responsibility to preach to every creature. Many Christians have adopted this view as a way around the simple but powerful preaching of the gospel.

Charles Parham, on the other hand, left a much greater heritage of spiritual fruit. Both men were from Topeka, Kansas. However, Charles Parham started Bethel Bible College where students studied the phenomenon of speaking in tongues. When some people there actually spoke in tongues during a prayer meeting, a new move of God was birthed. Later when Mr. Parham opened a similar school in Houston, William Seymour attended and was affected so strongly that he was instrumental in the Azusa Street Revival which started the Pentecostal movement—now nearly 600 million strong world-wide and Christianity's fastest growing branch.

Of course, it is good and right to remember the poor, to feed, and help them. But Jesus didn't command us to feed the poor, He commanded us to preach to them. To illustrate how easily this shift of thinking can happen, let's just look at two recognizable examples, of whom I personally admire, to illustrate this point.

The Salvation Army was birthed by the powerful desire of William Booth to get out of the pew and into the streets to "preach the gospel to the poor." Booth was considered a heretic by some because he wanted to preach and declare the gospel message and take the Scriptures outside the church building. He said: "While women weep, as they do now, I'll fight; while little children go hungry, as they do now, I'll fight; while men go to prison, in and out, in and out, as they do now, I'll fight; while there is a poor lost girl upon the streets, while there remains one dark soul without the light of God, I'll fight, I'll fight to the very end!"[1]

This gospel ministry began with fiery street preaching to the downtrodden and was accompanied with aid to the poor. The goal was to preach to the poor and give aid with a view to directing them to churches. There was no way they could preach to the poor without wanting to assist them with their daily struggles with hunger, shelter, and clothing. In time it became apparent that the street people they won to Christ did not feel comfortable going to the churches that existed at the time, so the Salvation Army opened churches and even houses to take care of the homeless and hungry. Eventually, they set up centers in every city where they were preaching.

Street-preaching workers reaching the lost were replaced by bell-ringing workers eager to receive offerings. This historic, and revolutionary, evangelistic ministry has become more of a social service organization for the poor than a gospel preaching ministry. It has morphed into an exceptional social service agency, one of the largest on earth.

While their kindness is legendary and they have an honorable past, the spiritual fruit in their outreaches has become a by-product instead of the goal. This is no indictment of the Salvation Army but a realization that the pure and simple effectiveness of preaching the gospel in power can quickly be cast aside by the sheer success and the fruit it produces. How do you deal with such a harvest?

## Be Nice or Tell the Truth?

We in America have an aversion to coming across as "nice." Yet there is not one example in Scripture where Jesus taught about being nice or acting nice. Jesus never said in the Sermon on the Mount, "Blessed are the nice...." *Being nice* is not the same as preaching the gospel.

At a conference a few years ago, I heard the incredible testimony of a Bulgarian apostle who had been beaten, arrested, and deported for preaching in his homeland before the fall of Communism. He had amazing stories about miraculous protection from horrific persecution he and the Bulgarian church experienced under Communist rule. As he was preaching, he asked, "What is it with you Americans about being nice? Nice is not a fruit of the Spirit and Jesus never said, 'Go and be nice.'"

This really got me thinking! We Americans are so concerned when we share the gospel that we might "turn someone off" or "offend them" that we forget the power the authentic gospel has to set people free and set them on fire for God! Dumbing-down our message to make it palatable is cowardly, compromising, ineffective, and produces bad results! The lesson is obvious—God's ways are just really not our ways.

## Good Motives Alone Aren't Enough

We have been taught that if we do good things and our motives are good, God will bless it and us. That is not true. The truth is, Jesus only did what the Father told Him to do and what outwardly may appear to look effective, kind, and good may not be fruitful or even helpful!

Jesus said things like, "preach the gospel to the poor." He also said, "Blessed are the poor in spirit, for theirs is the kingdom of heaven." Jesus followed a pattern as revealed to Him by the Father, and it worked. We need to see that the methods He used and the way He preached were always superior and bore more fruit than any way to present the gospel we might dream up.

Another example is much more current. The Vineyard was established in 1974 by John Wimber, a converted professional musician from California whose teaching on healing, signs and wonders, and power evangelism drew attention to the fact that the saints were supposed to be "doing the stuff" instead of just a few elite preachers. His courses on signs and wonders and power evangelism at Fuller Theological Seminary drew thousands from all over the world. In addition, his lack of a religious spirit and his desire to stay above religious politics allowed him to bring forth a fresh revelation of timeless truth.

His books, as well his regular publication, *Equipping the Saints* spawned a movement that numbered hundreds of churches around the globe and affected thousands. While I personally never met John Wimber, I have known and fellowshipped with many Vineyard pastors and church members over the years. I admire him greatly and respect for his original vision, and The Vineyard could not be greater. In fact, his books on power evangelism and power healing are so devoid of dated content and timeless in their revelation that they can still be used as textbooks.

Because he was treading into new and volatile territory at that time, he inevitably became a target for controversy and persecution. From an outsider's perspective, it appears to me that John Wimber was such a pioneer, like many who came before him, that he never fully realized the complete and ultimate vision God gave him. His vision to raise up churches in which everyone was equipped in their spiritual gifts and "doing the stuff" was not fully accomplished.

The Lord gave Wimber great international influence, and many people vied for his ear and his endorsement. Due to the great favor the Lord placed on him, he was soon surrounded by advisors who got his ear and diverted him from his original purpose and vision. Because of his lack of religious acumen, in time, he came under the influence and the counsel of ambitious, and sometimes even unspiritual, men.

For instance, some of his church leaders began an outreach emphasis which was appealing, but had little basis in scriptural model or practice and would not pass for gospel preaching. Books were written, seminars were presented, and much endorsement was given to this whole line of thinking. Looking back years later, I believe this outreach was a huge diversion of resources and focus from the simple beginnings of authentic gospel preaching. In time it opened the door to the acceptance of a seeker-friendly emphasis.

The initial foundation of preaching the gospel of the Kingdom with signs and wonders, healing, church planting, and discipleship, was replaced with "novel" ideas for outreach. For instance, one idea was to stand on street corners and hand out cold water and church fliers on hot summer days to suburbanites who were sitting in air-conditioned cars waiting for the traffic light to change. It is obvious this could not be confused with authentic preaching.

While this kind of activity was attractive to believers too afraid to share their faith, it ultimately had little effect in bringing souls into the Kingdom and making disciples. Since the proponent of this philosophy was allowed such a high platform in the movement and had close proximity to leadership, this "evangelism" emphasis helped open the door to bring the social gospel into the movement. In a short time, simple but power-filled gospel preaching was replaced with seeker-sensitive meetings.

Only a few years after John Wimber died of cancer in 1997, the movement looked little like its supernatural beginnings—the only remaining emphasis being worship and church planting. Teaching the Kingdom, healing, signs and wonders, and discipleship faded away or turned into something else. In the beginning, signs and wonders and the power and fear of the Lord were always present in their meetings. But in just a few years, the intense awe and presence of the Lord had vanished, replaced with seeker-sensitive services and attempts to be "relevant."

New ideas and outreach gimmicks were no match for authentic signs and wonders, so some churches left The Vineyard, feeling it had strayed from its fruitful roots. Nevertheless, the Lord allowed this movement to spawn two worldwide moves of God. The Vineyard has had more impact around the world in a 20-year period than many denominations have had in 200 years! I believe that God will give the movement at least a second chance to finish what it started. While some of my Vineyard friends might disagree with my assessment, many would not. The Lord decides these matters, and He is much more forgiving than any of us. Jesus told us that fruit should be our criteria to measure these kinds of things.

*Abide in Me, and I in you. As the branch cannot bear fruit of itself, unless it abides in the vine, so neither can you, unless you abide in Me* (John 15:4).

Whatever we think about these movements, the big lesson is that staying on message with the simple power of preaching the gospel can easily and absolutely be overshadowed by its own sheer success that mechanisms to handle the fruit become the priority.

## So What Would Jesus Do?

If Jesus was on the streets right now in 21$^{st}$-century suburban or urban America, would He hand out wristbands, give away sandwiches, and pass out cold water on street corners? Or would He cast out demons and heal the sick? Would He demonstrate against a woman's "choice," would He go on television, would He pass out tracts, or would He bring life and freedom through His uncompromised Word? I think in our hearts we know the answer. Jesus would do what we saw His Father doing and what we read about all through the New Testament. Many of our attempts at ministry are, in many ways, missing the point.

*Jesus therefore answered and was saying to them, "Truly, truly, I say to you, the Son can do nothing of Himself, unless it is something He sees the Father doing; for whatever the Father does, these things the Son also does in like manner. For the Father loves the Son, and shows Him all things that He Himself is doing; and greater works than these will He show Him, that you may marvel. For just as the Father raises the dead and gives them life, even so the Son also gives life to whom He wishes* (John 5:19-21).

## Jesus' Priorities

If you are still unclear about this, then look at the priorities of Jesus, or how He spent His time in ministry. Was His ministry primarily one of "feeding the poor" or "preaching to the poor"? They are *not* the same.

Did He pass out meals and water? What about the feeding of the 5,000? Jesus did that but only *after* those folks stayed around for three days listening to Him teach and preach about the Kingdom! I think He felt it was the least He could do after they showed Him such commitment.

And what about the time when Jesus said to Peter three times, *"feed my sheep"*? (John 21:17). Did He mean for Peter to literally give His followers food or, was He referring to the real food He had already referred to in the gospel—to do His Father's will?

*But He said to them, "I have food to eat that you do not know about." The disciples therefore were saying to one another, "No one brought Him anything to eat, did he?" Jesus said to them, "My food is to do the will of Him who sent Me, and to accomplish His work"* (John 4:32-34).

If you wonder what Jesus would do, then just look at how He spent His time and the priorities He lived by. A simple analysis shows He spent approximately one-third of His ministry time preaching and teaching the gospel of the Kingdom mainly to His disciples; another third He spent casting out demons and doing miracles; and He spent a third healing the sick.

Instead of the latest politically correct Christian fads found on local Christian bookstore shelves defining What Jesus Would Do, we should let the Word of God define it for us. Even if "everyone" is reading it, that doesn't make it true. There is so much information coming at Christians today it would benefit most of us to go back and read the *Bible*. We have become so spiritually lazy that we are dependent on others telling us the meaning of things. But Jesus said that the things of the Kingdom would be so simple a child could understand them!

The following Scriptures teach us what Jesus *really* did. They are exceedingly clear.

*You know of Jesus of Nazareth, how God anointed Him with the Holy Spirit and with power, and how He went about doing good, and healing all who were oppressed by the devil; for God was with Him.* (Acts 10:38).

*And as Jesus passed on from there, two blind men followed Him, crying out, and saying, "Have mercy on*

*us, Son of David!" And after He had come into the
house, the blind men came up to Him, and Jesus said
to them, "Do you believe that I am able to do this?"
They said to Him, "Yes, Lord." Then He touched their
eyes, saying, "Be it done to you according to your
faith." And their eyes were opened. And Jesus sternly
warned them, saying, "See here, let no one know about
this!" But they went out, and spread the news about
Him in all that land. And as they were going out,
behold, a dumb man, demon-possessed, was brought to
Him. And after the demon was cast out, the dumb
man spoke; and the multitudes marveled, saying,
"Nothing like this was ever seen in Israel."*
(Matthew 9:27-33).

*Now when He was in Jerusalem at the Passover, dur-
ing the feast, many believed in His name, beholding
His signs which He was doing* (John 2:23).

*And a certain man was there, who had been thirty-
eight years in his sickness. When Jesus saw him lying
there, and knew that he had already been a long time
in that condition, He said to him, "Do you wish to get
well?" The sick man answered Him, "Sir, I have no
man to put me into the pool when the water is stirred
up, but while I am coming, another steps down before
me." Jesus said to him, "Arise, take up your pallet,
and walk." And immediately the man became well,
and took up his pallet and began to walk. Now it was
the Sabbath on that day* (John 5:5-9).

*And for this reason the Jews were persecuting Jesus,
because He was doing these things on the Sabbath. But
He answered them, "My Father is working until now,
and I Myself am working."* (John 5:16-17).

*Wow!* It certainly appears by these passages that Jesus performed a great amount of signs, wonders, and miracles which He refers to as His "good works." Is it possible that because of the wrong emphasis that the church and society has put on this "social gospel" that the definition of good works by the average Christian has now become defined as handing out turkeys, giving away hot dogs, and mowing yards instead of preaching the gospel with God attesting to it with signs wonders and fruit? It certainly seems that way to me.

> *But realize this, that in the last days difficult times will come. For men will be lovers of self, lovers of money, boastful, arrogant, revilers, disobedient to parents, ungrateful, unholy, unloving, irreconcilable, malicious gossips, without self-control, brutal, haters of good, treacherous, reckless, conceited, lovers of pleasure rather than lovers of God; holding to a form of godliness, although they have denied its power; and avoid such men as these* (2 Timothy 3:1-5).

Wouldn't this be exactly how the enemy operates? To water down the truth about these "good works" of power? From healing the cancer patient and delivering the drug addict to preaching the good news? Why *wouldn't* the enemy's number 1 strategy be to get Christians debating about preaching the gospel and even arguing over how it is done! The enemy of our soul has taken captive entire denominations and movements with this delusion, some even label anyone truly "doing what Jesus did" as deceived or into the occult. How sad they can't see the truth!

The enemy has sent the church on so many bunny trails that I wrote a chapter about it in this book titled, "Beating around the Bush." There are so many ministries pursuing anything and everything *except* preaching the good news of the

Kingdom! And there are even more diversions, detours, and excuses for not doing it that it makes you wonder if there isn't something or someone propelling all this fruitless activity forward. There is. The enemy. He wants the church caught up in obsessive activity that leads nowhere and accomplishes nothing. He is more than happy to encourage us in those directions.

## What *Wouldn't* Jesus Do? (probably)

Instead of only paying attention to what is served up in Christian bookstores, pop culture and on television "feel-good" reality and talk shows we should be examining the New Testament and Jesus' life. Based on the gospel narratives of Christ's life, we get a clear picture of what he *wouldn't* spend His time doing. If He was physically here now in 21st-century America, Jesus could do a lot of things, but based on the gospels and His declaration of what His purpose was, He very *probably wouldn't* express His love for humanity by doing the following things—even as kind and as helpful as they may appear:

Bring a team to remodel your house.

Hand out glasses of cold water on interstate off ramps.

Wash your car.

Mow your grass.

Hand out turkeys on Thanksgiving and Christmas.

Give a bag of old clothes to the poor.

Give you His old furniture or shoes.

Sell donuts or cookies.

Pat you on the back.

Hand you a gospel tract.

Sew doilies and mail them to prisoners.

Give you a car.

Wash your hair and paint your nails.

Teach you English classes.

And a thousand and one other diversions.

The prime mission objective of the church is this: *preach the gospel and make disciples*. While all of these other things can be good and right, they are still *not* our primary mandate. Jesus preached with demonstrations of power present each time, not with slick communication techniques or feats of verbal acumen. Jesus healed the sick, cast out demons, and preached the message of the Kingdom. His message was crystal clear, His mission was without ambiguity, and His focus was laser accurate. He was born into our world as the first of a new race who could walk as children of God. He had power and authority over His circumstances and took dominion over everything He encountered. Unless the Father sent it, Jesus didn't receive it and wasn't distracted by it.

> *And we know that God causes all things to work together for good to those who love God, to those who are called according to His purpose. For whom He foreknew, He also predestined to become conformed to the image of His Son, that He might be the first-born among many brethren* (Romans 8:28-29).

While some theologians still hold to a view that due to our deep depravity He can scarcely share His divine character, the Bible is quite clear that God's prescription for our deliverance involves doing the works that He did. If looking to Jesus and getting our eyes off ourselves is a key to our transformation, than obsessing over our faults and failings is a dead-end street. The avenue of obsession over self-improvement is a road to nowhere. The way we change is through beholding and being transformed into *His* image, not by attempting to fix ourselves.

*Now the Lord is the Spirit; and where the Spirit of the
Lord is, there is liberty. But we all, with unveiled face
beholding as in a mirror the glory of the Lord, are
being transformed into the same image from glory to
glory, just as from the Lord, the Spirit*
(2 Corinthians 3:17-18).

Transformation occurs through beholding Him. The
Spirit changes us, not self-improvement techniques or discipline. Jesus never required His disciples to do anything but to
follow Him and imitate Him. He was mentoring them as they
beheld what He was and what He did. He modeled a new way
of living and He told us that greater things than He did, we
could do! Think about it—do you believe what He said and do
you want to obey?

**Endnote**

1. William Booth founder of the Salvation Army quotes -Thinkexist.com.

# CHAPTER 13

# BEATING AROUND THE BUSH

Have you noticed how much praying for revival has been going on of late and how little revival has resulted? The problem: we have been substituting praying for obeying, and it simply will not work. To pray for revival while ignoring the precepts written in Scripture is to waste a lot of words and get nothing for our trouble. Pastor and author A.W. Tozer wrote, "Prayer will become effective only when we stop using it as a substitute for obedience."

This chapter has been written by my son Ryan who is on staff with us. A prophet spoke over him years ago that his generation would not want to have anything to do with religion and would settle for nothing less than the real thing! He is definitely one of the "new breed" of leaders that the church needs in this hour.

If you are listening to and watching the popular theology and practice of the Charismatic church in America, you might be confused. Many new movements have cropped up, and I have watched one after the other hit the church, become enormously popular, ride it out for a couple of months (or years) and then see it fade into oblivion. Along the way, each of these popular movements or fads, captivates and enlists a large number of Christians as well as their time, energy, and finances, all the while promising personal fulfillment and a cataclysmic, worldwide revival. To date, none of these movements has accomplished what they said would happen if the church would mobilize around their ideal.

Sadly, the vast majority of Christians have at least a couple of these movements under their belt by now, and along with it the accompanying disillusionment, hopelessness, bitterness, and depression. It is depressing to invest vast amounts of personal resources in something that produces little fruit. The current state of much of the church is cynical, wary, and untrusting. They are cynical because what they have done hasn't produced anything in proportion to the amount invested.

They are wary because they have been lied to, at least in their estimation. Cynical, wary, and untrusting people are not fruitful people. The Lord requires us to be wholehearted, and it's impossible to be wholehearted while holding on to cynicism or bitterness. This has produced a fruitless, angry church. Nothing is more frustrating than to have your hopes dashed by false promises.

## In It for the Kingdom

Hopefully, we all got into this thing for the Kingdom, or rule and reign of God. We were told that the rule and reign of Jesus would produce life and peace for all who submitted to the King. We were told that the world, our cities and communities could be transformed through the power of the gospel. We were told that sicknesses and diseases would bow to the King of kings and Lord of lords. Even after all of the disillusionment and cynicism, most believers still acknowledge this truth. We still believe the basics.

The problem: applying what we know. Even a cursory study of the early church shows us a people walking in power and authority over sin, sickness, and disease. A brief glance at the life and message of Jesus promises the believer power, authority, and peace; so we can't say we don't know what is available.

The frustration: manifesting the promises. We have been promised to the gills, but we have seen few actual results. Because of this, some have doubted they even exist! I was talking to a guy a couple months of ago who was rescued by the Holy Spirit out of dead religion seven years previously. He attended Charismatic, spirit-filled churches, conferences, and meetings. He heard the talk of the power of God, healings, and miracles, but for seven years, he saw nothing. He was really starting to doubt if it was even real, and I don't blame him.

While a lot that is presently going on in ministries has more to do with the number of activities and conferences planned rather than genuine gospel activity, Jesus puts a huge premium on whether something is bearing fruit or not.

He said:

> *By their fruit you will recognize them. Do people pick grapes from thorn bushes, or figs from thistles? Likewise every good tree bears good fruit, but a bad tree bears bad fruit. A good tree cannot bear bad fruit, and a bad tree cannot bear good fruit. Every tree that does not bear good fruit is cut down and thrown into the fire. Thus, by their fruit you will recognize them* (Matthew 7:16-20 NIV).

Fruit speaks louder than words. Why? Because fruit has these certain characteristics:

1. It is visible and can be seen and measured.

2. It is in one of two conditions—good or bad.

3. No fruit leads to a serious spiritual problem.

Since the Lord told us not to look at what people say, but to what fruit is produced, let's look at a few of the current movements and the fruit produced.

## The Prayer Movement

Christians have logged untold hours of prayer for America and other countries. We have had one-hour prayer meetings, all-night prayer meetings, mid-day prayer meetings, and lately, 24/7 prayer meetings. We have been promised by these purveyors of prayer that the secret to a cataclysmic, world-wide revival is non-stop prayer, or having young people pray, or having old people pray, or having mothers pray.

The church has responded by investing millions of dollars in prayer rooms, prayer mountains, prayer retreats, and prayer conferences. The church has responded with personnel as thousands of people have been recruited to organize prayer events, prayer rallies, prayer groups, and some have even taken on prayer as a full-time job! These people call themselves "prayer missionaries." They pray a minimum of 40-50 hours a week and raise support to fund their praying. The church has also responded with time. It would be absolutely staggering to record the millions of hours of prayer logged by Christians for worldwide revival, citywide revival, church revival, etc.

But what about fruit? What has the church accomplished with its millions of hours of prayer? Has the world fallen to the gospel? Are the pygmies in Africa meeting Jesus sovereignly? Are all of the churches in the United States throbbing with revival? Has America turned to God? Has abortion stopped? Are all the political figures in America born-again Christians?

Nope. The stadiums aren't filled with the lost coming to Jesus and the streets aren't clogged with sinners coming to the Cross. The world seems completely immune to our millions of hours of prayer.

What's up?

## The Worship Movement

Christians have recovered the lost art of praising and worshiping God. The church has been swept up with a revival of worship. Great songs, original sounds, worship leaders, worship movements, recording companies, and worship conferences have virtually covered the church in America. The purveyors of the worship movement promise that if we will worship God for a protracted period of time, the spiritual climate of a community, city, and nation will change. If we just sing a few more choruses or get lost into spontaneous, prophetic worship, the glory will appear and all will turn to Jesus.

Like the prayer movement, the worship movement has been supplied with everything it needs. Millions of dollars have been spent producing and buying worship albums. Millions of dollars have been spent in organizing, promoting, and attending worship conferences. Millions of hours have been logged as people worship in their cars, on their way to work, first thing in the morning, before they go to bed, etc. Millions of hours have been logged by "worship missionaries" as they spend 40-50 hours a week worshiping God, again supported by church funding.

The result? Have the nations fallen into a trancelike state and marched into the church to be saved? Have the spiritual climates over major cities been changed by the power of our music? Have we unseated ruling principalities and powers?

Nope. In spite of the rather encouraging response of the church to the rally cry of the worship people, there has been little if any spiritual fruit to show for the millions of hours and dollars spent worshiping God other than the Body learning how to worship—which is essential. Somehow, the world is immune to our worship, energetic though it is.

## The Unity Movement

The promise: if we all come together in one accord, then the mighty power of God and an earth-shattering revival will rock the world. If we can get Blacks and Whites together.... If we can repent for the injustices done to African Americans, Native Americans, Japanese Americans, then the power of God will come.

According to unity people, all of the churches and world's problems can and will be solved if we will all come together. Their mantra: "They will know we are Christians by our love one for another. If the world sees our unity, they will come to the Lord in droves." If pastors stop jockeying for position and tear down the walls that separate church from church, if prophets start communing with teachers, if the White church will invite Black ministers, then America will fall to the gospel.

The church has responded. Pastors have prayed. White churches have had Black preachers in the pulpit. White people have said, "I'm sorry" to African Americans, Native Americans and the Japanese. We've held hands, prayed, worshiped, had meals and communion together. We've repented for everything under the sun and for a few things not under the sun.

What has all this produced? Does the church resemble a rainbow of colors, creeds, and denominations? Have the denominational lines fallen? Have the lost come running into the church? Have the nations repented? Have all problems been solved by the magic pill of unity?

Nope. Churches are still the most segregated places in the world. The world seems to be completely immune to our unity. They don't seem to care if we say "sorry" to each other. It's irrelevant to a lost person who attends religious meetings.

## It Goes On and On

There are more movements, including: 40 Days of Purpose, Lighthouses of Prayer, the Prayer of Jabez, Seeker-Sensitive churches, Healing Rooms, Spiritual Warfare, the Jezebel Spirit, The Restoration of Israel, Jewish Dance, etc. Many of these movements promise the revival we all want to see. The people championing these movements are tuned into what the church desires. We all want to see the world come to a saving knowledge of Jesus. We all want to see the lost get saved, the sick healed, and the oppressed set free. We want righteousness, peace, and joy to fill our homes, communities, cities, and nations. We want the rule and reign of God. Each and every one of these movements has revival at the core of their purposes.

They are all championed by godly, well-intentioned people. Although possibly misguided, I doubt that any of the leaders promoting these movements have anything but good motives. They all love Jesus, the world, the lost, and the church. This makes it extremely difficult to speak out against them or correct their errant course, although this is necessary. Jesus said check out the fruit; it has to be visible, not invisible! We can all have the best intentions and motives, but because of a lack of wisdom and guidance we can cause great harm to the Body of Christ.

The movements include good activities and beliefs, such as every Christian should live a lifestyle of prayer, worship, and personal devotion to Christ. And every believer should live their life in harmony and unity with others. After all, there is significant scriptural precedent for these practices, and the Lord and His disciples did so. But, an overemphasis of these activities quickly shifts the focus away from Jesus and His Kingdom.

Movements can become excuses for not preaching the gospel with signs and wonders following. They are elaborate disguises for lack of courage. All of these practices are encouraged to take place in private or in the church, promising the participant freedom from that pesky thing called discomfort.

Truthfully, the reason these movements are so popular is because they excuse the believer from living a crucified life. They give the cowardly Christian justification for their lack of boldness and power. They provide the believer with an activity where it is impossible to measure fruit. Who can *really* say what your prayers are producing? Who can *really* say what impact your worship is having? Who can *really* say what your unity is producing? Zimbabwe *may* be getting saved as a result of your prayers. People in Wales *may* be having sovereign encounters with God as a result of your worship. People in Chile *may* be set free because you said you were sorry.

## The Sad Truth

They probably aren't getting saved sovereignly as a result of your prayers. They probably aren't getting healed sovereignly as a result of your singing and clapping. They probably aren't experiencing inner healing because you apologized for your great grandfather's prejudice.

Sorry—you were well-intentioned, but misguided. You meant well but you were wrong. You gave your all, but you gave it to the wrong thing. I know it's depressing, but true. The fruit speaks louder than my words. Certainly, there have been many sovereign results of prayer, worship, and unity, but they have been on an individual level and a small scale. God is good and does nice things. But that is God's fruit, not yours. But the small scale events we see are nothing like we read about in the Book of Acts, as whole cities were turned upside down, and entire regions were shaken by the power of the gospel.

So what's the difference between us and them? What's the action that produces results?

## The Difference

They *said* something. They *did* something. They put everything on the line. They took their message outside, where it's needed. They took the power to the streets. If God didn't show up, everyone would know it. If it wasn't divine, then it would fail. If the God who invades the impossible was not active in the equation, people would die. People would be humiliated. They had courage. They had boldness. They had power. God was with them. Things changed. Cities fell to the gospel.

Folks, we are not going to get out of this without preaching the Good News of the Kingdom to all creation. He didn't say pray. He didn't say worship. He didn't tell us to say we are sorry. He told us to *preach the gospel*. He told us to heal the sick, cast out devils, and raise the dead. He told us to go into all the world, not stay in all the churches.

You know what to say and you know what to do. Why? Because you possess the Holy Spirit. You may not know what to say, but He knows. You may not know how to heal the sick, but He does. Put Him to work! Put a demand on the God who dwells within you! He will answer! It isn't complicated, and it isn't complex. The lost need a Savior. The sick need a Healer. The world needs Jesus. You have Him locked inside you. Give Him away!

It's as simple as obeying the Scriptures. Don't pray about it. You don't need to worship God for a month to understand this passage, and I doubt coming together with other Christians is necessary to accomplish its directive:

> *And as you go, preach, saying, The kingdom of Heaven is at hand. Heal the sick, cleanse the lepers, raise the dead, cast out demons. Freely you have received, freely give* (Matthew 10:7-8 NKJV).

As we are being provoked by the Spirit to bring God out of our boxes of religion, fear, and unbelief, I believe it is imperative for us to disarm and destroy every ridiculous and unscriptural excuse and rationale we create to let us off the hook in the area of healing. Allow the Lord to use this sort of primer on healing to disarm all the excuses, wrong teachings, and traditions that have held you back from believing the truth so you can follow in Jesus' footsteps.

Jesus said that certain teachers were *"making the word of God of no effect through* [their] *tradition"* (Mark 7:13). For centuries, human ideas, wrong doctrines, and doubt-filled theories have hidden or hindered the healing, deliverance, signs and wonders, and demonstrations of power that we see in the gospels from being proclaimed and acted upon as it was in the early church.

Worldly wisdom, fear of others, and compromise are so prevalent in our seeker-friendly churches today, that it is unlikely they will bring about a change of tradition without a powerful movement of God's choosing. Large crowds gather for motivational talks and self-help instead of preaching the crucified, but power-filled life! Instead of healing the sick, the old man is soothed and strengthened. Instead of confronting sin, people are told how to "handle their issues." Instead of casting out demons, the demonized are directed from the pulpit to get Christian psychological counseling and take medication. Even while these folks have large followings, the blind are not given sight, the deaf do not hear, and the lame do not walk. People are dying of sicknesses and diseases while the self-help preachers tell us to "be happy."

We as the people of God must be confident in the Word of God and the will of God regarding healing the sick. *"By smooth words he will turn to godlessness those who act wickedly toward the covenant, but the people who know their God will display strength and take action"* (Daniel 11:32).

The following are fallacies and traditions that need to be exposed, dealt with, and disposed of:

1. God wills some of His children to suffer sickness, and therefore many who are prayed for are not healed because it is not His will to heal them.

When Jesus healed the demon-possessed boy whom the disciples could not heal, He proved that it is God's will to heal even those who fail to receive healing. Furthermore, He assigned the failure of the disciples to cure the boy not to God's will, but to the disciples' unbelief. The failure of many to be healed today when prayed for is never because it is not God's will to heal them.

If sickness is the will of God, then every physician would be a lawbreaker, every trained nurse a defiler of the Almighty, and every hospital a house of rebellion instead of a house of mercy. Since Christ came to do the Father's will, the fact that He healed them all is proof that it is indeed God's will that all be healed. If it is not God's will for all to be healed, how did everyone in the multitudes obtain from Christ what was not God's will for some of them to receive? The Bible says *"he healed them all."* (Mark 9:14-27).

If it is not God's will for all to be healed, why do the Scriptures state: "by his stripes we are healed" and "by whose stripes ye were healed" (Isa. 53:5, 1 Pet. 2:24 KJV)? How can anyone be declared healed, if it is God's will for some of us to be sick?

Christ never refused those who sought His healing. Repeatedly, the Gospels tell us that He healed them all. Christ the healer has never changed. Only one person in the entire Bible ever asked for healing by saying, "If it be Your will" (Mark 1:40). That was the poor leper to whom Jesus immediately responded, "I will; be clean."

2. We can glorify God more by being patient in our sickness than by being healed.

If sickness glorifies God more than healing, then any attempt to get well by natural or divine means would be an effort to rob God of the glory that we should want Him to receive.

If sickness glorifies God, then we should rather be sick than well. If sickness glorifies God, Jesus robbed His Father of glory by healing everyone, and the Holy Spirit continued doing the same throughout the acts of the apostles.

Paul says, *"For ye are bought with a price: therefore glorify God in your body, and in your spirit, which are God's"* (1 Cor. 6:20 KJV). Our bodies and spirits are bought with a price. We are to glorify God in both. We do not glorify God in our spirit by remaining in sin. We do not glorify God in our body by remaining sick. John's Gospel is used by some people to prove that sickness glorifies God; but God was not glorified in this case until Lazarus was raised up from the dead; the result, *"many of the Jews... believed on Him"* (John 11:45 KJV).

3. God heals some; it is not His will to heal all.

But Jesus, who came to do the Father's will, *did* "heal them all." If healing is not for all, why did Jesus bear our sicknesses, our pains, and our diseases? If God wanted some of His children to suffer, then Jesus relieved us from bearing something which God wanted us to bear. But since Jesus came to do the will of the Father, and since He has borne our diseases, it must be God's will for all to be well.

If it is not God's will for all to be healed, then God's promises to heal are not for all. That would mean that faith does not come by hearing the Word of God alone, but by getting a special revelation that God has favored you and wills to heal you.

If God's promises to heal are not for all, then we could not know what God's will is by reading His Word alone. That means we would have to pray until He speaks directly to us about each particular case. We could not consider God's Word as directed to us personally, but would have to close our Bibles and pray for a direct revelation from God to know if it is His will to heal each case.

God's Word is His will. God's promises reveal His will. When we read what He promises to do, we then know what it is His will to do.

Please note this very important statement: Since it is written, *"Faith comes by hearing the word of God"* (see Rom. 10:17), then the best way to build faith in your heart that God is willing to heal you, is for you to hear that part of God's Word which promises you healing.

Faith for spiritual healing comes by hearing the gospel: "He bore our sins." We are to preach the gospel—that He bore our sins—to every creature. We are to preach the gospel—that He bore our sicknesses (Isa. 53:4)—to every creature.

Christ emphasized His promise, *"If you shall ask anything in my name, I will do it,"* by repeating it twice. (See John 14:13-14). He did not exclude healing from this promise. *Anything* includes healing. This promise is for all. Healing is for all. Otherwise Christ should have qualified His promise such as: *"Whatever you desire* [except healing], *when you pray, believe that you receive it, and you shall have it."* (Mark 11:24) But He did not. Healing, therefore, is included in the *whatever.*

This promise is made to you. If it is not God's will to heal all, His promise would not be dependable when Christ said, *"If you live in me, and my words live in you, you shall ask what you will, and it shall be done to you"* (John 15:7).

James says: *"Is any among you sick? Then he must call for the elders of the church; and let them pray over him, anointing him with oil in the name of the Lord: and the prayer offered in faith will restore the one who is sick, and the Lord will raise him up..."* (James 5:14-15). This promise is for all, including you, if you are sick.

4. Some people have believed that if we are righteous, we should expect sicknesses as part of our life. They quote the Scripture: *"Many are the afflictions of the righteous"* (Ps. 34:19), but this does not mean sickness as some would have us believe. It means trials, hardships, persecutions, and temptations, but never sicknesses or physical disabilities.

It would be a contradiction to say, "Christ has borne our sicknesses, and with His stripes we are healed," but then to add, "Many are the sicknesses of the righteous, which He requires us to bear."

To prove this tradition, theologians quote, *"But God of all grace, who has called us to his eternal glory by Christ Jesus, after that you have suffered a while, make you perfect, establish, strengthen, and settle you"* (1 Pet. 5:10 NKJV). This suffering does not refer to suffering sickness, but to the many ways in which God's people have so often had to suffer for their testimony. (See Acts 5:41; 2 Cor. 12:10.)

5. We are not to expect healing for "certain" afflictions. People quote the Scripture, *"Is any among you afflicted? let him pray"* (James 5:13 KJV). This again does not refer to sickness, but to the same things pointed out above: trials, hardships, persecutions, and temptations.

6. God chastises His children with sickness. The Scripture quoted to support this fallacy, *"Whom the Lord loves He chastens..."* (Heb. 12:6-8). God does chasten those whom He loves, but it does not say that He makes them sick. The word *chasten* here means "to instruct, train, discipline, teach, or educate," like a teacher "instructs" a pupil, or like a parent "trains and teaches" a child. When a teacher instructs a student, various means of discipline may be employed, but never sickness. When a parent trains a child, there are many ways to chasten, but never by imposing a physical disease.

For our heavenly Father to chasten us does not require that He smites us with a disease. Our diseases were laid upon Christ. God could not require that we bear, as punishment, what Jesus has substantially suffered for us. Christ's sacrifice freed us forever from the curse of sin and disease which He bore on our behalf.

7. The age of miracles is past.

Even unbelievers believe in miracles. There are even television shows about them. For this statement to be true, there would have to be a total absence of miracles. Even one miracle would prove that the age of miracles has not passed. Anyone who claims that the age of miracles is behind us denies the need, the privileges, and the benefits of prayer. For God to hear and answer prayer, whether the petition is for a postage stamp or for the healing of a paralytic, is a miracle. If prayer brings an answer, that answer is a miracle.

If there are no miracles, there is no reason for faith. If there are no miracles, prayer is mockery and only ignorance would cause anyone to either pray or expect an answer. God cannot answer prayer without providing a miracle. If we pray at all, we should expect that prayer to be answered. If that prayer is answered, God has done it; and if God has answered prayer, He has performed something supernatural. That is a miracle. To deny miracles today is to make a mockery of prayer.

Also, the age of miracles has not passed because Jesus, the miracle worker, has never changed: *"Jesus Christ the same yesterday, and today, and forever"* (Heb. 13:8).

When Jesus sent His disciples to preach the gospel, He told them: *"These* [supernatural] *signs will follow those who believe"* (Mark 16:17 NKJV). This was for every creature, for all nations, until the end of the world. The end of the world has not yet come, so the age of miracles has not yet passed. Christ's commission has never been withdrawn or cancelled.

When we preach that it is always God's will to heal, the question is immediately raised: "Why then do we die?"

> *God's Word says: "You take away their breath, they die, and return to their dust"* (Ps. 104:29 NKJV). *The Bible says: "You shall come to your grave in a full age, like as a shock of corn comes in its season"* (Job 5:26 KJV).

For us to come to our full age and for God to take away our breath does not require the aid of disease. God's will for your death as His child is that after living a fruitful life (see Ps. 92:14), fulfilling the number of your days (see Exod. 23:26), you simply stop breathing and fall asleep in Christ, to awaken on the other side and live with Him forever. *"So shall [you] ever be with the Lord"* (1 Thess. 4:17), Indeed, this is the blessed hope of the righteous.

People believe unbiblical things about healing and miracles because they have been taught this through the message, lifestyles, and model of the vast majority of American and Western Christian spiritual leadership. These leaders were wrongly taught by mentors or professors who themselves were filled with skepticism, unbelief, and doubt about these subjects, Rather than acknowledging what they did not know, they came up with an excuse, usually based on one Scripture pulled out of context to justify the deception they are under.

Consequently, students became like their teachers, full of unbelief yet willing to communicate grand and pious messages for their lack of power and authority in the realms of healings and miracles. Rather than saying, "I don't know," they say, "I don't know nor do I know anyone who has seen a miracle or a legitimate healing. Therefore I have concluded the age of miracles has ceased." What pride!

To assume something based on only on hearsay or one's own lack of firsthand experience is the height of arrogance. Unfortunately many of these professors are professing their unbelief to generations of well-meaning ministers who take their words as truth.

While oceans and seas cover over 75 percent of the earth's surface and many of us have had an opportunity to see a beach, most of us have little or no knowledge firsthand about what really goes on under the oceans. Ninety-eight percent of the oceans' vastness have never been penetrated by humans, let alone explored. Even a vast expanse of the world's land mass has never been explored by humans. For example, Australia is so vast and wide that only a small portion of it has been inhabited by civilized men. People live in modern, coastal cities, yet there are vast regions of the Australian outback and desert yet to be explored.

Therefore, an accurate assessment or judgment cannot be made on a subject like healing based on a person's or even a group's subjective experience or experiences. The truth about this area can only be uncovered and discovered when we choose to explore these unexplored realms with open minds, willing to learn new things. While there is some comfort in holding onto the familiar, no one will discover the truth unless they are willing to believe *all* the truths in the Word of God. These truths can't be ignored or deleted from our Bibles.

There is a mass deception over much of the American evangelical church on the subject because of the doctrine of cessationism. As mentioned earlier in the book, cessationism is the belief that God has ceased to perform works of power, and the gifts of the Spirit we see in the Bible are somehow unnecessary and unneeded today. How completely illogical and nonsensical! How can you accept one passage and throw away another?

Just 500 years ago scientists said the world was flat. But it took Magellan and other explorers who had the courage to be pioneers in areas never before explored. Experiencing the reality of regular miracles, healings, and supernatural activity as part of a believer's day-to-day life has recently gained acceptance by some Christian leaders, based on the experiences of Christians worldwide who have been healing the sick, casting out demons, seen hearing and sight restored, and even raising the dead.

**Endnote**

1. "Traditions of Men that thwart Healing"-TL Osborn, used by permission.

# CHAPTER 14

# WE'RE ON THE SAME TEAM, RIGHT?

While what I am going to cover here may offend or trouble some of you, it must be addressed and admitted to for the church to ultimately move forward into her purpose. We should treasure the truth more than religious idealism, some utopian concept of unity or our own sacred cows or pet doctrines. We should love the power, glory, and prestige of God rather than flowery words or slogans. We should value the anointing of the Holy Spirit more than talent, gifting, or good ideas. And we should value the integrity of truth over a politically correct brand of Christianity that is fruitless and void of authentic spiritual success.

We have all heard that unity with other churches is absolutely paramount, and that if we would all agree to disagree and focus on a few main things, such as "we all love Jesus," we can effectively win our cities and communities *together*. Supposedly, the one and only thing holding back authentic revival in our land is God waiting for us to come into unity; that if all the racial and ethnic divisions would be unified there would be a nationwide revival. Right?

While we have been exposed to a preponderance of this teaching primarily from prayer groups and unity movements, at this point in history there is little if any scriptural evidence, apostolic precedent, or clear doctrine in Scripture that validates this theory. Of course, there are principles in Scripture revealing the power in unity and agreement—these are huge. But there is some kind of idealism that Christians succumb to that moves them to believe that unity is the main gospel truth when it really isn't. Some Christians believe vehemently many things that are sideline principles of Scripture, and reject core principles to which the Bible gives much higher priority. Some things are true, others are truer. What we learn in second grade is true, but what we learn later is truer.

Before I challenge the sacred cow of unity, I truly desire for you who are reading this chapter to understand that I have no chip on my shoulder when it comes to Christian leadership. I am part of that leadership myself! I have spent much of my Christian pastoral experience attending pastors' meetings, councils, and presbytery gatherings. I love my brothers and sisters in the faith, and I applaud any one in any denomination who has accepted the calling to serve the Lord in a full-time capacity.

I am not angry at pastors. In fact I have hosted many leaders' meetings in more than one city and hosted monthly prayer meetings for years in my local area. I have fasted for revival, hosted unity gatherings, washed my brother pastor's feet, prayed for interracial unity, and prayed for and declared the wall of separation between men and women, youth and old, Israel and the church, and the haves and the have-nots to be torn down. Those were not wasted experiences, nor do I feel they were mistakes. But the truth is, we just didn't see the fruit we were all hoping and longing for.

Psalms chapter 133 is the main, but not the only, Scripture used to promote these theories. While this passage says that unity can and does command a blessing, it implies it is possible but not guaranteed. This one isolated passage actually implies more accurately this: It is good and pleasant for brothers to dwell in unity and God can bless that. Isn't that just common sense? And what about believing only this one avenue of blessing when there are so many more in Scripture? And to achieve this one blessing, should it require us to abdicate other truths or compromise and water down the integrity of the Word of God to pursue it? Isn't this line of reasoning, "come together at any cost," fueling the seeker-friendly church movement with things such as:

- a desire to come together under a wide, all-inclusive banner that requires little to nothing of its followers;
- the wholesale rejection of key passages of Scripture to accommodate the fears of the masses;
- accommodating the uncommitted in the name of bringing everyone in?

The bottom line: much of what has been accomplished through this "brand" of church is that we have now perfected a way to get the unconverted and irreligious to attend church, but they only hear just enough truth to make them think they are converted; then they go home without being offended. All the hope for the unbelievers is placed in whether or not they respond properly to our services. While getting them "in the church doors" can be good, what are we delivering to them? Is it possible many are now becoming immune to the authentic gospel by receiving such an inconsequential dose of it through these ministries? To receive an "immunization" is to render someone immune to something by giving them a minute dose; just enough for them to build up a resistance to it. Have we now made people think they are "saved," when in reality many have only received a minute dose they are now resistant to the real thing?

## False Unity

> *I do not ask in behalf of these alone, but for those also who believe in Me through their word; that they may all be one; even as Thou, Father, art in Me, and I in Thee, that they also may be in Us; that the world may believe that Thou didst send Me. The glory which Thou hast given Me I have given to them; that they may be one, just as We are one; I in them, and Thou in Me, that they may be perfected in unity, that the world may know that You sent Me, and loved them, even as You have loved Me* (John 17:20-23).

The other key passage used to promote unity is Jesus' famous prayer also found in John chapter 17. But if you honestly and soberly read it without prejudging, it is obvious to see that He is praying what the end result of our maturity looks like— that we would all look like Jesus as Jesus looks like the Father and the world would see that love and that we are all one. Awesome! I agree with that wholeheartedly. Who wouldn't? But again, like all supernatural transformations we see in the Scripture, it can't be accomplished with natural means and won't come about simply because we all sit in the same room and sing together.

## Unity Is the Effect, Not the Cause

The unity of the Spirit that Paul mentions in Ephesians chapter 4 is the same thing—a state of maturity and wholeness which the church comes to when the vast majority of the Body is operating in and obedient to the faith working in them to ful-fill their callings and use their spiritual gifts without reservation. It is the *effect* of this maturity, not the causal event creating it! It also implies walking in obedience to the Spirit's promptings on a daily basis.

Unity of the Spirit isn't event-centered. It doesn't revolve around pastors' prayer meetings or any kind of false or forced love and unity. By its very description, the unity of the Spirit does *not* emanate from anything we can do, or any doctrine we declare, or any call to unity or supposed mandate in the Scripture; but it is instead the effect of the Spirit's brooding over a place or situation or revival.

If you study past revivals and moves of God, you will see evidences of the "unity of the Spirit" occurring. In the Welsh Revival in 1904, one of the distinctive earmarks of this move of God was the way the congregation sang together in perfect unison or were completely silent for long periods at a time. That was caused by the unity of the Spirit. Yes, the people had to submit to it, which they willingly did. In 1906, the idea of Blacks and Whites worshiping together was unheard of until the Azusa Street Revival in Los Angeles. The idea that a White man, Frank Bartleman, and a Black man, William Seymour, would ever work together other than in a cosmetic fashion was unheard of. At that time it appeared unnatural, and it was unprecedented to have Black and White believers worshiping together.

Only God could have orchestrated such an event. History proves that the great humility demonstrated in the lives of leaders such as Bartleman and Seymour played a significant role in allowing the Spirit to do great things among them. Most revivals are not helped by man but ended by his involvement. As a human response, humility was the greatest key that allowed this. We need to respond the way He has called us to do and let God do the things He alone can do. A humility movement would certainly take us farther than any unity movement could.

## Babel Means Confusion

Ever since humans have been on the planet, we have attempted to unite to get to God. Man has always attempted to get to Heaven without God's help. The tower of Babel in Genesis chapter 11 is a poignant picture of man's attempt to get to Heaven without God. In doing so, God confused their languages so that the building was halted. The result of these attempts to reach God without His involvement always produces the same result—confusion, then scattering.

While we want unity, bliss, and harmony, the path must be God's way—through the Cross. A form of church that accommodates the uncommitted and diminishes the conversion process to becoming absorbed in their programs is not God's way. Instead, we must equip the saints of God—help them grow up, get them out of spiritual diapers, put them in the whole armor of God, and get them into the battle! This is the only path to maturity.

## The Emperor's New Clothes

As a sign of these politically correct times, there are doctrines and programs that have permeated the church. But if anyone attempts to point them out or hold leadership accountable for bringing these things in, they are branded as being against unity or being divisive and angry. Do you remember the fable of "The Emperor's New Clothes"? Everyone was afraid to tell him he was naked. So it is within many of the churches today.

> Because you say, "I am rich, and have become wealthy, and have need of nothing," and you do not know that you are wretched and miserable and poor and blind and naked... (Revelation 3:17).

What if someone sees that the Emperor (the present seeker-smitten churches and leadership) has no clothes (Clothes representing fruitful, effective gospel ministry) and is parading himself around as if he is clothed? The world picks up on this faux pas faster and better than Christians. As I mentioned earlier, statistics indicate there are people coming and going in churches- "church-hoppers". Is that just a "sign of the times" or an indication that there is nothing real for them there?

We have been preaching the gospel with signs and wonders in the streets and neighborhoods of our city for well over two years now with hundreds of miracles, conversions, and healings as evidence of the Lord's favor and His kindness to the lost. Yet it isn't the pagans, witches, meth dealers, or gang leaders who are the main source of some of our greatest antagonism. Instead, people who attend the local denominational megachurch have proved to be our greatest source of opposition.

Remember, Jesus said that not all will rejoice when the Kingdom of God is displayed and revealed. Because God's power is not evident and doesn't fit into their religious grid, they are quick to criticize our methods and results. Many would rather argue than see the good fruit of it. No matter what Christians have been told to the contrary, the unchangeable, incorruptible Word of God is clear that the power of God with signs, wonders, miracles, healings, and supernatural activity is the *normal and expected result* of preaching and teaching the gospel of the Kingdom.

## Jesus Wrote the Book!

Because we now have access to the Scriptures, the Bible, some believe we no longer need the apostolic power and supernatural enablement which was the lifestyle of the New

Testament church. Because we have access to a printed copy of the Bible some believe there is no longer any need for God to do anything more. Does this mean that toting around a King James Bible has more power than faith in His name? Do some believe that the Trinity really means the Father, Son, and the Holy *Bible*, rather than the Holy *Spirit*?

Jesus is the author of the Word of God and *is* the Word of God. *He is alive today* and "the same yesterday, today and forever." Doctrines of demons and traditions learned in seminaries and proclaimed in pulpits invalidate the very Word of God. This thinking limits God!

Salvation means much more than we have been told. Well-meaning folks say they believe strongly that Jesus saves, but to them that means going to church, hearing a message, and praying a prayer. Later they are baptized and "saved." That is only a cursory understanding of salvation.

The word *salvation* in the Greek means "to be saved from the pit, delivered, healed, rescued from death, and many other implications." To "be saved" is to become a new creation, to be born again into a different Kingdom. To believe that the gospel is only good to save a soul from hell but that it can't heal, deliver, or bring miraculous change is a great delusion fostered by wrong teachings.

While most evangelicals are OK with the supernatural exploits of Jesus, they wig out when someone says that Jesus told us that we can do likewise. Many think that the early church had a supernatural burst of power that got the church going, but that now it is not necessary or needed. How crazy is that?

> *And all the people were trying to touch Him, for power was coming from Him and healing them all*
> (Luke 6:19).

Jesus said we can have this power too. The twelve had it...

*And He called the twelve together, and gave them power and authority over all the demons, and to heal diseases. And He sent them out to proclaim the kingdom of God, and to perform healing* (Luke 9:1-2).

*Behold, I have given you authority to tread upon serpents and scorpions, and over all the power of the enemy, and nothing shall injure you. Nevertheless do not rejoice in this, that the spirits are subject to you, but rejoice that your names are recorded in heaven* (Luke 10:19-20).

The 500 followers of Jesus who saw Him after the resurrection were promised it...

*And behold, I am sending forth the promise of My Father upon you; but you are to stay in the city until you are clothed with power from on high* (Luke 24:49).

And all of the 120 in the upper room received it... and were promised even more of it...

*but you shall receive power when the Holy Spirit has come upon you; and you shall be My witnesses both in Jerusalem, and in all Judea and Samaria, and even to the remotest part of the earth* (Acts 1:8).

*And suddenly there came from heaven a noise like a violent, rushing wind, and it filled the whole house where they were sitting. And there appeared to them tongues as of fire distributing themselves, and they rested on each one of them. And they were all filled with the Holy Spirit and began to speak with other tongues, as the Spirit was giving them utterance* (Acts 2:2-4).

Paul said it was good to boast about God's power knowing it comes from God and not ourselves...

> *Therefore in Christ Jesus I have found reason for boasting in things pertaining to God. For I will not presume to speak of anything except what Christ has accomplished through me, resulting in the obedience of the Gentiles by word and deed, in the power of signs and wonders, in the power of the Spirit; so that from Jerusalem and round about as far as Illyricum I have fully preached the gospel of Christ* (Romans 15:17-19).

> *And my message and my preaching were not in persuasive words of wisdom, but in demonstration of the Spirit and of power, that your faith should not rest on the wisdom of men, but on the power of God* (1 Corinthians 2:4-5).

The gospel is not self-help, philosophy, or mental assent, but receiving the Spirit of God Himself. When we say, "receive Jesus," do you we know what that entails? It is receiving *all* that Jesus *is* and *has*! In us is the same *Spirit* that raised Jesus from the dead.

> *But I will come to you soon, if the Lord wills, and I shall find out, not the words of those who are arrogant, but their power. For the kingdom of God does not consist in words, but in power* (1 Corinthians 4:19-20).

> *...in the word of truth, in the power of God; by the weapons of righteousness for the right hand and the left,* (2 Corinthians 6:7).

> *for our gospel did not come to you in word only, but also in power and in the Holy Spirit and with full conviction...* (1 Thessalonians 1:5).

The emphasis on false unity comes out of the notion that if we will just throw away differences and embrace similarities there will be power. This is summarily untrue and doesn't leave any room for diversity or authentic integrity of identity. The bottom line in all of this is that just because we say or declare we are Christians and are believers, doesn't necessarily mean we are truly on the same team. How can two walk together unless they be agreed? We have seen the folly of attempting to work with and walk with kind, well-meaning people who don't think God heals today or that the Holy Spirit gifts are working.

Unless there is a huge amount of humility and agreement on the goals, we end up debating which stops the progress of getting anything accomplished. Nothing can prove more unfruitful than religious debate about clear points of Scripture. On the other hand, different groups can effectively get things done if they each have the same common goal. Jesus identified those who were "with Him" this way: *"Now John answered and said, 'Master, we saw someone casting out demons in Your name, and we forbade him because he does not follow with us.' But Jesus said to him, 'Do not forbid him, for he who is not against us is on our side'"* (Luke 9:49-50 NKJV). Jesus' instructions are clear—if folks we run into along the way are not against us, they are for us.

Another instruction that Jesus gives clarifies family relationships. It also reveals what the Lord felt about church family relationships or "brothers and sisters."

> *And a multitude was sitting around Him, and they said to Him, "Behold, Your mother and Your brothers are outside looking for You." And answering them, He said, "Who are My mother and My brothers?" And looking about on those who were sitting around Him, He said, "Behold, My mother and My brothers! For whoever does the will of God, he is My brother and sister and mother"* (Mark 3:32-35).

Jesus didn't say, "Can't we all just get along?" Jesus emphatically said, "Follow Me." Paul even refers to "false brethren" in Second Corinthians 11:26. Both these passages strongly suggest that just because someone implies they are a believer or calls himself a brother or a Christian, doesn't necessarily mean he will jump on board, attempting Kingdom exploits with you and endorsing them.

Whenever Jesus performed a miracle or there was a demonstration of God's power, it was also an invitation to make a decision whether to bow the knee to Jesus or not. Before the miracles, many called Him Rabbi; after they saw His power, they called Him Lord. People respond when the supernatural is obvious. But don't assume all will embrace it when God shows up. Our ministry had to adjust to negative responses when our idealism was challenged—you will too. Many times division occurs because the miraculous forces people to choose what sides. Remember Peter? He called Jesus Lord when He performed the miracle of the huge catch of fish! That miracle "hit home" with Peter, the fisherman.

## God's Pattern

Everything God asks us to do or He wants done adheres to His design and pattern. God is the God of order and perfect design. His ways are perfect. He is the Creator of all things, and they are good. (See James 1:17.) All creation is held together by His perfect, orderly, and synchronous plan. God is holding all things together and everything that exists comes from Him and in Him all things are held together.

Hebrews 1:3 says: *"And He is the radiance of His glory and the exact representation of His nature, and upholds all things by the word of His power."*

Colossians 1:16-17 also describes this force emanating from God that holds all things together in this way: *"For by Him all things were created, both in the heavens and on earth, visible and invisible, whether thrones or dominions or rulers or authorities—all things have been created by Him and for Him. And He is before all things, and in Him all things hold together."*

## Scientific Theories

Please bear with me through some scientific explanation that may seem off course, but is indeed important.

Particle physicists label forces, or a field of force, that are holding things together as the Grand Unified Theory (GUT). This theory is the fundamental and foundational principle of all quantum physics. While Newtonian physics is only the study of gravity, velocity, and other forces which study the way matter interacts with other matter, quantum physics is the study of this on the very small or molecular level.

An excellent example of regular physics and how it works can be seen in the effect gravity and electromagnetism has on our own planetary orbit. Earth is the third planet from the sun in our solar system. It spins around on its axis every 24 hours, hurtling at over 67,000 miles an hour in an elliptical orbit around the sun, accomplishing this orbit annually. Earth's rotation on its axis every 24 hours gives us each day and the larger orbit, the four seasons.

The speed earth travels and the rotational circuit it makes each day creates the precise gravitational pull and centrifugal forces that keep each of us standing on the ground, not hurtling out into space. If our planet would veer just a degree off its axis or the speed would increase or decrease, all of Earth's inhabitants would become airborne!

While Newtonian physics can suitably describe the orbit of the planets or the energy transformations during a game of pool, quantum physics describes how electrons surround the nucleus of the atom and other subatomic actions. Both sciences explain how matter interacts with other matter. The difference is that the common laws of physics begin to deteriorate on small scales. Quantum physics needs complex math to explain the behaviors and properties of small particles because the world of these subatomic particles is a bizarre one, filled with quantum probabilities and organized chaos. Normal rules don't apply. The atomic and subatomic is studied with a completely different set of probabilities.

## Intelligent Design

Since this wasn't meant to be a physics primer, let me summarize by stating that the small beginnings of understanding the reasons involved in the theory behind what's holding all things together is still almost too complex to be understood, and only a small number of scientists are working on it. It's a complex field of study involving precise calculations. To suggest that the creation of our world occurred by happenstance or accident after the "big bang" and without involvement of an intelligent design is ludicrous.

Many of the greatest minds in science are reconsidering the evidence of intelligent design. Some who have assumed Darwin's theory is truth are beginning to question it. Since the rules that govern Newtonian physics have been usurped to understand quantum physics, scientists may more seriously study the evidence of intelligent design. Physical science and all creation is clearly attests to the truth that humans and this planet came about because of an Intelligent Designer.

In recent years there has been a discussion in public schools about whether or not teachers should be permitted to teach the theory of intelligent design. The Bible is clear that the wisdom of God is better than our foolishness. Unfortunately, for decades Darwin's theory has been taught with no mention of the Creator. Hopefully, Christians in every community and sitting on every school board will correct the wrong, and teachers in the United States will give equal time to teaching the intelligent design.

*For who among men knows the thoughts of a man except the spirit of the man, which is in him? Even so the thoughts of God no one knows except the Spirit of God. Now we have received, not the spirit of the world, but the Spirit who is from God, that we might know the things freely given to us by God, which things we also speak, not in words taught by human wisdom, but in those taught by the Spirit, combining spiritual thoughts with spiritual words. But a natural man does not accept the things of the Spirit of God; for they are foolishness to him, and he cannot understand them, because they are spiritually appraised. But he who is spiritual appraises all things, yet he himself is appraised by no one* (1 Corinthians 2:11-15).

## God as Designer

In Genesis, one of God's first designs was to build an ark to rescue Noah and his family. Everything about that was purposefully and specifically measured to achieve the desired divine result. God also described the architectural design of the Tabernacle, each detail had a specific reason. And when God described the Ark of the Covenant, He gave us a model, something we could understand and comprehend; a container which, in symbolic nature only, would house His presence. God can and does reserve the right to design boxes. And He does a good job, just look at the infinitely complex design of the human body!

God has always had to lower His bar to get to us. Because our understanding and spiritual comprehension was so darkened due to the Fall, we largely have been unable to even fathom how great or limitless in power He is! In spite of all this, from the very beginning God has longed to walk with us in the cool of the day. He never wanted to be contained or put on the shelf until Sunday morning. God doesn't want to be up on the mountain accessible by only a few. God wants us to enter with Him into the land and possess our inheritance! We have access to the throne 24/7 through the blood of Jesus Christ.

> *Moses My servant is dead; now therefore arise, cross this Jordan, you and all this people, to the land which I am giving to them, to the sons of Israel. Every place on which the sole of your foot treads, I have given it to you, just as I spoke to Moses* (Joshua 1:2-3).

## Me-Centered God

Since God is the Master Designer, Architect, and Builder of all things, how could we ever consider packaging God and all that He is into a manmade cage, box, or building? What incredible arrogance and amazing audacity to imagine that the creature He created could contain Him. But isn't that what has been done in the church as ministers preach a me-centered gospel message with me-centered ministries declaring a me-centered God who exists to take care of me, me, me? No, wait. That's the Santa Clause Gospel. You know the one, where God only exists to bless us with whatever we want if we are good? Whatever it is called, it's just another package that we have created in our own image that limits the greatness of God.

Almighty God can't be put in our containers—He determined to be housed in His creation through His plan of salvation. Through our receiving and then believing in the gospel of the Kingdom, the end result is that we are to take dominion over His creation through Jesus Christ in us, who is our hope of glory. That is and will always be His plan for us.

In the New Covenant we are to be the carriers and containers of His glory, housing His presence wherever we go. To be a container for God's glory is the most awesome promise we have! It is that treasure Paul spoke of in Second Timothy 1:14: *"Guard, through the Holy Spirit who dwells in us, the treasure which has been entrusted to you."*

With such an awesome God and the wonderful promises we have been given, why has God gotten such bad reviews in our culture? When asked about Jesus, most people have good or at least positive things to say about Him, yet when non-Christians mention the church or religion, they immediately regress to making comments like, "the church is full of hypocrites," or "why are Christians so intolerant?"

I would go so far as to say that one of the church's prime failures is that the people of God haven't represented Jesus well. We Christians haven't allowed people to see a God of the miraculous, of the impossible, of unimaginable good, and of incredible love. Instead, we have shown the world an intolerant, impotent, angry God. We have shown them a God who requires us to become qualified and perfected for many years before He can use us in His ministry. We have shown them a God of the possible—a god of hypocrisy and false hope. We have promised and never delivered.

We need people to see Him in all His beauty, goodness, and power! We need to unashamedly stand up for Him. He wants us to accurately demonstrate His love and mercy and grace. We must tell the world about His healing nature, His miraculous creation, and His desire to welcome them into His forgiving arms.

Until the church sees Him more clearly, we can't represent Him accurately. We need to open our spiritual eyes to see Him as He really is. All our unbelief and wrong concepts and wrong doctrine must be replaced with a passionate and true knowledge of God. We need people to see the reality of Jesus, not just our caricature of Him. We owe people a supernatural encounter with this God that we declare we know so well. Bobby Connor said, "Many Christians are far too familiar with a God they barely know!"

> *I pray also that the eyes of your heart may be enlightened in order that you may know the hope to which he has called you, the riches of his glorious inheritance in the saints, and his incomparably great power for us who believe...* (Ephesians 1:18-19 NIV).

## See Me and Be Changed

We (the church) tell people that they need to get fixed but then we don't show them how through His supernatural power or demonstrate His ability through the miraculous. We declare to sinners to, "Change," "Get fixed," "Become like me," yet we don't show people how. We promise power but then hand them churchianity, religion, and rules; telling them the power is coming, yet it rarely and usually doesn't. We end up forcing them to jump through hoops we call spiritual foundations, "Alpha," and new member classes, when they first truly need a divine encounter with a supernatural God! We tell them to look to Jesus, but within a few weeks we position them to look to themselves to change—leading them down a dead-end street.

## Follow Me and You'll Change

Jesus never said, "Change, then follow me." Instead, He says in Matthew 4:17: *"...Repent, for the kingdom of heaven is at hand"* and two verses later He says, *"Follow Me, and I will make you fishers of men."* God never insists that we be qualified or able or astute or educated enough to accomplish His work. He gives His called all they need to fulfill their effectual purpose. It takes a supernatural encounter with God to accomplish supernatural ministry. The greatest part of that passage in Matthew is His promise to us: *"I will make you."* We will not make ourselves, but *He* will make us into what we supposed to be!

Supernatural ministry will never be accomplished with natural means but only by a supernatural, revelatory encounter with an out-of-the-box God! For example, look at the supernatural revelation encounter that a woman has with Jesus recorded in John chapter 4:

On the way to getting water… *And He had to pass through Samaria. So He came to a city of Samaria, called Sychar, near the parcel of ground that Jacob gave to his son Joseph; and Jacob's well was there. Jesus therefore, being wearied from His journey, was sitting thus by the well. It was about the sixth hour. There came a woman of Samaria to draw water. Jesus said to her, "Give Me a drink." For His disciples had gone away into the city to buy food.*

She questions why He would talk to a woman who is a Samaritan… *The Samaritan woman therefore said to Him, "How is it that You, being a Jew, ask me for a drink since I am a Samaritan woman?"* (For Jews have no dealings with Samaritans.)

He gives her prophetic revelation about salvation and Himself... *Jesus answered and said to her, "If you knew the gift of God, and who it is who says to you, 'Give Me a drink,' you would have asked Him, and He would have given you living water." She said to Him, "Sir, You have nothing to draw with and the well is deep; where then do You get that living water? "You are not greater than our father Jacob, are You, who gave us the well, and drank of it himself, and his sons, and his cattle?" Jesus answered and said to her, "Everyone who drinks of this water shall thirst again; but whoever drinks of the water that I shall give him shall never thirst; but the water that I shall give him shall become in him a well of water springing up to eternal life." The woman said to Him, "Sir, give me this water, so I will not be thirsty, nor come all the way here to draw."*

He bestows words of knowledge on her, telling her secrets only she and God know... *He said to her, "Go, call your husband, and come here." The woman answered and said, "I have no husband." Jesus said to her, "You have well said, 'I have no husband'; for you have had five husbands, and the one whom you now have is not your husband; this you have said truly."*

She freaks out... *The woman said to Him, "Sir, I perceive that You are a prophet. Our fathers worshiped in this mountain, and you people say that in Jerusalem is the place where men ought to worship."*

Then the Lord reveals a revelation about worship and the Father... *Jesus said to her, "Woman, believe Me, an hour is coming when neither in this mountain, nor in Jerusalem, shall you worship the Father. You worship that which you do not know; we worship that which we know, for salvation is from the Jews. But an hour is coming, and now is, when the true worshipers shall worship the Father in spirit and truth; for such people the Father seeks to be His worshipers. God is spirit, and those who worship Him must worship in spirit and truth."*

He reveals Himself as the Messiah... *The woman said to Him, "I know that Messiah is coming (He who is called Christ); when that One comes, He will declare all things to us." Jesus said to her, "I who speak to you am He." And at this point His disciples came, and they marveled that He had been speaking with a woman; yet no one said, "What do You seek?" or, "Why do You speak with her?"*

So she just can't stop talking about her encounter with Him... *So the woman left her waterpot and went into the city, and said to the men, "Come, see a man who told me all the things that I have done; this is not the Christ, is it?"* (John 4:4-29).

## God in the Open

To release God's power, we have to be willing to bring Him out in the open! The subject of God and His miraculous power mustn't be relegated to a Sunday school story for kids. To feel that your relationship with God is a "private matter" is not only untrue it is also unscriptural. Jesus is on the move! And wherever we go, the lost and needy are all around us—waiting to hear about Him.

This story of the woman at the well is a great example of God breaking out of the temple or synagogue box. It illustrates how Jesus met her, a sinner in need of a deliverer, on the way to get a drink of refreshing water. This dramatic, supernatural power encounter with God did not happen at the customary place at the customary time the customary way. God visited her because Jesus was willing to be a vessel the Father could use to do His works through, without hesitation or reservation. He said that doing His Father's will was "His necessary food."

On the way to quenching His thirst, Jesus ended up quenching her thirst as well. Her spiritual thirst was satisfied forever! Jesus told her who she really was. Nobody had ever done that and even if they knew who she really was, they wouldn't have said it to her the way He did. He spoke to her as if He had always known her, which comforted and assured her. She felt as if she was safe near Him.

He then revealed a divine mystery concerning worshiping the Father and how one must truly worship—one of the "thoughts of God" that can only be received through the Holy Spirit. Then better than that, Jesus reveals Himself to her, and she is changed in an instant. There is nothing so fulfilling as having an encounter that you know is with the One, the Only, Living God! She was instantly transformed and goes to tell everyone in her town about Him. She can't keep silent about what happened.

The Father demonstrates His love and mercy through Jesus in this and many other God-encounters recorded throughout the Gospels, Acts, and New Testament. We see a God not made with human hands. When God is out in the open, He pushes away the darkness of our limited, finite world, and invades it with the light of the Kingdom of Heaven.

**Endnote**
1. "Church Hopping" by Amand Phifer "Faithworks" used by permission.

CHAPTER 15

# THE BOLD AND THE RECKLESS

*He answered and said to them, "Well did Isaiah prophesy of you hypocrites, as it is written: 'This people honors Me with their lips, But their heart is far from Me. And in vain they worship Me, Teaching as doctrines the commandments of men.' For laying aside the commandment of God, you hold the tradition of men; the washing of pitchers and cups, and many other such things you do." He said to them, "All too well you reject the commandment of God, that you may keep your tradition. ... making the word of God of no effect through your tradition which you have handed down. And many such things you do" (Mark 7:6-9,13).*

## Power is God's Idea

Scripture teaches that to neglect or reject the Word of God so that we may hold on to our traditions, invalidates or makes the Word have little or no effect. Maybe this is why people who say, "I don't believe in healing" see so little of it. Or those who say, "I don't go for all that emotional stuff and speaking in tongues and prophecy and all that. I just don't believe that's for me."

When we hold on to what we were, we may never become who we really are. The woman at the well had her identity wrapped up as an immoral woman who had lived with as many as five different men in her life. When Jesus came along, He tells her who she really is. He defines her as a worshiper, not as an immoral woman. He prophesies over her the identity and testimony she has in Him. Revelation 19:10 says, *"...For the testimony of Jesus is the spirit of prophecy."*

Our past theological underpinnings can actually defy and undermine the truth of God's Word if we hold to them more than the truth. Power and the gospel are God's ideas, but denominations and traditions are humankind's ideas!

There are many people who were raised in mainstream-denomination churches who hold on more tightly to traditions than to Jesus. God is cut off from many of His own people because they would rather practice religion and traditions than live life with God's power? There are also Pentecostal, Charismatic, and non-denominational church folks so engrained in their traditions and belief systems that it is as if the Lord of the universe has to ask their permission before He can do anything they don't understand. Power is God's idea not the devil's. To credit the devil or the occult for anything and everything supernatural is arrogant.

A large segment of the American evangelical church sees miracles and Holy Spirit gifts as an optional, even undesirable, part of the Body of Christ. Through the writings of some of their popular authors and leaders, they have denigrated and downgraded the gifts of the Spirit, making them out to be something only ignorant and unlearned people believe in. They go so far as to say that miracles and gifts are some kind of aberration of Christianity.[1]

Even though Paul commanded us to *"earnestly desire spiritual gifts"* in First Corinthians chapter 14, some have rejected outright significant passages of the New Testament to keep their wrong doctrine working. How can one part of the Body say they don't need the other parts? This attitude serves to keep followers ignorant and even hostile toward the gifts of the Spirit operating today. When we make a decision to believe that God no longer perfo rms miracles, healings, or signs and wonders through His people, we eliminate or limit His effectiveness in the world.

> *But woe to you, scribes and Pharisees, hypocrites, because you shut off the kingdom of heaven from men; for you do not enter in yourselves, nor do you allow those who are entering to go in* (Matthew 23:13).

## Join the Club

The disciples also attempted to keep people out of "the club" that they thought was exclusively theirs with Jesus. Elitism and exclusivism have no place in the Kingdom. Jesus dealt with His disciples when they tried to enforce this kind of cliquishness after they found and "caught" someone doing something that wasn't with them:

> *Now John answered Him, saying, "Teacher, we saw someone who does not follow us casting out demons in Your name, and we forbade him because he does not follow us." But Jesus said, "Do not forbid Him, for no one who works a miracle in My name can soon afterward speak evil of Me. For he who is not against Me is for Me"* (Mark 9:38-40 NKJV).

Not only did Jesus allow this guy into the club, He affirmed him. It is not those arguing against Holy Spirit gifts operating today that Jesus holds as those who are "for Him." It is not those demonstrating against abortion He describes as "for Him." Rather, Jesus says those who "work a miracle in My name" are "for Me, not against Me."

We do not get to choose who is in the club. I want to be found as one who is working for God. It is one thing to ignorantly make a mistake and miss doing God's will or end up not doing something His way. Jesus clearly states that power and miracles are a validation of God.

> *Jesus answered, "I did tell you, but you do not believe. The miracles I do in my Father's name speak for me…* (John 10:25 NIV).

## Uneducated and Untrained

Does one have to have a theological degree to be used of God? Do we have to be a part of the "original twelve"? Does one have constantly do 40-day fasts and commit himself to a life of supreme devotion for God to use us? Does God only work supernaturally in deepest, darkest Africa or China? No! God uses ordinary people to do extraordinary things and he has only two qualifications: faith and boldness!

> *Now when they saw the boldness of Peter and John, and perceived that they were uneducated and untrained men, they marveled. And they realized that they had been with Jesus* (Acts 4:13 NKJV).

God is not impressed with our educational credentials, Bible knowledge, or our experience in "church." He doesn't concern Himself with whether or not we were trained in a prestigious Bible school or not. What people say is true about God is something that God is not especially worried about or something that keeps Him awake at night, as if He needs to sleep. In fact, I believe that God sits in Heaven and laughs at all who define Him. He must think their attempts at limiting Him are humorous!

> *Why are the nations in an uproar, and the peoples devising a vain thing? The kings of the earth take their stand, and the rulers take counsel together against the Lord and against His Anointed saying: Let*

*us tear their fetters apart, and cast away their cords from us!" He who sits in the heavens laughs, the Lord scoffs at them* (Psalms 2:1-4).

In fact, God makes it a point to use the most unlikely people to prove that it is He who is working to do these great things, not the person or vessel. God desires to use anybody and everybody who yield themselves for His purposes. Faith and boldness are all that is necessary— faith to hear and believe Him, and boldness to follow through and get it done. There has to be an action that corresponds to the hearing and believing!

Power is not the problem. God will strongly back up anyone willing to look foolish to make God look great! God is looking for those whose hearts are fully His to strongly support. The power of God comes when there is a boldness to preach, declare, and act.

*For the eyes of the Lord move to and fro throughout the earth that He may strongly support those whose heart is completely His...* (2 Chronicles 16:9).

These are days of both great darkness and great light! God is light and in Him is no darkness. He desires for His light to shine through us into all dark places. We are the key to letting His light shine. It is through believers exercising their faith and doing bold exploits that darkness is shattered. Psalms chapter 112 says that the people who fear the Lord will be mighty on the earth, their children blessed and abounding in wealth and riches.

*Praise the Lord! How blessed is the man who fears the Lord, Who greatly delights in His commandments. His descendants will be mighty on earth; The generation of the upright will be blessed. Wealth and riches are in his house, And his righteousness endures forever.*

*Light arises in the darkness for the upright; He is gracious and compassionate and righteous. It is well with the man who is gracious and lends; He will maintain his cause in judgment. For he will never be shaken; the righteous will be remembered forever. He will not fear evil tidings; His heart is steadfast, trusting in the Lord. His heart is upheld, he will not fear, until he looks with satisfaction on his adversaries.*

*He has given freely to the poor; His righteousness endures forever; His horn will be exalted in honor. The wicked will see it and be vexed; He will gnash his teeth and melt away; The desire of the wicked will perish* (Psalms 112:1-10).

## Mighty Warriors on the Earth

The passage in Psalms is declaring a day when those who fear the Lord will be mighty. Mentioning his descendants, the Bible says they will be *"mighty on the earth."* That is an important phrase because Jesus says in Luke 18:8: *"However, when the Son of Man comes, will he find faith on the earth?"* It is also important because faith, victory over the enemy, and exercising dominion is an exercise needed *not* in Heaven, but on the earth. Faith can only be exercised in this earthly realm where there are all the limitations of the world, the flesh, and the devil. In Heaven there is no cancer, sickness, bondage, or oppression. It is on the earth that these things exist. And God put us here to do away with them! That is why Jesus prayed in The Lord's Prayer for God's will to be done *"on earth, as it is in heaven,"* not "In heaven as it is in Heaven."

Earth is the battleground for our conquest of faith. We are told in the Psalms 115:16, *"The highest heavens belong to the Lord, but the earth he has given to man"* (NIV). It doesn't say he gave the earth to the devil, the boogey man, or any other such person, but to man. We and our children are to be mighty on the earth! The Hebrew word for "mighty" in Psalms 112 is *gibbor*. It translates 103 times as "mighty," 31 times as "warrior," and 5 times as "mighty warriors." The operative words are "mighty warrior."

So this Psalm of David prophesies a day coming when the end-time people of God aren't wasting away, just waiting for their social security checks and the rapture. Instead they are mighty warriors and dread champions of God on the earth destroying darkness and crushing the enemies of God beneath their feet!

## Three Types of Warriors

This whole concept of the warrior has a unique natural application as well. At a prayer gathering in Alabama in 2005, I met warrior chief of the Creek peoples, Nigel Bigpond. We talked about Native American warriors, and he told me that there are three kinds of fighters: the soldier, warrior, and mighty warrior.

Soldier. These men have been trained but have not experienced battle; they have trained with their weapons but have not used them. They are ready for battle.

Warrior. These soldiers have been trained and have been in battle. Most have used their weapons, possibly even killing the enemy.

Mighty Warrior. These are the warriors who are experienced in battle and regularly kill and defeat their enemies. These are battle-hardened men who know how to win. Victory is theirs, and they are confident of their success in battle!

We are called to be the Lord's mighty warriors on the earth! But just because we are God's children, that alone doesn't guarantee our victory. Obviously boldness or audacity is a big factor in winning. Jesus made a distinction between those who were His friends and those who knew Him at a distance when He said, *"You are My friends, if you do what I command you. No longer do I call you slaves, for the slave does not know what his master is doing; but I have called you friends, for all things that I have heard from My Father I have made known to you. You did not choose Me, but I chose you, and appointed you, that you should go and bear fruit, and that your fruit should remain, that whatever you ask of the Father in My name, He may give to you"* (John 15:14-16).

## Separating Men from Boys

It is obvious that Jesus' friends are given the good stuff. They are not slaves but friends, and He reveals to them all that the Father is showing Him. In addition, He wants them to bear fruit. While being a friend of God is a great thing, there is something else that separates the haves and have-nots—boldness. The haves are those friends of God who don't just love God, they also believe that He is able to do for them whatever they ask. So they ask and demand and even pester God until He gives them what they are asking. They don't just ask for themselves, they ask big bold things for others. In the process, they are personally taken care of and their needs are met.

*Then he said to them, "Suppose one of you has a friend, and he goes to him at midnight and says, 'Friend, lend me three loaves of bread, because a friend of mine on a journey has come to me, and I have nothing to set before him.' Then the one inside answers, 'Don't bother me. The door is already locked, and my children are with me in bed. I can't get up and give you anything.' I tell you, though he will not get up and give him the bread because he is his friend, yet because of the man's boldness he will get up and give him as much as he needs* (Luke 11:5-8 NIV).

The key thing to see here is not that the man who goes to his friend's house at midnight gets what he asks, but *why* does he get what he asks. Answer: Because of his blatant audacity, boldness, and persistence! It is not because he is the friend of the homeowner that his request is fulfilled, it's because of his boldness that "he will get up and give him as much as he needs."

Wow! That may burst a bubble or demolish a sacred cow for you, but I didn't say it, Jesus did. It seems as if Jesus honors our boldness of faith more than our friendship with Him. So this blows out the assumption that friendship by alone won't necessarily give me "carte blanche" in the Kingdom! Being a citizen by right doesn't mean you will take advantage of all the benefits of that citizenship, especially if you don't know what they are. God responds to faith, not our needs or our view of Him. He will meet our needs but we must apply even a little bit of faith to get it done. It is our boldness, our persistence, and our audacity to ask in faith that gets this kind of stuff done!

*Do not fear, little flock, for it is your Father's good pleasure to give you the kingdom* (Luke 12:32 NKJV).

While this passage reveals God's desire to give us His best, it is not even the Father's desire to give us the Kingdom that secures it for us. It is our boldness in going for and pursuing it that releases the results!

Like it or not, God does not primarily respond to:

- our needs
- our vision
- our works for Him
- diligence in ministry
- excellent character

- Christian vocabulary
- our lack
- lamenting prayer
- whining prayer
- our past accomplishments
- sicknesses
- pitiful situations

While God absolutely wants to give us the keys to the family business and do all those things we have always wanted, our boldness absolutely helps get it for us! Stepping out and believing God by asking and pleading always kicks over something that gets God's attention and releases His power! God likes us to ask Him in faith. The only two prayer meetings we read about in the Book of Acts that worked were those where they asked for boldness to preach!

> *Now, Lord, look on their threats, and grant to your servants that with all boldness they may speak Your word, by stretching out Your hand to heal, and that signs and wonders may be done through the name of Your holy Servant Jesus. And when they had prayed, the place where they were assembled together was shaken; and they were all filled with the Holy Spirit, and they spoke the word of God with boldness* (Acts 4:29-31 NKJV).

There are at least five types of people who ask things of the Lord, and only one of those gets something consistently. Why? James makes it clear that to have another mind about a matter when we pray and believe, only leads to frustration with no results.

> *But when he asks, he must believe and not doubt, because he who doubts is like a wave of the sea, blown and tossed by the wind. That man should not think he will receive*

*anything from the Lord; he is a double-minded man, unstable in all he does* (James 1:6-8 NIV).

Take a look at these five different types of people.

1. The Proud. They know Him *from afar*. While the proud may think they are God's favorites, they need to humble themselves to obtain His best. Psalms 138:6: *"Though the Lord is on high, Yet He regards the lowly; but the proud He knows from afar."*

2. The Ashamed. They are *at a distance*. These people might have been very close to Him at one time but due to their failure or lack of faith or cynicism are now distant. Matthew 26:58: *But Peter followed Him at a distance to the high priest's courtyard. And he went in and sat with the servants to see the end.*

3. The Backslider. Those who love God and serve Him, but not enough. They may start right, but they finish poorly. A good example is Solomon. He loved God but not enough and not when it mattered. He didn't love Him enough to be obedient.

4. The Regretful. They know God but don't do what He says. Those who call Him friend and even know what He is doing (see John 15:15), but aren't doing it with Him. They give excuses: "It's not the right time now," "It's the wrong season," "I'm waiting on God," etc. They can be whiny and blame others for their lack.

5. The Bold and the Reckless. These are His friends who are bold enough to believe Him and want to do what He is doing *now!*

*And they went out and preached everywhere, the Lord working with them and confirming the word through the accompanying signs...* (Mark 16:20 NKJV).

*But Jesus answered them, "My Father has been work-*
*ing until now, and I have been working"*
(John 5:17 NKJV).

We need to be the *Bold and the Reckless*! Being cautious, wise and extra careful might keep us safe, but it gets us next to nothing. There is a subtle danger in getting to the point of needing to minister and allowing others to do the ministry. Retirement is an American concept, not a Kingdom one. Unless we are equipping the saints in some fashion, we don't really have a ministry.

King David had two occasions when he got in real trouble for doing things he shouldn't have done.

The first was an adulterous affair with Bathsheba that happened because he stayed back in Jerusalem instead of fighting the battle.

*It happened in the spring of the year, at the time when*
*kings go out to battle, that David sent Joab and his*
*servants with him, and all Israel; and they destroyed*
*the people of Ammon and besieged Rabbah. But David*
*remained at Jerusalem* (2 Samuel 11:1).

The fruit of his affair and murdering her husband was for him to remain at war all his life; his wives were taken from him, and Bathsheba had a baby named Absalom who caused him lifelong problems.

David's second mistake happened after a great victory against the Ammonites that blessed him financially. This "blessing" caused him to submit to pride, and he numbered the people.

*...And Joab defeated Rabbah and overthrew it. Then*
*David took their king's crown from his head, and*
*found it to weigh a talent of gold, and there were*

*precious stones in it. And it was set on David's head. Also he brought out the spoil of the city in great abundance* (1 Chronicles 20:1-2 NKJV).

The fruit this time was the death of over 70,000 people by a plague.

I admire people involved in front-line ministry—folks like Rolland and Heidi Baker, Bob Jones, and David Hogan. They don't speak of 10- and 20-year-old stories about miracles, but have new stories every day about the supernatural things God is doing. They love doing the "dirty work" of ministry. They have not excluded themselves from or graduated from doing the work of winning the lost, casting out demons, or healing the sick. They routinely accomplish the will of God. They have few resources because their main focus is to do His ministry. Their lack of published books and materials may be missed after they're gone, but it doesn't stop them from doing their ministry.

They have financial prosperity without begging for money because as long as they are busy doing what the Lord says, He is committed to taking care of them. They may have needs or challenges, but there is something to be said for their devotion to remain "in the heat of battle." They aren't beyond praying for someone or delegating ministry to others. At the same time, they are each discipling many who are modeling what they are *doing* not theorizing.

Referring again to Luke 11:5-8, several aspects about boldness are evident:

1. Don't expect the Lord to bless you just because you are His friend. Being friends is wonderful, but we want to do things together with Him. It is because of your boldness that He (our friend) will get up and give us as much as we need!

2. He will give us boldness to preach the gospel and boldness to ask for provision. It takes boldness to ask God to heal a sinner who needs a healing as a demonstration.

3. We will receive boldness to speak; to open our mouths. It doesn't mean boldness to think, imagine, or even dream, while all these are important. Dreaming without doing is fantasy.

4. He will give us boldness to believe that what He says is true.

5. In boldness we will not only ask but will put others first in asking.

## Boldness Scriptures

Ephesians 6:18-20: *With all prayer and petition pray at all times in the Spirit, and with this in view, be on the alert with all perseverance and petition for all the saints and pray on my behalf, that utterance may be given to me in the opening of my mouth, to make known with boldness the mystery of the gospel, for which I am an ambassador in chains; that in proclaiming it I may speak boldly, as I ought to speak.*

1 Thessalonians 2:1-2: *For you yourselves know, brethren, that our coming to you was not in vain, but after we had already suffered and been mistreated in Philippi, as you know, we had the boldness in our God to speak to you the gospel of God amid much opposition.*

2 Corinthians 3:11-13: *For if that which fades away was with glory, much more that which remains is in glory. Having therefore such a hope, we use great boldness in our speech, and are not as Moses, who used to put a veil over his face that the sons of Israel might not look intently at the end of what was fading away.*

Luke 11:9-13: *"So I say to you: Ask and it will be given to you; seek and you will find; knock and the door will be opened to you. For everyone who asks receives; he who seeks finds; and to him who knocks, the door will be opened. "Which of you fathers, if your son asks for a fish, will give him a snake instead? Or if he asks for an egg, will give him a scorpion? If you then, though you are evil, know how to give good gifts to your children, how much more will your Father in heaven give the Holy Spirit to those who ask him!"*

Ephesians 3:20-21: *Now to Him who is able to do exceeding abundantly beyond all that we ask or think, according to the power that works within us, to Him be the glory in the church and in Christ Jesus to all generations forever and ever.*

James 4:2-3: *...You do not have because you do not ask. You ask and do not receive, because you ask with wrong motives so that you may spend it on your pleasures.*

Just think about it a minute. Why do so many of us get so little when it comes to what we ask? Because we expect little, we ask small. We only get what we are asking for when we are bold. Provision comes to those who are bold enough to war and bold enough to ask. Boldness always brings ample if not excessive provision!

Keys to getting is asking boldly and asking boldly for someone else with pure motives. Also, know what the Lord cares about. It is one thing to know what He is doing and another to realize that we aren't participating with Him. I want to participate! I want to work together with the Lord!

*And working together with Him...* (2 Corinthians 6:1).

*Now He was telling them a parable to show that at all times they ought to pray and not to lose heart, saying, "There was in a certain city a judge who did not fear God, and did not respect man. "And there was a widow in that city, and she kept coming to him, saying,*

*'Give me legal protection from my opponent.' "And for a while he was unwilling; but afterward he said to himself, 'Even though I do not fear God nor respect man, yet because this widow bothers me, I will give her legal protection, lest by continually coming she wear me out.' "And the Lord said, "Hear what the unrighteous judge said; now shall not God bring about justice for His elect, who cry to Him day and night, and will He delay long over them? "I tell you that He will bring about justice for them speedily. However, when the Son of Man comes, will He find faith on the earth?"* (Luke 18:1-8).

There is something about the principle of putting God's interests first and taking care of God's concerns, and trusting He will take care of ours. He not only knows what we need but He delights in giving it to us. He says that we don't have because we won't or don't ask.

> *...You do not have, because you do not ask God. When you ask, you do not receive, because you ask with wrong motives, that you may spend what you get on your pleasures* (James 4:2-3).

The key: if we are busy doing the Father's business we will be amply supplied with all of our needs being met. As we are doing the Father's business and doing it well and with fruitfulness, we will ask for ourselves; but the Lord knows we can be trusted because we have proven ourselves trustworthy handling the true riches of the gospel.

> *I pray that you may be active in sharing your faith, so that you will have a full understanding of every good thing we have in Christ* (Philemon 1:6).

**Endnote**

1. Tape GC 90-52, titled "Charismatic Chaos" Part 1- Grace Community Church in Panorama City, California, by John MacArthur Jr. All of "Christianity in Crisis" by Hank Hannegraaf Harvest House Publishing.

# CHAPTER 16

# MIRACLE IN WAL-MART

Are you ready for the supernatural miracles of God to become commonplace and everyday occurrences? Would you like to see the demonstrations of power you read about in the Book of Acts become a routine part of your daily life? Well, I have good news and bad news. The good news: you *can* experience God's power because we are experiencing it in Woodstock, Georgia! Not in Africa, Argentina, or China, but this stuff is happening right here in suburban Atlanta, Georgia, U.S.A. The bad news: many believers who are unwilling to change their long-held views are probably not going to see it. Jesus addressed when He began His ministry. He said, "Repent, for the Kingdom of Heaven is at hand," or rather, change the way you think because I want to show you a new way of doing things.

We have been programmed to think that miracles occur in church meetings or healing services, yet a quick glance at Jesus' lifestyle reveals most of His miracles happened out in the open, on the road, or on His way to another place. He didn't go somewhere to perform miracles, He performed miracles on His way to preach the gospel!

We have discovered that it are far more likely to see a miracle after walking out of a church building and knocking on the door of a neighbor's house than during a typical church prayer line. There is a much greater likelihood of seeing miracles and signs and wonders in the home of an "ice" user in a trailer park than in a Sunday morning prayer line. The reason: *"where sin abounds, grace does much more abound"* (Rom. 5:20).

There is much greater grace poured out when there is much greater sin and need. The church seems to have forgotten who the gospel is for and has advocated the preaching the gospel to only an elite club of "evangelists," pastors or supporting crusades. As the church in the Book of Acts shared the life of God daily with all who would listen, we should also be sharing our faith daily with all those around us. The lost and needy are everywhere.

## Some History

Seven years ago, I was leading a successful Charismatic congregation of several hundred folks. We had been experiencing waves of renewal and revival lasting more than five years. We had seen some dramatic and miraculous things in our church meetings and had sent teams to several nations as a result. Some of these missionaries are still successfully ministering overseas today. But as the waters receded after this five-year move of the Holy Spirit, we were left with the knowledge that our church structures as we knew them had to be radically reinvented and changed to accommodate the next level that God intended.

At the prospect of this Holy Spirit-directed change, I realized I could not endure the task of leading a typical American mainstream congregation and church system that only allowed the tangible anointing to momentarily invade "our" services. The idea of facing more programs and activities t roubled me. To be "successful" in mainstream American church leadership, a pastor faces dozens of "compromises," many of which I deemed unfruitful. I was never wired by God to be a politician or accept an unscriptural outcome as Okay. The system of church I had been involved with for many years in many different levels—from church plant to mega-church– seemed to foster an attitude of "keeping things they way they are" rather than forcing change which causes fruitful lives.

Many of the folks who had been with us through this move of God expressed a strong desire that they wanted to be part of prototyping a "new way of doing church." I knew that many of them would have to leave behind their foundations and abandon their teachings and comfortable forms of godliness that they relied on. Much of their faith did not rest on the power of God, but on a mish-mash of convoluted beliefs that they brought with them when they arrived at our church. All of us, including myself, would have to repent and change—I was up for it and thought they were, too.

I met with a few core people to challenge them about pressing on into this new thing by looking at our present state of unfruitfulness, then looking forward to where we could be in a few years. When I presented them the opportunity for discussion, I quickly realized I had not prepared the people well enough for the effort it would take to make this huge transition. It would cost them everything! Most couldn't and some wouldn't risk it all. Some had turned away from the prophetic ministry and began rejecting power and the gifts of the Spirit and eventually returned to what they deemed safe, traditional churches. While it was sad, I had no choice but to continue on in my quest for the real. Only a few continued on and most did not stay by my side.

I came to realize that this task was not for the faint-hearted, and wanted to discover the authentic Christianity that men and women throughout history were willing to fight and even die for. While most of us would not die for what Christianity in the Western world looks like today, we would die for the gospel of the Kingdom that Jesus preached. What compelled people such as John Wycliffe to call down on his head the wrath of Rome and the Pope? What power did John Knox have that moved the Queen of Scotland to say that she feared him more than all the armies of England? That kind of power and authority is precisely what we began looking for and pursuing!

A short time later, our ministry was prompted by the Spirit to relocate, and we decided to go back to the drawing board of the New Testament to see what God's Word had to say about doing church. We realized our foundations had to be built on nothing less than the Lord Himself. Jesus Christ was, is, and always will be a stumbling block to religion when honestly revealed and communicated. When the Lord showed up somewhere, the result was always the same and very predictable. In the New Testament whenever the gospel of the Kingdom was declared and demonstrated with boldness, there was always one of two results: riot or revival! Jesus said, *"From the days of John the Baptist until now, the kingdom of heaven has been forcefully advancing, and forceful men lay hold of it"* (Matthew 11:12 NIV).

Whenever there is a clash of these two Kingdoms, sparks will fly! We had to make some strong decisions. Would we continue to entertain and accommodate the carnal and uncommitted, hoping they would come around? If so, wouldn't we have to clearly define what we believed about the Kingdom of God? You couldn't say one thing and do another. We had to have the results that God wanted and we couldn't manufacture miracles, healings, maturity, and fruit in the lives of people. Drug addicts can't get free without God's intervention. Diabetes can't be cured without the touch of God. Only God can produce this kind of authentic fruit. While the supernatural might be faked by a few, the works of God can't be manufactured or copied.

While I personally had been seeing miracles, healings, and deliverances most of my Christian life, I wondered, "could every believer truly operate in the power of God that we see in the life of the average believer in the New Testament?" Could we really see the dead raised, cancers leave when we cursed them, and could we actually win more than we lose? John G. Lake talked about this over 100 years ago. And John Wimber's vision to see the saints equipped and moving in power evangelism and healing was partially realized but largely unfulfilled. Was this transformation we were planning really possible? Could the activity of God seen in Nigeria and Argentina actually work in the United States? We thought, *yes*! And we pressed forward.

We decided to go all the way—to see the gospel of the Kingdom preached with signs, wonders and miracles, and actually see measurable, supernatural fruit. For a year we exposed ourselves only to those ministries that had real manifestations of supernatural power. We looked at our teachings and refined them to remove the excuses for the failure most of us have come to expect. You know, things like: "The reason the Lord didn't heal him was because it was his time to be with the Lord" because Scripture says, "My times are in your hands, Lord."

Then we began a ministry training school to train ordinary believers to do exploits of power. (See Daniel 11:32.)

The Saints School goals:

1. To remove unscriptural excuses and fears people inherited from past church cultures.

2. To have believers measure their effectiveness by spiritual fruit rather than the number of people they talked to or how many they prayed for.

3. To go for the miraculous and release people in their gifts with practical opportunities to believe and step out.

4. To train more through modeling than talking.

Jesus equipped the apostles by modeling ministry, then releasing them to do it. In the American church we do it backward. We allow teachers with no practical experience or fruit to teach things they only know about intellectually. No wonder we are bearing so little fruit! How can someone who has never healed someone of a cold talk or teach about healing? How can someone who has never mastered something be a master of anything?

Within a matter of months we had groups of two, four, and six folks going out to different places to share God's power. Our theme: this isn't rocket science, we can all do it! Our mandates:

There are no qualifiers except believing and stepping out in faith.

- You don't have because you don't ask.
- We have nothing to lose except our pride.
- We'd rather be fools for Christ than just fools.

Within a few days and weeks we started receiving reports about backs healed, cancers healed, skin diseases disappearing, and many instant healings like joint pain and even chronic arthritis and such! Nearly all were family members, people at work, people at school, and neighbors. The farther away from typical church meetings and services we went, the more miracles we saw! Sunday church meetings were filled with everyday moms and working people sharing their testimonies of what God was doing when they stepped out of their comfort zones and moved in faith during the other 166 hours of their week. Sunday mornings were no longer filled with the standard fare, but instead with amazing testimonies of people being used by God. Sharing what God was doing through them released encouragement and boldness for others to go out and make a difference in the world around them. The sense was: I can do this!

The following story is just one of the many wonderful examples how God longs for us to take Him with us everywhere we go and not be ashamed to declare His goodness in public.

It was a late afternoon and two young people were looking for an opportunity for God to do something. They were walking through Wal-Mart when they asked the Lord to give them something for the people in the store. They came upon a lady who looked to be in her 60s. All of a sudden the Lord spoke and gave the young man two words for the lady: *husband* and *money*. When they approached her, they asked if she was burdened with something concerning her husband and involving money. They introduced themselves and then told her that the Lord had sent them to her that day to encourage her.

She told them her name was Jesse, and then burst into tears and blurted out that she had just prayed a few minutes before they walked up, saying, "Lord I need to know you are here for me right now," and how her husband of many years had recently died, leaving her with immense financial challenges. She was fearful and depressed and said she was unable to sleep or think clearly. She also had been fighting many sicknesses.

They told her that the Lord had sent them to her to help, and when asked if they could pray for her, she agreed. When they prayed, the Holy Spirit showed up in Wal-Mart, lifting the depression and fear off of her. She cried, then smiled, then laughed as the Spirit of the Lord broke her oppression. Her countenance changed; and she looked completely different! The two got her name, address, and phone number and noticed she lived nearby. They asked her if they could visit her that week and pray for her again. She agreed.

When they arrived at her house at few days later, her married children were there and wanted to meet the people who had prayed for their mom in Wal-Mart. They were extremely grateful, thanking them profusely for being so kind to their mom and praying for her. Then they recounted to the prayer team how different Jesse had been since they prayed for her. They said she was feeling better physically and was completely free of the anxiety, hopelessness, and depression that had been clouding her life since her husband passed away. Praise the Lord for freedom! While this was a wonderful testimony, it had a much greater impact!

When the young lady of this prayer team shared the testimony in church that next Sunday, she was unprepared for the response. While the words they received from the Lord for Jesse were about both her husband and finances, they had been so overjoyed because of her deliverance from sickness, insomnia, and depression that they weren't necessarily thinking about helping her financially. But as soon as the young lady finished her testimony to wild applause and shouting, people began streaming forward and dropping money and checks on the floor! There was over $1,600 given that morning and within a few weeks another $5,000 came in for Jesse, the Wal-Mart widow who had an encounter with the Lord.

A few days later the prayer team went over and gave Jesse the money in cash. When they showed it to her and told her there was more than $6,500, she collapsed on the floor and then rose up crying and praising God for His goodness! The living room in Jesse's house was alive with tears of joy and became a praise service as the children, grandchildren, and Jesse were all praising God. The entire church got involved in this effort born out of the testimony shared of those two young people who decided to go to Wal-Mart and see God do something that afternoon. He truly did!

This is doing church in a way that makes a difference in people's lives. Not only did Jesse receive God's blessing, but all those involved were blessed because they were being used by God to His glory on earth.

# CHAPTER 17

# THE 166 FACTOR

*The boundary lines have fallen for me in pleasant places; surely I have a delightful inheritance* (Psalms 16:6 NIV).

*For none of us lives to himself alone and none of us dies to himself alone. If we live, we live to the Lord; and if we die, we die to the Lord...* (Romans 14:7-8 NIV).

All of us who consider ourselves born-again Christians should live our lives on this earth not just for ourselves but for the Lord. We are not here by accident so therefore we exist for the Lord's pleasure and to further His purposes. Our purpose in life should be to fulfill His destiny for our lives. We can't over emphasize the importance of making good use of our time while on the earth. We were given our lives, gifts, talents, and even our specific time slot in history for His purpose. The crucial question: are we serving God's purpose? Are we doing the task that only we can do? Are we ministering to the people the Lord has sent our way? Are we fruitful and productive, not just busy? Are we doing something that really matters and will extend His Kingdom on the earth?

Acts 13:36 says, *"For David, after he had served the purpose of God in his own generation, fell asleep, and was laid among his fathers, and underwent decay."*

## Each Generation's Purpose

The Bible declares that David, whom God described as *"a man after my own heart,"* served God's specific purpose in his allotted time on earth. To this end for us, it is essential that we understand the gravity of *stewardship*. It simply means that our time, financial resources, and assets and gifts are not our own, but exist solely to accelerate and advance God's purposes. We are not here simply to take up space and consume oxygen, but to make an impact for *Him*. All committed lovers of Jesus should want to do that.

But to make a difference, something fundamental and rudimentary in the way we view church and ministry must change. The foundation of our beliefs determines everything else that is built upon it. That is why Jesus said we must build our house (our life) on the rock (Him) rather than sand that easily washes away in a storm. (Matt. 7:24-27).

> *Therefore everyone who hears these words of Mine, and acts upon them, may be compared to a wise man, who built his house upon the rock. And the rain descended, and the floods came, and the winds blew, and burst against that house; and yet it did not fall, for it had been founded upon the rock. And everyone who hears these words of Mine, and does not act upon them, will be like a foolish man, who built his house upon the sand. And the rain descended, and the floods came, and the winds blew, and burst against that house; and it fell, and great was its fall* (Matthew 7:24-27 NKJV).

## Fundamental and Rudimentary

We must also change our understanding of church and ministry in a rudimentary way because of the impact on our daily routine and lifestyle. The word *rudiment* simply means, "a fundamental element, principle or skill, as in a field of learning."

I have been a drummer since I was 12 years of age. While I don't play as often as I used to, drumming is like riding a bicycle. I can pick it up with little effort just by taking time to review the basics. Why? Because when I first learned to play, I memorized and learned the 20 fundamental drum rudiments. Without learning these, I would have a hard time even remembering how to play. Rudiments have to be practiced daily as a lifestyle. They are not like a test you cram for to learn material that you will never use again.

As in learning to play an instrument through practicing the rudiments, there are basic and fundamental lifestyle elements of Christianity that need to be practiced so they become a part of who you are in Christ.

One overwhelming concern I have is that the time I spend here on the earth with my family, job, or doing ministry be fruitful, effective, and lasting. I don't just want to be a nice person or do busy work for Jesus; I want to help change history, I want to fulfill God's purposes for my life! Life is a gift, and we must not squander it.

Not only does each generation have its own specific slot in history, but each generation has a specific purpose to fulfill. Today humankind is more productive than ever—but we are also tempted to waste time. Because we are bombarded 24/7 with distractions, news, and entertainment, we could end up at the end of our short lives not accomplishing the goals God gave us. We must choose wisely those things on which to focus.

*But what things were gain to me, these I have counted loss for Christ. Yet indeed I also count all things loss for the excellence of the knowledge of Christ Jesus my Lord, for whom I have suffered the loss of all things, and count them as rubbish, that I may gain Christ and be found in Him, not having my own righteousness, which is from the law, but that which is through faith in Christ, the righteousness which is from God by faith; that I may know Him and the power of His resurrection, and the fellowship of His sufferings, being conformed to His death, if, by any means, I may attain to the resurrection from the dead. Not that I have already attained, or am already perfected; but I press on, that I may lay hold of that for which Christ Jesus has also laid hold of me* (Philippians 3:7-12).

## Changed Minds

This book is titled *It's the End of the Church As We Know It—The 166 Factor*. The number *166* describes the hours left in the week when we are *not* attending a two-hour Sunday church service. The word *factor* means "one that contributes in the cause of an action." In other words, the 166 Factor is the number of hours we have every week when we can declare and demonstrate the Kingdom of God to those who need to see God through us. We may be the only "God-in-skin" people will ever see! Jesus got off the throne of Heaven to reach us. Can't we get off the pews—and couch—to reach our neighbors, coworkers, community, city?

I believe that one of the first things Christians must be delivered of is a "meeting mentality." Otherwise we assume that what happens in our two-hour church meeting once a week is the only time we interact with God. What happens in our meetings may be wonderful and glorious, but we can't keep God in a church box. God is everywhere all the time, and is capable of anything, anywhere, and anyplace.

We need a "lifestyle mentality," to constantly and consistently live our life for God, not just during a few meetings a week. We are the Church; and the Church is the primary expression of the Kingdom of God on the earth. While the Kingdom is the rule and reign of God, we are the visible manifestation of that Kingdom. The Church holds several key purposes in the earth.

First, the Church should hold up the truth as a foundation for society. *"...if I am delayed, you will know how people ought to conduct themselves in God's household, which is the church of the living God, the pillar and foundation of the truth"* (1 Timothy 3:15 NIV).

There are important, fundamental issues facing our nation today and the church must stand up for the truth of God's Word. The most notable current issues include upholding the institution of marriage between one man and one woman, and rejecting homosexuality as an alternative lifestyle. If Christians do not take a stand on especially these two issues, society as we now know it will collapse. Every great society before us that tolerated perversion and licentiousness has come to an abrupt end.

If the church won't stand up for the truth, who will? We are to be salt and light in and to this world. Light never has to fight to dispel the darkness, it just does! Yet it must not be hidden—by saying and doing nothing, we allow the status quo of darkness and ignorance. Jesus said, "I am the light of the world." We need to reflect His light that shines in us at home, in our workplace, our community, and in our nation.

This is why the prophetic ministry must be brought out of the church and into the open. We can't keep the light of God's truth hidden in conferences and ministry times during church services. Remember the old gospel song that goes, "Hide it under a bushel? No! I'm gonna let it shine...". We can't hide what we have; our light keeps the world from plunging into even deeper darkness.

*And so we have the prophetic word made more sure, to which you do well to pay attention as to a lamp shining in a dark place, until the day dawns and the morning star arises in your hearts* (2 Peter 1:19).

Second, the church must visibly demonstrate the light of the Kingdom of God by preaching the gospel of the Kingdom with signs and wonders. While social works such as feeding the hungry, clothing the needy, and helping the unfortunate in practical ways is essential, there is a much greater need right now for the church to reveal God's glory through miraculous demonstrations of His power and love. Signs and wonders, miracles, and demonstrations of God's power are desperately needed to defeat the onslaught of darkness our culture is accepting and endorsing more and more each day.

There is no surer way to express God's love for us as when an individual has had their space invaded by God's delivering and healing power. God is truly a "space invader" who cannot sit by and do nothing as a person succumbs to the bondage of sickness, addiction, or torment. What kind of love does it show the world for Christians to ignore those we walk by every day who need a touch from Jesus? *How* to preach the gospel has been made too complicated by too many for too long—it is good to go back to the words of Jesus in Matthew which describe what preaching the gospel is by *His* definition, not ours. *"As you go, preach this message: 'The kingdom of heaven is near. Heal the sick, raise the dead, cleanse those who have leprosy, drive out demons. Freely you have received, freely give'"* (Matthew 10:7-8 NIV).

Where to go. Okay, this is not complex. First, Jesus says to preach: *"As you go...."* Most of Jesus' miracles happened on the way, and as He went. Jesus is on the move, we should be too.

What to say. Second, He tells us exactly what to say: *"The kingdom of Heaven is at hand (or near or here)."* We don't need to invite them to our Bible study or meetings. or ask them this or that.

What to do. There are five things we are told to do:

1. Heal the sick. This doesn't mean to anoint the sick with oil and have the elders pray. It means to heal them by saying, "Be Healed, in Jesus name!" We have seen many healed instantly when we say and do this.

2. Raise the dead. Command the dead to live again. We have had one instance of this in our church. In another church where I preached about raising the dead, a 16-year-old girl commanded a dead baby to live in a mother's womb. The doctor had told her that her baby was dead and surgery was scheduled; when she returned, the baby was alive and fine!

3. Cleanse those who have leprosy. This involves any and all kinds of uncleanness such as AIDS.

4. Drive out demons. Addictions and bondages cannot be counseled away; they must be cast out in Jesus' name!

5. Freely you have received, freely give. Whatever the Lord has freely given to us, we can freely give away to others. Whatever we have been freed from we have authority to free others from as well.

Can you imagine the pandemonium if believers started doing the works of Jesus in places like malls, video stores, or the grocery store? Wow! What would happen if someone in a wheelchair was pulled out of it and started to walk through the mall? What if someone was injured at work and a Christian went to him and healed him instantly right there in front of all his coworkers? Now doesn't that sound like fun? Doesn't that sound like what Jesus wants us to do?

Third, the church must express God's wisdom. Today most unbelievers view the church as an important but outmoded institution. Many of the seeker-friendly churches try to dispel that notion by showing them they are wired, hip, and contemporary. While we need to reach contemporary society, without a message that changes people's lives with the power of God, all we have is just another institution doing dead works.

We must not compromise the truth or lower the standard to reflect the times. While the church must stay culturally relevant and aware of societal norms, I believe we need to raise up our own culture where Jesus is King and the Kingdom of God is proclaimed and reflected. The gospel of the Kingdom is about God's supernatural power invading people's lives and destroying the works of the evil one. The wisdom of God is how we go about delivering the authentic message devoid of religious baggage and targeted in a way that is relevant.

> *to the intent that now the manifold wisdom of God might be made known by the church to the principalities and powers in the heavenly places according to the eternal purpose which He accomplished in Christ Jesus our Lord in whom we have boldness and access with confidence through faith in Him*
> (Ephesians 3:10-12 NKJV).

## Meeting or Lifestyle

The hypocrisy that comes with being a Sunday-only Christian can be replaced with reality as we consistently live the 166 Factor: Living for God the rest of my week. We can't "go to church," because we *are* the church! Yes we go to those meetings and activities at the buildings the church is using, but we must look beyond meetings to see that "being the church" means we *are* the church 24/7.

Ananias and Saphira had a meeting only, Sunday-only Christian mentality. It fostered a hypocritical life and got them killed. (See Acts 5:1-11.) Ananias and Saphira were known to the people in the church as big givers, they had some kind of reputation for that it seems. They were giving beyond the ten percent of tithing. Some scholars believe that when Barnabas, a newer convert came into the church, his generosity exceeded theirs and people heard about it so they were jealous he might steal their position as the big givers. The focus in this particular church was on giving—and giving publicly. Americans make a big deal about "bringing things out in the open." But what if we had that kind of openness regarding our finances?

What if every week churches published the dollar amount each believer gave? This would certainly rid people of financial pretense! Remember, we are only giving out of what we have and God doesn't demand blood from a turnip. Yet as long as people make the financial area off limits to the Holy Spirit, most people will be stuck in a meeting mentality, rather than a Christian lifestyle. I believe that what people do with their money tells more than any other area whether they are believers or not.

There are few poor people in hell, but there are many rich and wealthy. Some people think that God cares more about us being out of debt and owning our house than He does about using our resources to further His purposes. This is a lie perpetuated by hell to keep us in slavery to our possessions. When we have bills to pay, these are not God's fault, they are our problems. God wants to meet our needs; but He also wants us to learn about stewardship in the process.

God requires us to give Him all of our money and resources in one of two times: when we are alive or when we are dead. When we're dead is obviously not the time to negotiate with God about why we didn't let go of those things while we were still alive. Those who have more, will be held accountable to a higher standard. The time to deal with the money issue is now. None of us can take any of our financial assets with us to the next life.

## What Is Ministry?

Ministry is not simply preaching in church, on street corners, or on television; it isn't just singing gospel songs, praying over people, or leading a Bible study. While it can be all of those, that isn't primarily what Paul meant in Ephesians chapter 4 when he spoke of the saints doing the "works of ministry." Our concept and view of ministry and its purposes must radically change for us to truly make it part of our lifestyle.

Ministry is serving others and sharing God's power, love, and heart to anyone, anywhere, anytime, and anyplace. It is not entertainment or amazing preaching performances, done with colorful eloquence or passionate presentation. Today America has hundreds, maybe thousands, of great preachers and orators, but few have changed the heart or the atmosphere of even their own neighborhood, let alone region or country. Huge ministries can generate giant projects, employ many people, and spawn creative activities, yet most of even the largest have little real spiritual impact on a region and its atmosphere like we see in the Book of Acts.

> *And we pray this in order that you may live a life worthy of the Lord and may please him in every way: bearing fruit in every good work, growing in the knowledge of God, being strengthened with all power*

*according to his glorious might so that you may have
great endurance and patience, and joyfully giving
thanks to the Father, who has qualified you to share in
the inheritance of the saints in the kingdom of light*
(Colossians 1:10-12 NIV).

## Qualified to Minister

We need to see that God has qualified us in His Son to
be able to do these works of ministry. At the point of our conversion we are called to His service and we begin our faith
adventure. While the full ramifications of that may not be
understood for a time, as we are faithful to do as He has
requested of us, God gives us more responsibility and authority.
God is looking at what He is able to do in us, not what we think
we can do for Him! He qualifies us so He gets all the glory for
our success.

*For consider your calling, brethren, that there were
not many wise according to the flesh, not many mighty,
not many noble; but God has chosen the foolish things
of the world to shame the wise, and God has chosen the
weak things of the world to shame the things which are
strong, and the base things of the world and the
despised, God has chosen, the things that are not, that
He might nullify the things that are, so that no man
may boast before God* (1 Corinthians 1:26-29).

God desires for all of us to be busy about the business of
the Kingdom of God. This involves gospel preaching and evan-
gelizing as well as prayer, declaration, and taking ground for
God. There is an ample harvest and all of us will have our hands
full as we bring neighborhoods, communities, and cities into the
Kingdom.

## Full Employment in the Kingdom

The Scripture passage in Matthew chapter 20 you read earlier in this book regarding the workers hired throughout the day and receiving the same amount of pay is not about salvation or entering into heavenly bliss, but rather about the people of God being fully engaged and employed in the business of doing their ministry that the Lord has given them. It reveals the high priority that the Lord gives to "full employment" as a tenet of His Kingdom government, and that many will be hired at different times. It also shows us that there are people waiting around, looking for something to do but no one has offered them a job, even in the "eleventh" hour.

I believe we are in the "eleventh hour" on the Lord's prophetic "day," and that there are many standing around waiting to be "hired," yearning to be useful for the Kingdom. We must give every believer a job to do. This isn't about a couple of people doing ministry. It's about the Body doing the works of ministry to fulfill their destiny.

## Spirit-filled for a Purpose

From the very beginning God wanted fellowship with His creation so humankind would be like God on the earth. We are destined to be God's visible representation on the earth. God's command to Adam was, "...*Be fruitful and increase in number; fill the earth and subdue it. Rule over the fish of the sea and the birds of the air and over every living creature that moves on the ground*" (Genesis 1:28). That command remains relevant.

Our ultimate purpose as Christians is to be like God on the earth. We are called to exercise dominion over the earth and subdue it for God. Until we can heal the sick, raise the dead, speak to the mountain and move it, exercise authority over the weather and our circumstances, have no provisional problems, and do all this as a matter of our normal lifestyle, we are living below our birthright as children of God. We are called to be children of God.

We must embrace our destiny, which is one of warfare, conquest, and dominion rather than drinking tea and singing our favorite songs. While I like tea and love many contemporary Christian songs, there is more to Christianity than self-centered living. We can't have peace and love without taking dominion and subduing our enemies. My generation didn't want war they wanted peace and love. But when the enemy has already brought the fight to us, we must fight back or there will never be peace and love for all.

> ...*The Son of God appeared for this purpose, that He might destroy the works of the devil* (1 John 3:8).

## Supernatural Living

> *For in him we live and move and have our being...* (Acts 17:28 NIV).

> *Jesus answered, "It is written: 'Man does not live on bread alone, but on every word that comes from the mouth of God'"* (Matthew 4:4 NIV).

When we become born again we enter into a new way of living in Christ. We *want* to live according to His will for us. Our priorities, time commitments, and vocation shift after we give our lives to the Lord. If Jesus really is our King, our lifestyle should reflect a change from a Me-centered life to a Him-centered life. If we are truly living for Him and in Him, then even all the good things He gives us must be laid at His feet on a regular basis. Instead of living to protect ourselves, take care of ourselves, and serve our own self-interests, we should serve a higher and nobler calling for the glory of God.

*I press on toward the goal for the prize of the upward call of God in Christ Jesus* (Philippians 3:14).

If we are living in Him, moving for Him, and have our identity or being in Him, we will live a supernatural life. A supernatural life is a life in which God's spirit lives and breaths. It is a life in which believers are directed by prophetic revelation and walk in supernatural power. The supernatural unction of the Lord directs as the Spirit guides, and these believers witness miracles, signs and wonders as part of their lifestyle, attesting to their faith.

The impossible is the norm for these believers. They love a challenge and aren't afraid of the devil. They aren't surprised at opposition but actually see it as a sign of the Lord's favor. They are not downcast by persecution but see it as a signal of living for the glory of God. Those who live supernaturally have incomprehensible peace in the midst of storms. Learning to walk and abide in Him eventually leads to representing Him accurately to the world as we manifest His love, joy, and kindness. When we demonstrate His power through the His gifts, we manifest His likeness and nature. The fruits and the gifts of the Spirit will both be seen in us if we walk out a supernatural life.

Instead of living a life "by chance," a believer can live a life with purpose and direction and prophetic fulfillment. Our purpose can be to live and please the Lord as we live for the gospel. Instead of living for careers, hobbies, and interests, or even our family and friends, we live to further the plans and purposes of God. Selfless living is the beginning to this new way of life.

*I have been crucified with Christ and I no longer live, but Christ lives in me. The life I live in the body, I live by faith in the Son of God, who loved me and gave himself for me* (Galatians 2:20).

I have been married to the same beautiful woman for more than 34 years. We have five children and six grandchildren—I am a family man. God is too. However, Jesus says we are to live in such a way that all of our existence glorifies the Lord, and out of that we gain great fulfillment and pleasure. If we only live to enjoy time with our friends, that is not truly living for Him. If our life is devoted to our family, that is not truly living for Him. Many wives think that their prime calling in life is to care for their family's needs, but even that must be subject to the Lord's purposes. And living for the enjoyment of fellowship with our brothers and sisters in the church is not truly living for Him. When asked who His family members are, Jesus says: *"And someone said to Him, 'Behold, Your mother and Your brothers are standing outside seeking to speak to You.' But He answered the one who was telling Him and said, 'Who is My mother and who are My brothers?' And stretching out His hand toward His disciples, He said, 'Behold, My mother and My brothers! For whoever does the will of My Father who is in heaven, he is My brother and sister and mother'"* (Matthew 12:47-50).

Living for and in Him is a supernatural adventure. Jesus calls us His friends and we can work together with Him in our daily life here on earth. What a privilege! Yet, I realize that many believers are so caught up in so many different ways that most are unable to do God's will even if it is their highest intention. They became bogged down with ancillary issues and situations.

For example, as parents we should love, nurture, materially provide for, and spiritually train our children. But in our country today, there is an out-of-balance view about parenting that puts children's needs, desires, and even schedules above those of their parents. Mothers are running around from dawn to dusk taking their children to ballet classes, music lessons, soccer practice, boy scouts, girl scouts, and other activities. While these activities may help children learn and develop talent and character, they can also expend time and energy without really benefiting their future.

I believe that as Christians, there are four basic different styles of living. These are not the only ones but these four illustrate the ways many of us deal with things. I humorously labeled each to illustrate the point.

## Accidentally

The survivors—people who have experienced hardship in the past and have become fatalists. Their favorite song: "I'm a Man of Constant Sorrow." They regularly look for something bad to happen to them. When it does, they say, "The Lord allowed it." And if something good happens, while they might say "praise the Lord," they are probably more likely to think, "The Lord is blessing some area of my obedience." If too much good happens, they brace themselves and get ready for the bad. They seem to have more faith for the bad than the good. They actually look for something ugly to come their way. They live with a superstitious sense of timing. "The Lord works in mysterious ways," is their motto. They don't see the Lord as mysteriously good but mysteriously bad. Because they aren't secure in God's love for them and aren't scripturally clear on God's immense capacity to bless and reveal His goodness to people, they miss a lot of good the Lord has for them.

While it is fine and good to acknowledge the Lord at work in our lives, we are not to acknowledge Him as the source of our problems because honestly, He isn't. These folks live almost snake-bit, like they are cursed. They live without any prophetic purpose or plan just trying to survive. They either live in dread, waiting each day for the sword over their heads to fall, or in a giddy fantasy world hoping to win the big jackpot. Either extreme is not living in reality. When bad things do occur, they get introspective, wondering, "what did I do wrong?"

Living by accident means they live with little to no sense of God's purpose, plan, or reason. A Christian living accidentally will rarely accomplish what God wants from their lives because they spend a majority of time just trying to survive. Their favorite television program is "Survivor"—the "reality" show. They are always grappling with the reasons for their ups and downs, but do nothing intentional to take control of their lives—except maybe take a vacation.

## Consequentially

The grim reapers—people who are still living under the consequences of their own bad decisions. Their favorite question: "How could this be happening again?" A Christian who lives consequentially is always living behind the eight ball, never really getting out from behind the past. These folks never seem to get it right, mostly because they are daily dealing with the consequences of bad decisions. They continually reap their own bad harvest, but never quite figuring out why. To live consequentially is to live life looking for and going through easy "open" doors rather than kicking down the gates of hell or advancing into the territory God has given them in the Spirit. They spend a lot of time "checking things out." Jesus didn't say check all your options; He said, "Follow Me."

We all make some bad decisions, and we have to deal with the consequences. That is part of life and can actually be a good learning experience. But if we never learn and keep repeating the pattern, our life becomes inconsequential.

Sowing and reaping is a Kingdom principle we should learn to use to our advantage. We should be sowing Kingdom seeds, making wise choices, and reaping good benefits. Although we reap bad results because of poor choices, we can go to God and He will bail us out and deliver us from our mistakes and dilemmas. God helps those who are willing to break the cycle. "Grim reapers" can turn their lives around when they start making wise choices and start reaping the results.

## Circumstantially

"It's all good"—People who live their entire lives with their circumstances dictating the direction of their life. They live by the creed: "*Que sera, sera*; whatever will be, will be." Whatever comes their way, moves and directs their lives.

Things happen in life that are good *and* bad—and we have little control over many of them. These folks end up blaming their lack of vision and obedience (which sometimes facilitates the good and bad things) on the Lord, which is a wrong view of sovereignty. They live with an apparently huge level of faith, always asking God for huge things, but it is obvious they haven't earned how to trust Him for the little things—the things that may make the huge requests unnecessary.

For example, the Bible teaches, "husbands love your wives." If a man's wife is starved for love and the man is upset because his wife doesn't sense God's love, he may pray, "God show my wife love, show her love." But if the husband neglects to show his love for his wife, he is hindering God's blessing to his wife. First Peter 3:7 says, *"Husbands, live with your wives in an understanding way...so that your prayers will not be hindered."*
People who live circumstantially end up frustrated and blame everything on the devil or their amazing call of God or something

else, never quite seeing it might have something to do with their lack of basic obedience:

- If you don't work, you don't eat.
- If you talk all the time at work you will get fired.
- If you don't love your wife/husband she/he will feel unloved.
- If you don't pay your rent you will get evicted.
- If you buy a car you can't afford it will be repossessed when you don't make the payments.

These folks may be immature or lack common sense, but somehow they feel that God should do for them huge special things yet they haven't grown in little areas of faith. A major symptom of this type of living is that they have an incorrect understanding of the sovereignty of God and a false view of taking dominion. Many of these folks have even experienced something traumatic early in life and so think that bad or good can happen at any time, and when it does they will react to it—until then, they just let whatever happens, happen.

Isaiah 54:14-17 says we are not to put up with things like this coming our way without putting up a fight. It is a fight of faith. Many times they are "waiting for the Lord to do something" when in reality the Lord told them clearly in Scripture what they should do about it. Their favorite song: "Since I lost hope, I feel a whole lot better." Somehow they keep doing things wrong yet keep blaming the devil. If they bring order and obedience into their lives, they will see success.

## Supernaturally

These are the overcomers who live supernatural lives. They resemble the members of the Book of Acts church in the

21st century—more like an "X-Files" church, a church to be investigated! These are the ones who live supernaturally exciting lives. They don't put up with anything that comes their way if it is against and contrary to the Word of God and their prophetic destiny. They decree a thing and light will shine on their ways. They are the head and not the tail. They are faithful not flaky, yet have a Holy Spirit spontaneity in their lives and are living out the future God has for them.

They speak to the things that are not and bring into being the things that are necessary for their advancement. They do not fear a bad report when it comes because they know that is not the final word on the matter. The supernatural is a normal part of their lives, and there is an atmosphere of the miraculous and awe in their everyday lives. They live in an expectant atmosphere waiting for the goodness of God to come their way. Yes they have setbacks and yes they lose battles sometimes, but their victory is assured because His victory was already accomplished on the Cross. They are enforcing the mandate of His victory. It is a faith-filled, purpose-directed, and spirit-led life of fun and adventure. Every day they come home with blood on their swords because they live and move and have their being in Him, destroying the works of the devil wherever they see them. The devil has them on his dreaded enemies list and they make the devil nervous! Nothing is impossible for them and they live securely in the love of God knowing that God is sending good things their way.

*For whatever is born of God overcomes the world; and this is the victory that has overcome the world—even our faith* (1 John 5:4).

Sound exciting? It is not a pipe dream but a new way of living that every Christian can walk in. It was prophesied in Daniel that the saints would receive the Kingdom of God.

*But the saints of the Most High will receive the kingdom and will possess it forever—yes, forever and ever* (Daniel 7:18).

And then in Hebrews it says the same: *"Therefore, since we receive a kingdom which cannot be shaken, let us show gratitude, by which we may offer to God an acceptable service with reverence and awe; for our God is a consuming fire"* (Hebrews 18:28-29).

It is an easy thing to continually serve a Master and His Kingdom which can never be shaken and we are freely given to have His resources at our disposal by applying faith!. All these powers of the age to come are ours right *now* if we could just see how close they are! The passage in Matthew chapter 4 *"Repent, for the kingdom of heaven is at hand"* can be better understood this way: "Change your way of thinking, because there is another reality operating here right now where God rules and lives."

# CHAPTER 18

# THE PROTOTYPE

*Dreams without action are only a fantasy, but acting on your dreams fulfills your destiny.*

You read in a previous chapter about how I left behind a mainstream church to pursue a more biblical and fruitful model. I guess I am a reformer. Reformers are those who can't tolerate the unfruitful, so they decide to start over. There are two kinds of reformers: those who curse the darkness, exposing the wrongs, and those who bring light into the darkness. They want to build something rather than tear down. I had given nearly 22 years of full-time active ministry before I began a quest to pioneer a different prototype of church.

A *prototype* is an:

- original type, form, or instance serving as a basis or standard for later stages;
- original, full-scale, and usually working model of a new product or new version of an existing product:
- early, typical example.

As we see in this expanded definition, the church in the Book of Acts could be defined as: an early, typical example, as well as the form or standard to go by. But when I talk about prototype I am not only talking about going back to the Book of Acts for a baseline. There would be similarities because we would also use the original as a standard, but to have a new prototype of church would be more accurately defined by the second definition: a working model of a new product or new version of an existing product. The existing product is "church" but this new working model would actually fly, it would actually work according to biblical criteria.

There have been attempts to build a working model that is culturally relevant, but they have been unsuccessful—like trying to put new wheels on a 1927 Studebaker, or like Israel trying to move in the Ark of the Covenant in a new SUV.

Today's church entertains and uplifts but rarely corrects, disciplines, or trains—providing discipleship. And when today's church does make disciples, it reproduces dysfunctional ones with a faulty message and a lower standard. The Church is to be the bearer of truth but we can't give folks the good news of the gospel if we don't give them the truth—the bad news about their condition. You can't disciple people in the truth who are not born again by the Spirit of Truth.

Hearing a couple of Scripture passages will not change anyone, and while it is possible that people can be converted in our typical American Sunday morning service, it is questionable as to what are they being converted to. Are they now disciples of Jesus their King and Lord, or were they told, "Try a little bit of Jesus, He will be your buddy." Or "Join my church, it's a lot of fun." God's methods are always accomplished by the Spirit in a supernatural way. We cannot remove the Spirit and the supernatural and somehow expect a holy result.

Do we want huge churches filled with the unsaved but not filled with the Spirit? Do we want to cater to them so not to offend them? Or would we all rather hang out with real disciples of Jesus who don't just say they love Him, but truly act like and reflect Him? We get what we are declaring, and lately a lot of what is being declared doesn't produce good fruit.

## Constantly Changing

In our city there is one of the largest aerospace defense contractors in the nation. For the past seven years they have been developing the FA-22 Stealth Fighter aircraft for the United States Air Force. It initially was designed for air superiority but after the Cold War ended and the war on terrorism changed the mission, they have been slowing the pace of production. During the first several years of the program they built several of these aircrafts, then sent them to California for a year or so to test fly them every day. This flight testing exposes all the glitches that would not have surfaced in the design phase, and allows them to refine and perfect all aspects of the plane from avionics to weapon capabilities, and even its turnaround time.

One fascinating thing I learned as I heard about the way these planes were developed was the manufacturer's ability, by using on-board computers, to discover, document, and then correct thousands of things seen during the test flight of the first four fighters. Each subsequent aircraft built reflects all of the corrections and changes detected in the previous models. Every glitch or imperfection is captured on the plane's computers then downloaded back to the factory. The next plane off the production line is free of the problems—making each plane produced better than the one before.

Of course, to do this, it costs more in time and money but the product gets better and better. In this example we see how the prototype isn't the finished product, but rather a constantly changing design, being continually adjusted and perfected until it is a remarkable flying machine, perfect in nearly every detail.

In the same way, discipleship is an as-you-go process. I noted earlier that a large number of the miracles in Jesus' ministry occurred as He was on the way. We can't disciple the saints who are called by God to do works of ministry if we don't do works of ministry. If we aren't active—on our way—they won't have a model. Also mentioned earlier was the Greek mind-set that so captivates the church that we actually think that if we *hear* something taught, we become it simply by listening and learning. Unfortunately that isn't the way things work. According to the NTL Institute for Retention Rates, most people retain only 5 percent by hearing and maybe a little more by reading. But we retain over 75 percent by doing and 95 percent by teaching someone else by doing! This is called modeling or tutoring, and it obviously works.

Even if a stadium is filled with people and they hear the world's greatest communicators, they will only retain 5 percent of what is said and probably less if there are a lot of distractions. Maybe this is why expensive gospel crusades with huge crowds have less than 2 percent of their "converts" still walking with the Lord just six months later! How unproductive and wasteful this type of outreach is. Yet we hold on to our sacred cows of religious foolishness.

When we employ people to do their ministries without any qualifications—except to be born again—then all of their character flaws, wrong ways of thinking, and the like will surface quickly. In Luke chapter 9 we read the account of Jesus sending out the 12 and when they return they tell about "what they had done." They tell what they had *done*, not what they said or talked about. Preaching should always be about what is *done* rather than said. Have you ever heard the statement, "When all is said and done, there is always a lot more done than said"?

The disciples came back after their gospel preaching adventures and they were:

—having an argument over who was the greatest (Luke 9:46).

—trying to stop someone who was not with them from preaching the gospel (Luke 9:49).

—about to call fire down from Heaven to consume a Samaritan village (Luke 9:53-55).

In just a short time Jesus had to confront and correct selfish ambition, pride, exclusivity, and anger. Most of us would have taken them out of ministry and put them on the shelf while we made them take character classes for six months, but Jesus responds by being overjoyed; by Luke chapter 10 He is sending out 70 more disciples!

I doubt any of us would have handled these situations this way. We ought to admit that our ways don't work and we should use His methods. It is obvious that having people *do* ministry rather than just learn about it, is the quickest way to train and grow real disciples and watch them "fly."

Before we began to develop the new church prototype, we defined it according to the Word of God. The standard of measurement for success had to be biblical fruit such as; salvations, deliverances, miracles, healings, and the growth of disciples. This was Jesus' and Paul's criteria so it was good enough for us. It also had to be based on leaving a presence for the Kingdom of God to come back to. As we explored the Scriptures, I realized that we assumed a lot about what the church was.

Things the Scriptures say the Church is:

1. The Body of the Lord Jesus Christ. His hands, feet, touch of healing, representation on the earth (Colossians 1:18).

2. The pillar and support of the Truth
   (1 Timothy 3:15).

3. The Bride of Christ (Revelation 19:7).

4. The salt of the earth (Matthew 5:13).

5. The light of the world (Matthew 5:14) bearers
   of light (Ephesians 5:7-9).

6. God's new creation (2 Corinthians 5:17).

7. Warriors in God's army against satan
   (Ephesians 6:10-20).

8. An assembly of called out ones, a fellowship of
   witnesses to the faith (1 Corinthians 1:2).

9. The House of God's faithful (1 Peter 4:17;
   Colossians 1:2) (John 15:26-27).

10. Aliens and strangers in this world and ambassadors
    for the King (1 Peter 2:11; 2 Corinthians 5:20).

11. Ministers reconciling humankind to God
    (2 Corinthians 5:18-19).

12. Adequate, able, and competent ministers of the
    New Covenant of life (2 Corinthians 3:6).

While all these things seem idealistic, they are reality because whatever God says is true is truly reality. *"Let God be true, and every man a liar"* (Rom. 3:4).

The truth of God's Word is a higher reality, a truer truth than we have ever beheld. The truth of God's Word is more literal and real then most of what we see, feel, hear, and smell. There is a higher plane of existence that we can walk in and experience only if we "Come up here" to a higher place in God. This realm is accessed by faith and then by walking in and obeying the Spirit's holy voice unquestioningly.

*If then you have been raised up with Christ, keep seeking the things above, where Christ is, seated at the right hand of God. Set your mind on the things above, not on the things that are on earth* (Colossians 3:1-2).

So then what are these things Paul is talking about as "things above"? They are the things of the Kingdom, the true riches Jesus spoke of in Luke 16:11. It speaks of the Kingdom itself. It also speaks of the fruit and the gifts of the Spirit which far surpass worldly riches. A full stomach or a fat bank account cannot give anyone righteousness, peace, and joy! These true riches are the very things God wants us to strive to possess here on the earth.

We have access to the knowledge of God Himself! *"Oh, the depth of the riches of the wisdom and knowledge of God! How unsearchable his judgments, and his paths beyond tracing out!"* (Romans 11:33 NIV).

Every good thing bestowed and every perfect gift is from above. (See James 1:17-18.)

We in Christ are seated above with Him.

*...These are in accordance with the working of the strength of His might which He brought about in Christ, when He raised Him from the dead, and seated Him at His right hand in the heavenly places, far above all rule and authority and power and dominion, and every name that is named, not only in this age, but also in the one to come* (Ephesians 1:19-21).

*But God, being rich in mercy, because of His great love with which He loved us, even when we were dead in our transgressions, made us alive together with Christ (by grace you have been saved), and raised us up with Him, and seated us with Him in the heavenly places in Christ Jesus, in order that in the ages to come He*

> *might show the surpassing riches of His grace in kind-
> ness toward us in Christ Jesus* (Ephesians 2:4-7).

We can walk in the wisdom of God from above. *"But the
wisdom from above is first pure, then peaceable, gentle, reasonable, full
of mercy and good fruits, unwavering, without hypocrisy"*
(James 3:17).

We are empowered and have access to use the name that
is above all others—the name of Jesus! *"Therefore God exalted
him to the highest place and gave him the name that is above every
name, that at the name of Jesus every knee should bow, in heaven and
on earth and under the earth, and every tongue confess that Jesus
Christ is Lord, to the glory of God the Father"* (Philippians 2:9-11
NIV).

> *...those who have once been enlightened, who have
> tasted the heavenly gift, who have shared in the Holy
> Spirit, who have tasted the goodness of the word of God
> and the powers of the coming age...*
> (Hebrews 6:4-5 NIV).

In Him, we have all *now*!

- Enlightenment—our spiritual eyes are opened.
- We get to taste of the heavenly gift.
- We share in the Holy Spirit.
- We taste the goodness of the Word of God.

  Taste the powers of the Kingdom age.

We are empowered and led by the spirit to be children of God.
Children can taste from their Father's table. Children have
access to the family business. Children get to have all their dad's
stuff *and* their own!

## Two-thirds of God's Name is GO

Two thirds of God's name is GO! In the New Testament we see that the apostolic church was told to *go*, not stay. They were only told once to stay, as Jesus commanded them to wait in Jerusalem to receive power from on high. (See Luke 24:29.) But after Pentecost, they were to go around in all the villages and towns proclaiming the good news. Most of Jesus' miracles occurred on the way to here or there. Whenever we see in the Bible the following words or phrases: *going, going out, on the way,* and *as you go,* we also see a corresponding move of God happen. In the New Testament, Jesus and the disciples are doing ministry 166 times as they were on the move. Jesus is moving! By the very nature of the term, a "move of God" involves movement.

> *And Jesus was going about in all Galilee, teaching in their synagogues, and proclaiming the gospel of the kingdom, and healing every kind of disease and every kind of sickness among the people. And the news about Him went out into all Syria; and they brought to Him all who were ill, taken with various diseases and pains, demoniacs, epileptics, paralytics; and He healed them* (Matthew 4:23-24).

> *But they went out, and spread the news about Him in all that land. And as they were going out, behold, a dumb man, demon-possessed, was brought to Him* (Matthew 9:31-32).

> *And it came about while He was on the way to Jerusalem, that He was passing between Samaria and Galilee. And as He entered a certain village, ten leprous men who stood at a distance met Him; and they raised their voices, saying, "Jesus, Master, have mercy*

*on us!" And when He saw them, He said to them, "Go and show yourselves to the priests." And it came about that as they were going, they were cleansed* (Luke 17:11-14).

Have you ever thought that maybe we won't have a move of God unless someone is moving with the gospel? All throughout Scripture we see that apostolic, prophetic, evangelistic, and teaching ministries were going, on the way, and moving. The American model of "going to church" and "coming to services" is not the apostolic model revealed in the New Testament. While thousands of believers came to hear Jesus teaching the Kingdom, His preaching was done in and on the highways and byways, reaching the ones who needed it the most. The gospel was carried through the Mediterranean regions and Westward thanks to the Roman Empire's road system.

While many Christians may outwardly profess that they want to see a revival and a move of God, the vast majority are waiting for it to come to them on their time schedule, according to their lifestyle, and when it is convenient with their work and school schedules. While this attitude of a convenient, meeting-centric Christianity is common in the United States, it has been true of other cultures as well; but the lessons of history and reality prove that this "convenient revival" rarely occurs. Sunday revival is a misnomer.

While America has seen some church-centered revivals like the one in Brownsville, Florida, in the mid-1990s, the vast majority of society-reforming and sin-killing moves of God in American history not occurred "on the clock." God does not come to us on our terms, we must go to Him on His terms. He won't punch our clock. We work for Him, not the other way around. It is our *privilege* to partner with Him in doing His exploits! We all have a sense of adventure born in our hearts to work with Him!

## Light in the Darkness

The extraordinary miracles we hear about in the New Testament happened as the gospel went forth where it was needed, in Jesus' apostolic company. They carried the treasure with them wherever they went. The light of the gospel was taken to the needy and the lost sheep of Israel. Can you imagine what would happen if you carried a candle into a sports arena for a Saturday night basketball game? Do you think carrying a candle into the huge 18,000-seat sports arena would even minutely improve the lighting when it is competing with tens of thousands of watts of light bathing the place in white light? No, it wouldn't.

That is what happens when we hold massive believers' events. There is so much blinding light in the room, yet none of it is does anything to pierce the darkness *outside* just a few hundred yards away! While these gatherings have their place, are we so comfortable with the "found," that we are afraid to go after the lost? Can't we see that the power and light level increase only when there is a demand put upon them?

The deeper the darkness, the brighter the light. This darkness was prophesied about in Isaiah 60:1-3: *"Arise, shine; for your light has come, and the glory of the Lord has risen upon you. For behold, darkness will cover the earth, and deep darkness the peoples; But the Lord will rise upon you, and His glory will appear upon you. And nations will come to your light, And kings to the brightness of your rising."*

But *we* are the light bearers and the glory carriers. *We* are the ones who are capable of destroying the darkness with just a little bit of our bright light!

> *For God, who said, "Let light shine out of darkness,"*
> *made His light shine in our hearts to give us the light*
> *of the knowledge of the glory of God in the face of*
> *Christ. But we have this treasure in jars of clay to*
> *show that this all-surpassing power is from God and*
> *not from us* (2 Corinthians 4:6-7 NIV).

That is the nature of light. It only brings illumination and contributes where there is deep darkness. The deeper the darkness, the brighter the light will shine and bring light to and in it! A little light can change the atmosphere in a dark place! It doesn't take much light to allow sight in a dark room, just a few watts. And can the darkness fight to stay when you walk into a completely dark room and turned on the light? Darkness *always* flees in the presence of light, and this gospel of the Kingdom is the light in the darkness!

The gospel has much power and contains so much light that darkness must flee when confronted by the simplicity of it. When light meets darkness, there is a clash of two opposing kingdoms. In weather terminology, when a cold front meets a warm front, there is a violent storm; in Christian terminology there also always a storm when the gospel of the Kingdom is truly proclaimed to the kingdom of darkness.

## Allow Him to Define the Gospel

> *And as you go, preach, saying, "The kingdom of*
> *heaven is at hand." Heal the sick, raise the dead,*
> *cleanse the lepers, cast out demons; freely you received,*
> *freely give* (Matthew 10:7-8).

Take a look at this often overlooked passage. It tells us *who* should preach, *how* to preach the gospel, *what to say* when we preach, and even *what it should look like* when it is preached. Jesus says preaching is to:

- Declare.
- Proclaim.
- Herald like a town crier.

In biblical times and even in recent history the purpose of the town crier was to call out every hour, on the hour, the condition of things in the town. He would herald, "Three a.m. and all is well." The gospel was designed by God to be so clear and simple that a child could understand it, and the proud would probably miss it!

The Bible says *as you go* not as you stay. It says preach, not pontificate, elucidate, or extrapolate; It says to *say this*: "The Kingdom of Heaven is at hand", not:

"How about coming to Bible study?"

"Try Jesus."

"Are you saved?"

"Want to be born again?"

"Are you in a church?"

"Do you want to join our church?"

"Do you want to come to our church?"

"Want a hot dog and a blanket"?

Preaching the gospel is not necessarily setting up a tent and bringing a large conference or a mass meeting to an arena in a distant land. Preaching is not only done where there is a large podium, big black Bible, and a glass of water sitting beside it. Preaching is not necessarily hearing a lecture on the home, finances, or a Bible study of the Book of Ruth. While Bible studies have their place and purpose, Jesus defined none of that as preaching the gospel. While teachings on the home or classes about church membership probably won't provoke a clash of Kingdoms, delivering the gospel will!

*As he went along, he saw a man blind from birth. His disciples asked him, "Rabbi, who sinned, this man or his parents, that he was born blind?" "Neither this man nor his parents sinned," said Jesus, "but this happened so that the work of God might be displayed in his life. As long as it is day, we must do the work of him who sent me. Night is coming, when no one can work. While I am in the world, I am the light of the world." Having said this, he spit on the ground, made some mud with the saliva, and put it on the man's eyes. "Go," he told him, "wash in the Pool of Siloam" (this word means Sent). So the man went and washed, and came home seeing.*

*His neighbors and those who had formerly seen him begging asked, "Isn't this the same man who used to sit and beg?" Some claimed that he was. Others said, "No, he only looks like him." But he himself insisted, "I am the man." "How then were your eyes opened?" they demanded. He replied, "The man they call Jesus made some mud and put it on my eyes. He told me to go to Siloam and wash. So I went and washed, and then I could see." "Where is this man?" they asked him. "I don't know," he said.*

*They brought to the Pharisees the man who had been blind. Now the day on which Jesus had made the mud and opened the man's eyes was a Sabbath. Therefore the Pharisees also asked him how he had received his sight. "He put mud on my eyes," the man replied, "and I washed, and now I see." Some of the Pharisees said, "This man is not from God, for he does not keep the Sabbath." But others asked, "How can a sinner do such miraculous signs?" So they were divided.*

*Finally they turned again to the blind man, "What have you to say about him? It was your eyes he opened." The man replied, "He is a prophet." The Jews still did not believe that he had been blind and had received his sight until they sent for the man's parents. "Is this your son?" they asked. "Is this the one you say was born blind? How is it that now he can see?"*

*"We know he is our son," the parents answered, "and we know he was born blind. But how he can see now, or who opened his eyes, we don't know. Ask him. He is of age; he will speak for himself." His parents said this because they were afraid of the Jews, for already the Jews had decided that anyone who acknowledged that Jesus was the Christ would be put out of the synagogue. That was why his parents said, "He is of age; ask him."*

*A second time they summoned the man who had been blind. "Give glory to God," they said. "We know this man is a sinner." He replied, "Whether he is a sinner or not, I don't know. One thing I do know. I was blind but now I see!" Then they asked him, "What did he do to you? How did he open your eyes?" He answered, "I have told you already and you did not listen. Why do you want to hear it again? Do you want to become his disciples, too?"* (John 9:1-27 NIV).

One final thing in the description of preaching in Matthew 10:7-8 is the whole concept of it being "freely" given. One reason the gospel is "good news" is because it is free. The gospel is precious and a treasure, yet freely given and received. While it cost Jesus everything, the ability to give it away comes with no cost except on the part of the person giving it. Are we willing to be a fool for Christ to win some to Him?

## Our Treasure

*Guard, through the Holy Spirit who dwells in us, the treasure which has been entrusted to you* (2 Timothy 1:14).

We have a sacred trust given to us as believers. We have a treasure within us that includes Christ in us, the gospel, our destiny, and our purpose. Without understanding this, we won't understand or comprehend that what we have is exactly what the world needs. This amazing gift of Christ in us, the hope of glory, can be freely given to any and all who need Him. He is our greatest treasure and the precious message we have can flow out of us at anytime, anywhere, anyway if we will only allow Him. There is no hindrance that can hold God back from coming forth from us and bringing His Love, power, and light to a lost and dying world. The world needs God—a fully revealed heavenly Father. We can do nothing less than allow Him to shine through us and touch humanity with His tender grace and mercy.

The following quote and short story are two of my favorites—I pray they will be yours too.

"Some wish to live within the sound of church or chapel bell.
I want to run a rescue shop within a yard of hell." —C.T. Studd

"And They Called Themselves Fishermen"
—Author Unknown

A group existed who called themselves fishermen. There were many fish in the waters around. In truth, the whole area was surrounded by streams and lakes filled with fish. And the fish were hungry.

It came to pass that week after week, month after month, and year after year, those who called themselves fishermen met in meetings; they talked about their call to fish, the abundance of fish, and how they might go about fishing. They carefully analyzed what fishing meant, urged fishing as an occupation, and declared that fishing is always to be a primary task of fishermen.

These same fishermen built large, beautiful buildings for local fishing headquarters. Their plea was that everyone should be a fisherman and that every fisherman should fish. In addition to meeting regularly, they organized a board to send out fishermen to other places where there were many fish. The board was formed by those who had the great vision and courage to speak about fishing, to define fishing, and to promote the idea of fishing in faraway streams and lakes where many fish of different colors swam. Furthermore, the board hired staff and appointed committees and held many meetings to issue statements on fishing, to agree on what new streams should be thought about. Large, elaborate, and expensive training centers were built with the original and primary purpose of teaching fishermen how to fish.

Over the years, courses were offered on the needs of fish, the nature of fish, how to recognize different fish, the psychological reactions of fish, the various backgrounds of fish, and how to approach and feed fish. Those who taught had doctorates in *fishiology*. Further, the fishermen built large printing houses to publish their fishing guides. Presses were kept busy day and night to produce materials solely devoted to fishing methods and equipment. Meetings were arranged to talk about fishing. An expert speaker's bureau was also provided to schedule special speakers on the subject of fishing. Notwithstanding all this activity, it was noted that fishermen themselves did not fish; they pleaded for fishing. The boards did not fish; they planned for fishing. The teachers of Fishiology did not fish; they explained fishing. The expert speakers did not fish; they preached about fishing.

However, after one stirring address on "The Necessity of Fishing," one young man left the meeting and went fishing. The next day he reported that he had caught two outstanding fish. He was honored for his excellent catch and was scheduled to visit all the big meetings possible to tell how he had done it. In fact he quit his fishing in order to have time to tell about the experience to the other fishermen. He was also placed on the Fisherman's General Board as a person having considerable experience.

Now many of the fishermen made sacrifices and put up with all kinds of difficulties. Few were well paid for their service on the boards and training centers. Some lived near the water and suffered the smell of dead fish. They received the ridicule of some who made fun of their fishermen's clubs and the fact that they claimed to be fishermen, yet never fished. They had doubts about those who felt it was of little use to attend and talk about fishing. After all, were they not following the One who said: *"Follow Me, and I will make you fishers of men"* (Matt. 4:19).

It came about that one day someone made the outlandish suggestion that those who did not fish were not actually fishermen—no matter how much they claimed to be. Someone actually asked: "Is a person a fisherman if year after year he never catches (or even tries to catch) a fish? If he is not fishing, can he be following?" Those who called themselves fishermen, and their boards and committees and training centers and speakers, were all very hurt by that question.

*Jesus asked them, "Have you never read in the Scriptures: The very Stone which the builders rejected and threw away has become the Cornerstone; this is the Lord's doing, and it is marvelous in our eyes? I tell you, for this reason the kingdom of God will be taken away from you and given to a people who will produce the fruits of it." And whoever falls on this Stone will be broken to pieces, but he on whom It falls will be crushed to powder [and It will winnow him, scattering him like dust]* (Matthew 21:42-44 AMP).

**What's your excuse for not fishing?**

# ABOUT THE AUTHOR

Marc Lawson has been in ministry for more than 27 years and is founder of Mighty Warrior Ministries. He leads church at North Gate, a three year old church prototype that is attempting to "do church as *unusual*." Passionately committed to an atmosphere of liberty and seeing signs, wonders, and miracles by the Spirit, he desires to activate the Church to reject the present "mile-wide, inch-deep," spectator brands of Christianity and instead embrace doing Kingdom works of ministry.

He has been married to his wife, Linda, for 35 years and lives in Woodstock, Georgia, with two of their five children, Katie and Jordan. Their other children are married, and they have six grandchildren.

Contact info for Marc Lawson and North Gate Church is on their Website: www.info@ngca.org.

Additional copies of this book and other
book titles from DESTINY IMAGE are
available at your local bookstore.

Call toll-free: 1-800-722-6774.

Send a request for a catalog to:

**Destiny Image® Publishers, Inc.**
P.O. Box 310
Shippensburg, PA 17257-0310

*"Speaking to the Purposes of God for This
Generation and for the Generations to Come"*

**For a complete list of our titles,
visit us at www.destinyimage.com**